*The Flower Seeker*

# The Flower Seeker

An Epic Poem of William Bartram

PHILIP LEE WILLIAMS

**MERCER UNIVERSITY PRESS**
Macon, Georgia

978-0-88146-208-1 | H807 | Hardback | Limited Edition | Audio CD
978-0-88146-228-9 | H820 | Hardback | Audio CD
978-0-88146-221-0 | Paperback | P414


© 2010 Mercer University Press
1400 Coleman Avenue
Macon, Georgia 31207
All rights reserved


First Edition.

The letters in Canto 15 are from Documents Relating to Indian Affairs 1754-1765, ed. William L. McDowell, Jr.
(South Carolina Department of Archives and History, 1970/1992) and are used by permission.
The documents themselves are part of the collection at the South Carolina Department of Archives and History.

Books published by Mercer University Press are printed on acid free paper that meets the requirements
of American National Standard for Information Sciences—Permanence of Paper for Printed Library Materials.

Mercer University Press is a member of Green Press initiative (greenpressinitiative.org), a nonprofit organization
working to help publishers and printers increase their use of recycled paper and decrease their use
of fiber derived from endangered forests. This book is printed on recycled paper.

The interlinear images in the poem are from the USDA's Natural Resources Conservation Service online plant image gallery.
All these copyright-free drawings are of plants that Bartram could have seen on his trip across the American South.

Images on pages xi, 1, 41, 59, 199, 212-213, 237, 249, 282, 341, 361, and 419,
appear courtesy of American Philosophical Society, B.S. Delafield Collection.

Images on pages ii-iii, 21, 119, 145, 159, 185, 225, 261, 315, 329, 375, and 437,
appear courtesy of the Natural History Museum, London.

Library of Congress Cataloging-in-Publication Data

Williams, Philip Lee.
The flower seeker : an epic poem / by Philip Lee Williams. — 1st ed.
p. cm.
ISBN 978-0-88146-208-1 (hardcover limited ed. with cd : alk. paper)
— ISBN 978-0-88146-228-9 (hardcover : alk. paper)
— ISBN 978-0-88146-221-0 (pbk. : alk. paper)
1. Williams, Philip Lee--Travel--Poetry. 2. Voyages and travels--Poetry.
3. Nature--Poetry. 4. Southern States--Poetry. I. Title.
PS3573.I45535F66 2010
811'.54—dc22


2010020190


Book design by Burt&Burt

*For Adelaide Ponder,*
*Mentor, first publisher, friend*

Other Books by
PHILIP LEE WILLIAMS

NOVELS

*The Heart of a Distant Forest*

*All the Western Stars*

*The Song of Daniel*

*Slow Dance in Autumn*

*Perfect Timing*

*Final Heat*

*Blue Crystal*

*The True and Authentic History of Jenny Dorset*

*A Distant Flame*

*The Campfire Boys*

POETRY

*Elegies for the Water*

NON-FICTION

*The Silent Stars Go By*

*Crossing Wildcat Ridge*

*In the Morning: Reflections from First Light*

CHAPBOOK

*A Gift from Boonie, Seymour, and Dog*

William Bartram (1739–1823) was an American naturalist whose *Travels* (published in 1791 in Philadelphia) is one of the most important books ever written on natural history and Native American ethnography. The book describes Bartram's four-year trek across the American South from 1773-1777. *The Flower Seeker* is about William Bartram's life and travels, but many episodes are fictional, and those wishing the facts as Bartram wrote them are urged to read the *Travels*. This long poem in part follows that book and even uses some of its language but is not intended to be read as history.

I only went out for a walk and finally concluded to stay out till sundown, for going out, I found, was really going in.

—JOHN MUIR

·

In June as many as a dozen species may burst their buds on a single day. No man can heed all of these anniversaries; no man can ignore all of them.

—ALDO LEOPOLD

# PREFACE

*H*ERE *in the last summer of my last year,*
*Here in the moontide garden of my lives,*
*I stand to walk before I die. The dovecote*
*Fills with marbled wings. Our horses stamp*
*Near the coach house and the stone barn*
*With an aim toward adventure, a higher*
*Memory and one I now so desperately share.*
*This shade simmers with delicate shadows,*
*The architecture of swallowtails, a dancing*
*Buttress in the waning days of my life.*                    10
*Ice-pit, cold-cellar, greenhouse, shed:*
*I see the walls of one man's existence*
*Crumble to imaginary dust: the dust is me,*
*Though, old man in a sparkling season*
*Who trod the swamps for one azure bloom.*
*The names still fill me as the rain will swell*
*A droughty well:* tube-rose, painted bunting,
Quercus prinos, Keowee, *and* dyeing indigo.

*Here is the last river and my final flow,*
*A life of tramping woods and flower hunting,*          20
*The mounds where alligators roar and dwell*
*Rising from the page of this diurnal gloom.*
*The Schuylkill River has its route and reason,*
*From Valley Forge to Philadelphia then the sea.*
*I need to ride the rocky range of all persistence,*
*So I try to see the passage of the almost-dead*
*Backward to the Carolina days. I leave no wife,*
*No children, or their heirs to run along the prancing*
*Lawn; yet I am still the witness, meadow-*
*Green too bright for one old man to bear.*               30
*All my life when flowers rise, I sigher*
*Of beauty, form, and structure, solid urn*
*For ideas in their flittering flight, will camp*
*To suit their summons, petal by petal, boat*
*Moored to my solitary need. Bees in their hives*
*Hum. I see the sudden eyes of bird and deer.*

*Our father built the main house stone on stone*
*Here in Kingsessing's richly umber fields.*
*Four blocked rooms, one per season of the year,*
*The columned portico, the hand-carved window*
*Frames. Then year by year the structure grew*    40
*Like cypress-vine, feet-square, so carpentered*
*A leveled ball would scarcely roll. When Father*
*Died he left the house to John, and we described*
*A garden of such rare delights then grew it, seed*
*On seed. Ferns and wildflowers, Carolina allspice,*
*Witherod viburnum, medicinal plants, kitchen*
*Spices and herbs, common flowers: each stem*
*Spun from collecting trips—what owl-sung days*
*We had! We nabbed the native beauties in situ,*
*Sprung the rushes from their sinking swamps,*    50
*Dug up myrtle from its rusted hills. Larkspur,*
*Sing to me of muscled days; sail me once again*
*To the Crystal Basin and its jewelling rays.*

*Will my body also go to seed, all my days*
*Growing for a later man to pluck? Will a fen*
*On a river's course, an attitude of scales and fur,*
*Show the way, the unclear path between the stumps*
*Of my narrative? In these days I need to see into*
*The far country of my youth where lizards laze*
*On logs beside a waterfall, and a rolling rim*    60
*Of carriages sings my longing for the bracken*
*And the tiny cheek from birds and glove-gray mice.*
*I hear the flutter of parakeets, a swish of weeds,*
*A wild longing made so nectar-sweet, denied*
*For that reason alone. Restlessness is the mother*
*Of all travel, the rosined priest, the firm arbiter*
*Of all we learned and all we thought we knew.*
*But now there is only the river and this meadow*
*Left to me, a sweet enduring lack of wreck or fear*
*Of it. This fine day holds from my eyes then yields*    70
*A summer pale as ice but strong as boy's new bone.*

*I recall the day my hand knew drawing*
*Was its profession. At first it was the birds*
*Who called my name as I began to shape*
*The world to my new-spun boyhood eye.*
*Father took me to the Catskills, hills*
*Like heaven lit with feathers and so many songs*
*A man could not sing them. The animals came*
*Into my palette; turtles brought the world alive*
*With their profound deliberation. Wide oaks* 80
*Sheltered me in the heat of inspiration,*
*And in that shading all the world of nature*
*Broke open like a lovely light. Then I saw*
*The changing maple, jagged palm of peace*
*That took me days to understand. And I knew*
*A slow solitude was my life's due stride,*
*That I would traffic not in the shout of towns*
*But in wild streams and the deepest wood*
*Upon a continent, stroked with midnight's shimmer.*

*Now that I have grown into a dimmer* 90
*World, my eyes too old to see how spring could*
*Dress a Carolina river into soft and icy gowns*
*Of fog, and what is left of youth's sharp pride*
*Has vanished with each petal, each day's blue*
*Victory over storms, I take my old man's ease*
*With things. Now the only way that I can draw*
*The world is through memorial days, my future*
*Clouded as it is with distance and its passion.*
*A rain comes up and in this garden shakes and soaks*
*Each spindle and its nodding flower that thrives* 100
*On such ecstasies. I say, to rose, my simple name,*
*My* William *and the story for which it longs.*
*And in those now-lost echoed rills*
*I bring the view from such sweet high*
*Places I have roamed. I recall the cape*
*And my Uncle William's warming words*
*And the trail where wildcats showed their pawing.*

*God grant me space or time—can there be*
*A difference to an old man? I need to show it,*
*How eagles spread their eyes into bright sparks*                110
*Of flint-struck fire on the streams, how we ate*
*The* Prunus Chickasaw *with its purple gratitude;*
*The crossed and disappointed nights, my restless*
*Nature in the hold of its divine contemplation.*
*What, I wonder now, was in my care those days,*
*In my control to keep and shape? Can I bring*
*Back the islands of the Georgia coast, alive*
*As dew on a boy's camping cloak? Grant it,*
*God, that incandescent wonder at the coves*
*I claimed, the pulsing Cherokee heart,*                         120
*The gliding fish in the still, clear waters.*
*Grant me the airy days when alone I tramped*
*The fluttering groves, inhaled the new life.*
*I will walk among the genius of all green,*
*And resurrect the man that I once knew.*

*For decades now I've barely stirred, true*
*To my nature as minor lord this garden, seen*
*By ministers and presidents. All the strife*
*In their eyes faded, and on them stamped*
*An indelible mark of nature's sweetest daughters.*              130
*If I ever thought I might prepare to start*
*On another journey, I delayed. These old groves*
*Are enough to keep a seedless man, a plant*
*Purveyor, in check. I have come to thrive*
*In both what howls and what can learn to sing,*
*To value all cerulean blues and clouded grays.*
*I have found in turtles' eggs an inspiration*
*For men like me who leave the world nestless*
*Creatures. I have found the perfect latitude*
*For botanical days, the path, if seen quite late,*              140
*For my trek back to the lynxes and the larks.*
*In a garden, greatness cannot be to grow it:*
*It is to know it, as one sails the deepest sea.*

# CANTO ONE

*N*ow we plunge into the froth of sea,
The *Charleston Packet* dipping gracefully,
Porpoise of the pleasant light, our companion
Ship, the *Prince of Wales*, not far astern.
Delaware behind us, the sun to strong port,
I stand the prow and watch our lip of froth
Fold back, the joyous sea-birds crying
Out their genus, stuttered clouds, shame
Of all darkness. Together we shall sail
To Cape Henlopen on this strong gale, 10
The men shouting with strong, taut joy
As the sails chuff and strain behind it.
All afternoon our stream is fair, brute
Breakage of the death-knell sea shipped
Out to other latitudes, our captain firm
At the tiller-wheel. I am bound for Florida,
Called by Dr. Fothergill of London to search
For the rare and useful products of nature,

Chiefly of the vegetable kingdom, the nurture
Of the ivory flower, a priestless church 20
In a world without name. That sunny corridor
Will open her shade for me, and each berm
Will breach for my inspection. I have clipped
Wildflowers in the Catskills with pale chutes,
And now to the South I've seen, to find it
Newer than the gangling stride of nature's boy.
In the April-tide of our slide and breaking sail,
With wind that shapes within my heart or grail,
I exult. I have been a man without a name
Who wants to speak his day before the dying 30
Comes to call his time. The sea's green broth
Peels back. The bruise of clouds cannot abort
Our passage. I am bound for riverlight and fern,
For tramps along each waterway and canyon,
And so I love this swift and silver pace to sea
We plow, faster than the hive's call to its bee.

A full day passes and the Captain leans to tell
That storms lie on our path, wild breaking skies
With forks of lightning that snap down to tear
The ocean waves apart. I come on deck, sailors          40
Run like ants around a kicked-up hill, knowing
What to do and yet fearing it. They speak recipes
For God's salvation, touch omens, scratch scars,
And sip the long-remembered duty they have known,
Most of them for years. The cabin boy is half-mad
With glee for the coming fearful blow. Others know
Too well the terror of the sea at rage. At first I think
We might skirt the worst of purpled clouds that rank
Us, but soon there is no compass-point to bear
That might let us breach the storm. "Mr. Bartram,        50
You might head belowdecks soon," says Captain Wright,
But I bid to stay. Disorder spreads. The waves turn
To mountains, peaked with indigo crests, and birds
Vanish and leave us to our coming sea-floor dash.

There is, in nature's firework-spark and splash
A greater magnificence than I can put in words,
A greater violence than a quilled hand can earn.
It shapes the sudden eye of iris, the deeper flight
Of seabirds from a storm. Thunder's hard drum
Can bang a blister on the current then sharply dare      60
Us to breathe. I see it come and want to shout, thank
God for this shift of fortune. A young man, no blink
At this possible calamity overwhelms me. For I know
That only in youth can such disaster bring one bad
Tidings and joy at the same time. I am not yet grown,
Not really, so I watch the waves in their sculling scars
And feel their power charge me. If such sight is disease,
Let me sicken quickly into the invalid bed. A glowing
Slips into the low sky, winds rip our sails. We tailors
Of the deep take a terrible shaking. Cabins wear         70
Their furniture in a tipped-up corner. Rich lies
Begin their lives now, old stories cast their spell.

For two days and nights the sea, high church spires,
Splashes over the gunnels, state-rooms all shattered,
Deck-work disarrayed. Then comes a lively wind
From the northwest, and Captain Wright, who smiles,
Says, "Mr. Bartram, is this how you prefer the sea?"
I reply, "I would not have missed her heaving shriek
For anything on this Earth." We notice then to port
The *Prince of Wales* is gone from us. No matter. She          80
Will appear in better times. He speaks it, so I believe,
But as I watch the flat expanse I am unsure now what
One must believe. Then, on the tenth day, the boy
Aloft spies a sail, and we come astern and see it is
Our joyful companion. He had made port safely
At Cape Hatteras; alongside, he throws us ten bass
He caught in harbor. He sails on ahead then
To Charleston (we having reached Henlopen before
The storm), and we come into port that next morning
Near eleven, shivering with anticipation for the land.          90

Now watching the cobbled streets come close to hand
I pause to consider the magnificent rose sky dawning
Over this New World, the seabirds as they wheel, soar
Above the earth and ocean depths. The luminous fin
Of light paints the water into a luminous scale, a cast
Daily showing me the sublime conflict so chastely
Glittering as the porpoise leap, the fine, rich fitness
So bold and at the same time in all this light so coy
That transmutes a liquid into silver, gold, the old hot
Vector of glimmers and transitions we can conceive,          100
Delight of transitory things. If I were a whale, the sea
God of all swimming things, I could not love the sort
Of waves and wind the more. And when air wreaks
The sky and buoyant water-way, I know that I can be
The sort of man who peels away adventurous miles
As if they measured inches. I know that when the end
Comes in this life, I will see what really mattered
Between the pain of ice and the pride of ancient fires.

Charleston: Harbor sharp with morning's ache

I stride the streets in search of Dr. Chalmer                           110
For assistance and counsel for my inland trip,
A gentleman, I'm told by my worthy patron,
Intelligent and clear-eyed, filled with worthy aims
For a youth in love with flowers and hawk's blood.
And so I stand before the cipher of wind and leaf,
Gone from the riptides and solitary ship-watch,
Now feeling the mysterious lift of navigation
Toward new sights, tropical splendors, the stars
And moon glowing over Carolina's birdsongs
And green glories. Now in cool April, I decide                          120
To sail south to Georgia, to the garden streets
Of Savannah, fine capital of the state, so I board
A coasting vessel. Birds soar and sing over us,
Raucous gulls that shriek their appetites astern.
Governor Wright and the Assembly welcome me.
A few days, a good horse, and I am on my way.

Now I ride astride my mount down Sunbury-way,
The gnarled and gentled land to right, to left, the sea.
Fifteen miles south of the great Ogeechee River, I turn
To the town, a shady, moss-bearded place, the dust                      130
Of many men moldering in the cemetery now adored
By widows who keep it greenly neat. There to greet
Me are genteel ladies and gentlemen, who abide
The sea-storms with cheer. But I am bound for strong
Sights and aromas. The next day I ford the channel bars
And hike a coastal island in delight. I have no intimation
Of prior thought: all lies before me to know and write, hatch
Of turtle and songbird eggs, seashells on the crust of reef,
Heaped-up mounds made by the Indians of old, and a flood
Of plantations with their potatoes, corn, indigo. The same             140
Mounds from Indians spill with broken pots, an atrium
Of live oaks overhead, basket-marks in clay, rough grips
To hold it on a cooking fire. And I am the young helmer
Of it all. I fear I will shake my head in shade then wake.

And rich before me stands the fruit of old Linnæus,
*Pinus taeda, Quercus sempervirens, Ilex aquifolium,*

*Prinos varietas*, the prickly palmetto leaves, wide lawns
Of sweetgrass, and the evergreen water oak, scatteringly
Planted by Nature. Cinereous-shaded clay holds the loamy
Surface, nursery for hatchling plants, magnitude, stability                    150
The nurseryman's delight. Roebuck dash and dart in fresh
Giddiness among the majesty of evergreen shadows,
Yet also on this island roam the tyger, bear, and wolf,
The fox, the hare, but no moles, for I have not espied
Their neatly tunneled lines. I see enormous rats scurry
Over pottery-strewn mounts, and in the hidden terraces
Of clay the rattlesnake, coiled, clattering with its threat,
Glass snake, coachwhip, serpents of each scale and stripe.
And O the wings, the superlative eagle, execrable tyrant,
Prone to rapine and violence, extorting tribute from every                    160
Feathered nation. Also the lark, the fishing-hawk,
The finch, Catesby's ground doves, soft, chaste, small.

Who were these men and women who lived in the halls
Of this island's live oaks? Did their children gawk
At the natural world, filled with such delight the very
Moon or sun caused them to dance? Did subtle sirens
Of birdsong flute them to sleep at night? I see a pipe
Lit by the fireside, chiefs quiet on mounds, and yet
I wish there could be singing, an absence of heresies
And their worries, guilts. I want to know that worry                          170
Was not part of that life they led. The cultured deride
Such men, but I am unsure whom Nature chooses, gulf
Between the green world and we *moral* men, meadow-
Strides afraid of serpents and not prone to grip and mesh
With what the world alone provides. This tranquility
Should be all we could half desire. I dream the homey
Thatch-beds on which they slept beside the tattering sea,
The sip of hummingbirds and bees in their gentle drones;
No more great days were ever seen in ancient Ilium,
And the dead can only give us gifts and never betray us.                      180

Off the sweet and densely dappled island, I roam
Back through Sunbury and join friends who head
To Midway for church service, hear a sermon

From Rev. Osgood: "Nature may not exceed in kind
Her delicacy." How odd in this nave of shadows
To hear the high church groan solicitudes. Still,
I shake the hands of those who touch this pilgrim
On his green tour. Now I go north in a level country,
The Midway and Newport rivers from deep marshes
And swamps to rice plantations with their sunken fields.                    190
And write the delights before me: *Magnolia grandiflora*,
*Andromeda nitida*, *Glycine frutescens*—vines, shrubs,
Bands, and garlands, pyramidal laurel and plumed palm.
The arbors arch those who live near the straight road.
Moonlit nights fill with fantasias of the mockingbird,
Warbling nonpareil, and turtledove. What animated
Dance lies before me. Here is the door of Mr. Andrews
Who begs a stranger with all grace into his singing home,

So I must tell the stories that I know. A wee gnome
Of a squirrel scampers on the porch rails. "What news                        200
Do you bring from the world?" he asks. "Storms decimated
Us at sea . . ." I begin, then tell those days word to word.
He shows a new machine. Duties stowed,
We fish on a bank shaded by sweet bay trees, a cool balm
Of myrtles, magnolias on the creek. "A bite!" I kneel, grab
The flipping fish with pleasure—large as a hand, this agora
Giving us the market of fins' delight. The water yields
A red-belly, so-called, oval, its topside olive. I search
The rest to find silvery, pearl-glint sides, and then I see
Its bright scarlet stomach, darting up rays of fiery scrims                   210
Into pearl on each side. We eat to our delighted fill.
But in morning I strike once more along the meadows
Toward the towns on the Altamaha, curving to benign
Darien as the roads turn muck. I cannot yet determine
If I am on the right path or not. I see many dead
Animals, not lost as I become. This is now my home.

What is it to be lost in this world? I recall my father
In his day's delight among the cultivation of our land,
And I remember Florida-days earlier when almost a boy
I tramped the wild and roaring land. And yet the old fear                     220

Of lostlings bears me forward in the dwindling light
With fear I cannot stop. I want to know the rivers'
Source and wide-mouthed flow-point to the salty sea,
To be the translator of avian language, its human voice
Upon the Earth, to describe the flowers in green days
As no man ever has before. Where, Navigator of us all,
Have I strayed? *There.* I see it now. A glimmering light
That leads me to a house. The gentle farmer bids me sleep
There for no reason that I know. How kind his wife treats
A roaming stranger in wandering boots. I turn my horse          230
Now, confident, toward Darien, through the swamp
And along snake-hung oaks, a wildcat screech, first flits
Of a butterfly in the overhung weeds. Here's a plantation,
Small but neat with delight. The owner's name: McIntosh.

No scene of primitive simplicity ever grooved its rush
Along stream bank as this farmstead does. Sensation
After sensation envelops me. An old, gray-haired man sits
Among the berms and breaths of wind, stands to pump
His hand in friendly ways. "Welcome, stranger. Of course
Come in on this sultry day." Roasting venison greets          240
Me with its deep smoky richness, as a storm with deep-
Purple sheets of violent clouds rises, giving a fright
To horses in their pens. After eating, we stand in the hall
Before the door, watch the lightning crash, the ways
It strikes from cloud to cloud or to Earth, hard choice
Of animals for shelter in the blow. "Awesome as the sea,"
McIntosh says, sucking on his pipe. A sharp flash slivers
The pine tree before us, sets it afire. The raging light
Ascends twelve feet into branches, flames and nears
Spreading, goes out. Rain floods. We stand with joy,          250
We stand to hear the rake of water lip the spongy land,
We stand to see the roebuck and the rising feather,

To see what Nature's hand endows. A plump turkey,
Beyond the storm's strong surge, struts, a stately
Bird, dark brown coat of copper-tipped feathers.
"Here it glows like burnished gold," I tell my host,
And he nods, smiles. "We reared it from an egg found

In the forest," McIntosh says. Intrigued by such scenes,
I leave my new friend in the cool, salubrious air, ride on
To Sapelo Bridge where the salt tide flows, stop at Bailey's,                    260
Deliver letters from the Governor, move along the road
Faster on my journey. Now I press to the riverside home
Of Lachlan McIntosh (of the same Scots' name). What
A friend he is! How can one account for that sharp turn
Of affection? That in meeting we know a bond grew
That could not be torn? Such grace and dignity he
Shows me. He walks beside, says, "Friend Bartram,
Come under my roof, make my house your home as long
As you need. From this moment, you are part of my
Family, and I will warm your stay." His son, John, he                           270

Says, will be glad soon to join my journey, a free
Boy of virtuous habits. How can one repay such high
Honor? I rest for three days, and begin a new and strong
Adventure. I ride north among the stirring soft drum
Of my mount's stride toward Barrington, past the filled lea
Of farms on the waters of Cathead Creek, then as I draw
Near the Fort I see beautiful shrubs in sweet graces earn
My eye. Is one the *Gordonia* with larger and more fragrant
Flowers? The other is beautiful and singular, grown
Not as a vine, but like a tree, with large panicles, a load                     280
Of blue tubular flowers flecked with crimson inside, a daily
Light for all to see. From that warming distance, a bride
Could hold clusters of possible roses. In my dreams
I have seen such flowers, in the air or on the ground,
Umber or sienna brown. After fifteen miles I coast
Toward the ferry at the Fort. A bluff here. The weather
Is mild. The ruins of an Indian town. Not lately,
Children ran its paths, on mounds were priests speaking.

A Creek rows me slowly over the river now, and I see
The large tall trees, *Nyssa coccinea*, before us, growing                      290
On the banks of the river, in the water, near the shore.
The leaves are oblong lanceolate and entire, hoary
Underneath, upper surface a full green, petioles short.
I land on the bank and mount my horse, follow the road

To the ferry on St. Ille, passing through the wilderness.
Now I go from cultivated settlements to dark and grassy
Savannahs, high pine forests, and I see a new species
With large white fragrant flowers whose stems are small
And almost feeble, with little ovate, pointed leaves,
Ending with a simple raceme or spike of flowers,                    300
Salver-formed, deep rose red. And so I also see here
Dens or caverns dug in the sandhills by the great
Land-tortoise they call the Gopher. These castles
Are retreats in daytime for the creatures that come
Forth in the night in search of prey. Such mounds
Resemble those of the ancient men of these streams,

And I pause to wonder who has copied the others' dream.
I stay the night with new friends, share cheese, pounds
(It seems) of fresh butter, and milk. The next day some
Pines form a promenade into flowery plains. Thistles              310
Scrub my trouser fabric as I clop along. Then late
In the day I pass through a swamp where many deer,
Herds of horned cattle and horses roam. In bowers,
*Chironia* and *Pillcherima* perfume the air and please
The eye. I also see a species of lupine in that hall,
With green lingulate leaves. I know no true antecedent
For it; turkey, quail, other brightly speaking birds pass
Through my sight. In the evening, with no distress,
I come to St. Ille to lodge; in morning, bags stowed
For the crossing, ferry to St. Mary's. The days purport           320
To enliven my step, but I find serene evening, soaring
Wind, fragrant pine, all silent and enchanted. Like a door
Opening in a dream, an Indian appears ahead, glowing
In the sunlight, rifle in hand. My heart snaps within me.

*Who are you, old man, who sits to know his passing*
*Days? How can sweet spring find my garden when all time*
*Has grown autumnal around me? The pale grandeur*
*Of age is overrated; I have no gift of prophecy, seer-*
*Like qualities for the pilgrim. All I own is memory*
*And this green and flowered acre, this old serenity*              330
*In the time of my hermitage. The businessman, the trade,*

*The ledger books all fade. Now my currency is sunfall,*
*My music made of mill-race and the quiet adoration*
*Of hurtless things. I strain to bring back my boyhood*
*Days, the river-crossings, botanical adventures, faces*
*I could not in my own fancy imagine. I recall the loud*
*Insect uproar of the night, the shady vespers, the supreme,*
*Sabbath-loud shouts of swamps in the deepest darkness.*
*I want to travel past this much-earned melancholy to roads*
*Of seasonal delight. I want to be almost innocent in the way*          340
*My eyes seek to curve around the dusty paths before me.*
*Who are you to ask more than his simple passing days?*

*I was the Flower Seeker, the pioneer of sands and clays,*
*Of crystalline pools more splendid than the deepest sea.*
*I rode in the reflected genius of Nature, felt the spray*
*Of Nature's rhythms and it's codes,*
*Of waterfalls on my face, inhaled the liberty that startles*
*Even free man. Shakespeare could not have dreamed*
*It all: islands roiled with brambles, seashells, rose clouds,*
*The hazel canopy of live oak. In my young man's races*
*I never found such animal riot. Rivers, sulfurous blood*          350
*Flowing from swamps, and on those trails the impatient*
*Youth mad for species, genus, the pleasure of one tall*
*Pine rigid with rapture in the breeze. What have I made*
*In this life? What knowledge gained, what old enmity*
*Forsaken? I want to bring back the strong and sensory*
*Equations of those days when I found no real fear*
*In each day's awakening, an old man's right to be sure*
*Of one sure thing, the sweetness of the rose and the lime*
*That lift me up to trails I have no hope for surpassing.*

*I must not live with losses, the natural man's shoal*          360
*Of remembered innocence. I must not strike against age*
*As if it were the enemy. I have come to bloom again,*
*To feel the flesh of flowers against my stubbled cheek,*
*Aroma from buttercup and desire. In a garden, green*
*Is the prayer, yellow the genuflection. In a garden, rain*
*Gilds rose, and the scent of life is the scent of all roses.*
*If I can no longer be young in the shale, the sediments,*

*I can rouse myself to the necessity of geology, the larger*
*Picture, the parson of precision, a gnat's pin-eye,*
*The millipede's creep. Memory is my richness and lecturer,*          370
*The Crystal Basin, clear as if it flowed from my bent hands*
*Into the river that glows past these blooms long beyond*
*The terminal date of my stone. I am buoyed by treasure*
*I can barely stand to tell in fear it will never come again*
*On a summer afternoon. No man can feel what I know.*
*And yet I strain to shock my sentence into absolution,*
*The commutation that time gives even unsainted men.*

*Give me strength for a day, sinew without a sin,*
*Memories of solemn light, sanctified Revolution*
*Against what oppresses. Let me learn to sow*          380
*My last faint furrows with the purse of palmate fern,*
*Leaf to leaf with emerald light. Let me learn to measure*
*What measures me. Walk with me to the delight of pond*
*And stream, the curling calyx of flower days. See lands*
*Of boyhood brightness bloom. Who cares if conjecture*
*Has the ring of truth? The brown-branched wren cries*
*Loud enough to leap its folio doom. My horse charges*
*Through parapets of possibility, a leaper of pediment*
*And bright embodiment of all I see before Nature closes.*
*I want to tramp the stones and woods of that world again,*          390
*To stand taller than any mortal man has ever seen.*
*I cannot know more love than those nights of which I speak,*
*But I want to have a day for these memories to mend.*
*Give me the time of an oracle, slow stride of the sage,*
*The golden glow of seasons in my golden bowl.*

The Indian with a rifle sees me. I slow, hide behind
A knobbed tree. Unarmed, I freeze. He gallops toward
Me, and I prepare to die and yet become so tranquil
That a peace shifts slightly in my bones. A confidence
Spills into capillary and blood. The bronze, scowling          400
Emissary stops suddenly and seeing no fear blow
Through me like a sail before a squall, he rides up,
Thrusts out his hand. In that holy mist we shake
Like brothers, and his horse walks onward through

The tasseled shadows as if striding in a book.
"Do you know the path to the trading house?" He
Stops on his mount, turns. The day before he had been
Beaten from that doorway, treated as a rough man treats
An animal from his campside. Still, he gives me
The way without revenge, and ten miles further I find                410
The St. Mary's River, its trading company. A man says,
"See yourself lucky; the Indian you saw is a murderer
Outlawed by his tribe. We took his gun and broke it up

I WILL SING THE SONG OF THE MAN OF BATTLE
I WILL SING THE SONG OF THE LORD . . . .
I WILL SING THE SONG OF HIM
      WITH THE WELL-PROPORTIONED LIMBS, THE MAN OF BATTLE.

And beat him senseless. Yet he got another rifle, struck
His fist in the air, said he would kill the first man to stir
Among his footsteps or stop his hunt for venison or bread.          420
You are lucky to be alive." But what does this sound
Mean to me, each stir and strike of man or shadow? I see
No truth in his words or those of an Indian who meets
Me in unripe shade. Is there one whose naturalized sin
Is obvious for all to know? Between mountains and sea,
I cannot say. Between great plains and the baited hook
Of possibility, I do not know. Trying not to think (I do
Not know answers in this gentle age), I pass a nook
Notched with peach trees, along with a rich crop
Of cotton, indigo, corn, rice—I note the soil, true                 430
Loam, its flower and verdure—now beds with cowling
Of violet, amaryllis, and mimosa. Their sweet sense
Of contact with the world enchants me. Like a sandal
Of a prince, the slipper-rose delights. If an eagle soared
Just now, I'd rank it lower than all the ilex I could find.

The St. Mary's flows from the Okefenokee Swamp,
Three-hundred miles around. In the wet season
It seems to be a lake, knolls of high land, and one
Place may be an earthly paradise. Indians live there;
The women are incomparably beautiful. Many, when          440

Nearly lost hunting in the swamp have been found
By these lovely girls called Daughters of the Sun
Who give them oranges and corn cakes, then send
Them away, for their husbands are cruel to strangers.
Those who live in that land twist among labyrinths
Like an enchanted land that appears and then vanishes
As the traveler moves through. Outside Indians rush
To invade, see the slow magic but then, lost and fearful,
Barely slip out into the world with their lives and stories.
Yet when they try to find the spot they never can,                    450
Its power to vanish its greatest magic. Can they be
Fugitive remnants of the ancient Yamasees who escaped
Massacre during the Creek war? No man alive knows.

I only see that from this mystic setting rivers flow
Outward through a plain and pine forest, scraped
By shell and scudding winds down to the blue sea.
Now, with regret and fecundity at my back, I scan
The knobs once more then turn and return to glories
Of the Altamaha on the road that took me in. Tearful,
Though not showing it, I arrive back, a singing thrush                 460
Giving welcome at the home of McIntosh. Sun's varnish
Glistens on the trunk of every tree, I dream hyacinth
And rose-fields as I stay here three days. A manger,
Filled with hay, serves my hungry horse well. And, pent
With the passion of boys, John, son who will now come
With me on adventures, readies. We set forth on ground
Of our choosing; the earth receives two strong men
To stride for petals and stems. We head to Savannah, air
Damp with anticipation, and I send ahead in this sun
My collections to Charleston, and we need no reason                   470
To delay: we head north to Augusta, stamping our luck.

What clear days! The air fills with wildflowers,
The river road firm, weather rich with rain's delay,
We ride, John and I, north through earthly delights.
As if cultivated by a magnificent arborist whose eye
Can stretch leagues, we catalog by word and deed
*Quercus sempervirens, Liriodendron tulipifera, Halesa.*

Small rivers and branches spread like a liquid forest
Across spring-struck land, limb to limb with groves
Of such magnificent density we stop, love the songbirds'                    480
Cries. Every swamp is filled with rivulets and rills,
Which spring like myth from banks along our route.
Every copse glows greenly with *Magnolia grandiflora*,
And then the covetous glory of the azalea and smilax,
And multitudes of trees and flowers less conspicuous.
"The earth, you see," says John, "is black and soapy
At the surface." I commend his eye. He clops alongside
Me. I teach Linnæan nomenclature. He laughs the Latin
into shreds. We come to a bank of considerable height

That runs parallel to the coast, the sandhills, and light                   490
Of sifting qualities plays over them and leads a satin-
Like plain to the eye, savannas with ponds, beside
Which grow clumps of viburnum, and long and ropy
Vines that sway in the least breeze. A quite ridiculous
Fear comes over me as I stand the stirrups, gaze tracks
Of deer and feral cat. We learn what landscape we adore;
We learn if seashore or mountain is what we are about
As visionary travelers. This country, sun along our sills,
Illuminates me; makes me strain for artwork or words
Others might know. The smell, like fresh-cooked loaves                      500
In the early sun, replenished by sandy rivulets, the dearest
Fragrant hills of life, the rocky precipices not falsely
Falling one inch but cascading brightly, carrying seed
For the season to another plot of rising. Yet a sigh
Admits the climate to be hot and sultry. But all frights
Of moonless eventide can't make us halt or slow to stay
Away. The strong man does not flinch, never cowers

When rough sound wakes us in the feasting night.
So we come to Augusta, village of the fertile plain.
Its buildings line the river banks, bricks to full flow                     510
Of water. In summer when the river is scudding, low,
Cataracts are five feet high; I make the crossing
Five *hundred* yards here. We wait three days, then
Creeks and Cherokees arrive for treaty talks, merchants

Smug, demanding two million acres for their debts
Of longstanding aid. But the Creeks, proud and in their
Own land and that of their fathers' fathers, strut off a rage,
Threaten, cry their grating grief. The old men grow weary
And the young men dream damage. Yet the presents
Before them turn their heads. "Will they regret selling          520
Their country for so little?" John, pensive, asks. I tell him
That men sell brothers for less, pawn their best-loved
For the glimmer of a coin. The Governor, though,
Recommends me to the protection of the Indians,
And Colonel Barnett, chosen to enforce the deal, asks us

To go with him to the villages. May turns the rust-
Colored hills green. The woods breathe winds at once
Filled with fragrance and warning. We see the true
Principles of vegetative life, the hills and well-grooved
Slopes, lovely lawns, meadows. Augusta, well-trimmed          530
And ordered, cannot hold my restless step. I am felling
My own interior forest with each step, and my presence
Is needed by the flowered fields I describe. I do not fear
What may occur. As a boy I could not wait to turn the page
Each day toward a wilder world. I step in the sweeting air
Of spring and see my first rhododendron, its rich jets
Of perfume filling the land around it. I would purchase,
So to speak, this cerulean *Pancratium fluitans*, spend
A day with *Philadelphus inodorus*, that pale embossed
Bloom I catch. But all that must be a memory. The flow          540
Of the river is behind us. John and I join it, the slow
Motion of chain-carriers, guides and astronomers laying
Notions of sweet stars and eclipse before us, fine light.

Summer flows over us. The air is insufferably sultry.
Now, we set off for the Buffalo Lick on the ridge
That divides the Savannah and the Altamaha, eighty miles
From Augusta. There, the surveyors will split into three
Companies to measure land with chains and clear eyes.
The second day, John says, "I see a village, don't I?"
And I say, "Men see many things before them in wild          550
Country that is not true—visions of heaven, citadels,

Ruins of the ancients." But we ride closer and I see he
Is correct: Wrightsborough, built by Quakers, settles
In the light, welcomes us with hospitality creed binds
Us to. We scout the soil and trees, write down clear
Lineages, depths, bark-types. Now we go through
Fertile plain and trees of vast growth. What trunks
Come before us! Like Greek columns they rise
In clarity, and we pace them, each more magnificent
Than the last. "No one would believe it," I say. One                    560
Of our surveyors nods, too stunned to say much more.

Tulip, black oak, liquid-amber: these trees soar
Thickly through the fields, a giant's garden, hot sun
Sharp. Father, Father, I would surely halt and repent
Of every sin to see such sights. Now before us also rise
Monuments of the ancients where the devoutest monk
Might genuflect, a stupendous conical pyramid, dew
Blazing on tetragon terraces, a sunken area quite near
Sheltering earthbanks, evidence. John kneels and finds
A hand-sized pottery shard, their clay-fired kettles.                   570
What strong nation danced here? We travel on, kneel
To collect flowers, and see mounds. Not infidels
Who built them, buckets of black soil, and each child
Helping to make holy sepulchers of the woodland eye.
Did the old ones cultivate these trees with their maize?
The delight of shell-bark hickory now softly creeps
Among amazement. Such domestic life within the wilds
Stops us: from these trees come hickory milk. Sedge
Burnishes the open spaces, but trees make this country

A kingdom of shade and usefulness. Four days farther,                   580
And we reach the Buffalo Lick, amazing to all senses,
Several acres near the Great Ridge. The earth as deep
As we could dig is clay-white with strong saline vapors.
I cannot taste salt but imagine its tart tang. Horses,
Horned cattle eat of it. We camp here, adjust and plan
The survey. John's eyes go wide. Now one man
Sets up surveying instruments, and suddenly an Indian
Appears and cries against this work. Only by hand

Can you find this thing, he signs. The instrument lies!
The Creek will be cheated of land! And, amazed,                                                   590
We find he is right, the surveyor wrong. Can you regain
The trust of one who thinks himself so badly cheated?
The Indians, who have come with us ready to turn back
Toward Augusta, and yet the others speak them out of it.
What trouble awaits us here? If the compass no longer
Works between men of honor, what will? I feel an edge
Of danger, look to the boy in my keeping and wonder

If the clouds in storms will fear the old thunder
When it comes. Finally, the chief set the wedge
Of fear aside and tells the men the stronger                                                      600
Of the instruments, the compass, is not truly fit
For a man's keeping. This worrisome and black
Time lifted, everyone settles. Rancor has retreated
Long enough for two companies to pack and strain
Toward unknown regions for surveying. Strike tents,
Un-hobble the horses, douse the last of the fires,
For we are bound north for the Broad River land
Along the Great Ridge. Now many rivulets bend in
Sweet succession around us, and Indian Olive, fans
Of *Trichomanes*, the elegant Indian Lettuce. Sand                                                610
Hills grow astonishing varieties of greenery. Courses
Of streams caress the root systems. Plumes taper
Toward the light; broad, lanceolate, obtuse, I keep
Reminding myself of my other world, but no fences
Hold here. I think of him, my first guide, my father.

*The mirror, that great deceiver, shows me a man*
*I do not know, somewhat like my father but not*
*Him, either. Can I find the boy who tramped among*
*The wild places in that great adventure from youth?*
*I cannot even keep the line-lengths straight as I speak*                                          620
*Those days aloud here in the greener glories of garden*
*And genuflecting earth. I feel the light sipping nectar*
*Of the next life as a hummingbird settles down upon*
*A spring-sweet blossom. I want to calm myself to see*
*The great Buffalo Lick, the tribes in their paint, glare,*

*And pride; I want to know why I never took a wife.*
*Keep telling yourself the same story, I think, repeat*
*It with the variations of old age until it then seeps*
*Into another's memory, as if he had gone south to sing*
*Of viburnum and azalea. Father, I want to know what*                    630
*You did not or at least one thing that I can then leave*
*To my friends and the fronds here before me. Can I be*
*A river of flowers floating through the countryside?*

*I rest in the shade now. Old men must dream a wide*
*Path to the past, or the lasting night rises like the sea*
*Over them, perpetual wonder but an eternal heave*
*Of regret and lost rapids from the wildest streams that*
*Any boy ever skipped. I tie up my bones with old string*
*That breaks at the slightest strain; into memory creeps*
*Amazing sights from the natural world. Botanical deceit*            640
*Enraptures me; I am a man with more than one life*
*To live and die. I want my remembrances to be spare*
*Some days and as exuberant as gardenias when I see*
*A summer garden before me. I have tried to be a son*
*My father would finally shed his nod upon. One acre*
*Is enough for one my age to stroll, but my burden*
*Is greater. I am the keeper of fern and mound and beak,*
*One who knows what is and what cannot be the truth*
*Of things. And just as the night sky is finely strung*
*With stars, I am netted by acceptance of my given lot.*              650
*Take my word on it, friend. Then take my offered hand.*

# CANTO TWO

*You who travel with me cannot know flowers*
*From the stamen out, nor do I, propped as I am*
*Among the daylilies and spicy air of Pennsylvania,*
*Wayfarer among my age and impatience to get on*
*With maps and compasses. You cannot go back*
*With me to the Mosquito River with my father,*
*Or know whom I knew: DeBrahm, surveyor*
*Of highlands and arrogance; Benjamin Hawkins,*
*A commissioner who kindly understood the Indians*
*And their abraded world; Old McIntosh, good soul*　10
*Among well-meaning men. I have not yet described*
*The lovely Broad River or an Indian spearing a trout*
*With his reed harpoon. I have days, years, to share*
*And yet how can I re-sleep the dream? For it seems*
*Like a drowsy humming-afternoon's adventure to me*
*Now, a tale told by children in a riverbank's idling*
*Time. Now I wonder of geography and place names,*
*What I may have mistaken, what days I have mislaid*
*In narrative. No matter. The trail is there if we are not.*

*In the acreage of each life there is an enduring plot*　20
*Of ground none else may enter. Before memory fades*
*Entirely, I want to tramp again through it, play games*
*With other boys, skip a board writ in sand, guiding*
*Me back and backward. And you, who hope to see*
*My life whole, I ask patience for my frosty dreams,*
*For the distance from limb to limb and den to lair.*
*I want to believe in the truth that I was then about*
*Marvelous things, to know how Spanish moss allied*
*With oak limbs to create all poetry, green whole*
*As all colors in the light. I want to see my mendicant*　30
*Days restored; to find joy and new eyes gawking*
*At that rivered land before me. I am no soothsayer.*
*I am a man of many steps, one who would bother*
*To kneel before a passionflower, slip it in my sack*
*For later times among my quiet-day specimens. Gone*
*From me is the strong stride of those hours, the mania*

*Of kingdoms, the princely petals, the words of lamb*
*And lion. I sit in my garden now and watch for showers.*

We camp by the river waters, and I leave to hike up                    40
A rocky slope and, reaching for a shrub, slip down
And tear it leaf by root. The air fills. The pure aroma
Of cloves and spicy perfumes surrounds me, and though
I've bruised my arm, delight packs me back to camp.
There I find my philosophical companion McIntosh
Sitting by waters on an eddy shoal, staring at small
Gravelly pyramids whose summits almost break
The surface of the flow. "Look, William, they're made
By small crayfish that swim nearby," he says. "This is
Their citadel, their fort for retreat from their enemy,                 50
The goldfish, where their young can come to hide
Before attackers draw close." We watch, see veteran
Crayfish venture out to hunt, and when they do, outlier
Goldfish flash brilliantly into the pyramids in search
Of young to devour. "The elders rush back to defend
Their own kind!" cries my friend. "So this kind of war
Must be continual." I rejoice in such a green delight.

And yet there is more: the broad streambed bright
With reflected liriodendron, hickory and oak, oars
Of seed pods paddling down-current where they blend                    60
With rhododendron shade. I thought we had a fat perch
Presented for dinner by an Indian who slogged the mire
And gave it to us. But it was the salmon-trout, the sun
Glowing orange on its speckled flanks. The fish died
After our friend stood beside the bank with reed-stem
Harpoon in his hand and thrust it sharply down. Splash
Followed splash until he pulled it in. He asked no trade,
Just gave it, fifteen pounds of fish, for supper. We take
Turns praising such ingenuity as we eat. Night birds call,
And we pause to listen to their brilliant melodies, a rush            70
Of notes octaves wide. Night comes and its old stamp
Of delight and fear, but we have earned our sleep due
To adventures today. From fire I see the stream foam,
The water putting on for sleep its lovely dressing gown.

I take my last sip from nature's bright and flowing cup.

We leave this place, and the land rises sensibly in hills
Then mountains, and each day our ride grows slow
And slower, and yet we do not care. *To be young*
*And slow is not the same as being old and deliberate,*
*I now know.* At the river our hunters bring venison                    80
And turkeys for a camplit feast; we speak the tales
Of old adventures with bright delight. Next day I see
What rocks and fossils I can find, and there are quartz
And mica, but no marble or limestone. We find here
Great piles of friable white stone in side-split masses
And made with pulverized seashells, as if by the hand
Of Neptune on a day of yawning creation. But buffalo
Are now gone as are elk, and yet the rattlesnakes spit
In masses like warnings from the Garden they inhabit.
Bears, panthers, bobcats, and wolves, though, wander                   90
Freely in these woods, and we hear their scream,
Count their stealthy paw-steps with morning's delight.
But now we must head back beneath the purchased stars.

We journey back to Savannah but a fever mars
My pace toward Darien. At first I feel a prickly fright
That comes with illness, then the shuddering dream,
The night sweats, the time to make my plans and ponder
If I will be given time for plans at all. I'm given rabbit
Roasted to perfection, strong meat from a cooking pit.
A grouse that once froze to nod his head and ruffle so                 100
No dread predator would come near goes cold, bland
On my plate. I think that fear and shame surpasses
Such a death, but I am too sick to care. I sip cool beer
When propped to see the window's light. A new torch
Comes in—it's night, I see—then I fade as if the old sea
Closes over me. I know now why men speak of whales
In their rush to understand utter interior darkness, one
Room where light is not remembered. I consider it
Rude when they say I'll recover. I am convicted, hung
By disease from a bed-cloth gibbet. Then I start to know             110
I shall recover, and I sit to touch the glow along the sills.

THE UNWILLING HERALDS ACT THEIR LORD'S COMMANDS,
PENSIVE, THEY WALK ALONG THE BARREN SANDS.

When well, with no clear trails to follow out among
The lilies and viburnum, I spend several lovely months
With my hollowed cypress canoe, poling waterways
For specimens: seeds, roots, and flowers. And more
(And many days the better) I sit in quiet places to draw
What I see before me. Clouds of tropical incense drift
Around as I sketch a bowl of petals blooming on a vine         120
Or watercolored pines along a slope. My brush blesses
A surface with shapes of green magnolias, and I fix
With my draftsman's hand images of *Myrica, Laurus,*
*Illicium,* and a dozen more. I step among the elegance
Of groves and meadows, stride the high, distant forests
With strength I can only claim by pencil-line or sable brush.
There comes a time when grandeur becomes the sublime,
And more than once I feel that power rush through me
Like a rich cascade of water powered by Nature's guile.
I lose myself mile by mile, stopping to freely feast           130
On sights never seen by an artist's shaping eyes.

I descend a peaceful stream, check out the prize
Of wildflowers. But I stay within my boat, at least
As happy as ever; I stroke the water mile to mile
Then stop and find a camping grove. I tie off to a tree
My canoe, ascend banks to an Indian field, a time
Of timeless sight in what's left of light and deep, lush
Shadows. The grass is succulent. Beyond is terraced
With swaying pines. I collect firewood at once,
Build a welcoming blaze, spread blankets. The forest          140
Cries aloud with diversity and all desire. Sticks
Flare in the camplight. Now come divine stresses
And sub-stresses from the poetry at Nature's spine,
And light from our old and honored sun begins to sift
Toward darkness. A mockingbird sings wild and flaw-
Less melodies. I have opened this land's new door
Into a world of green rooms. It seems beyond praise
This afternoon. The moon rises in eclipse. Just once

Let me feel full grace, the forest's warmest song.

My fire burns low. Blue smoke barely rises above                    150
The moistened embers. Thick clouds claim the stars,
And toward morning a storm begins to unfold along
The streambank's greenness. The river's surface
Roils reflections into strangeness, then the creatures
Race for caverns. From my tent-fly I watch it all
Explode about with utter unwriteable delight. Fear
Cannot find me. Orchestras of rain string the open
Places, making musical cutlery of sticks and bones.
The thunder moves east and ebbs. The white tide
Of lightning goes seaward past the rocks. A wind             160
Comes from the west, drying off the flowing hair
Of the woods around me. The water grows calm.
I need a small taste of that suffering violence
But not much. I am a flower seeker, and I need quiet
Places, shelter from moral uncertainties. Is virtue
A discoverable land? I only hope for cool release
From despair in time, the limits of human power.

The inhabitants fascinate me. In their strongest hour
The Creeks could have taken *armies*. The disease
Of travel has ended in their line. They came to new       170
Lands from beyond the Mississippi where a small riot
Of wilderness holds. On their journey they sensed
The horrors of suffering beyond pain. With no Psalm
To cheer them, they fought tribes, stalked lairs
Mad with claws and bloody teeth. When could it end?
They knew when they found the river and the wide
Plain, the shell-struck pasture and the field. Drones
Of insects must have lured them to a stop. Hoping
For calm and finding sickness must have come near
To ending them. Still, they issued an enduring call        180
To confederacy for allied tribes; they came, features
Untrustful but then accepting. There is a purchase
Of stability with freedom's loss, the way all strong
Men delight in survival. The English came with bars
Of gold, cinnamon, a conqueror's wariness of love.

As they moved east, English came, settling Carolina
And building Charleston on a peninsula between
Two rivers that set to sea. The Creeks sent deputies
To form alliances, and that treaty remains inviolable.
And yet these strong-faced bronzed men never cease          190
Warring against others: they slash out against
The Yamasees, the Ogeeches, and so many more
That one by one they vanish entirely or fade into
Other people with a sigh. They chase the Yamasees
To the gates of St. Augustine, howling mad delight
As they beg the Spanish for open gates. And they say
No, we cannot let you in, and slaughter begins, rivers
Foaming in blood, bright with slashed bone. I consider
This story of a people's sorrow and let it unsteady me.
It is time to leave this path, and I head back toward        200
Broughton Island since Cherokees in their current rage
Will not allow a man to ride northwest into Carolina's
Mountain ranges. So I turn to that earlier trail

With my father in Florida that year. I fail
To forget rich vegetation and the calm Designer's
Love of it all. So I resolve to turn my road's page
For Florida, write off to London. The gill and gourd
Will clap and clatter on horseback. The deep sea
On my left, I shall clop for that wild and widowing
Land; alligators' clacking roar makes me shiver            210
With fearful delight. I must say what's in my head,
Admit the journey begins with a child's sharp fright,
And know the divine monitor within me. No promises
Made are always kept; I am at whim and then send to
God my resolution for an unhurried life. It's 1774
Now; I set off for Florida, wading off into the dense
Undergrowth on short excursions; streams crease
The land with sunstruck delight. The air is violet
With evening sights as I take the help I please
To have from a vessel. Into such a sweet scene             220
I ride, isle to isle, until the shores of St. Simon's.

"I carry on quite the trade with the tribes
Hereabout," says James Spalding, the fine
Merchant. "Explore the breadth and depth
Of this island with sea on one side and a channel
On the other, barrier of ocean's storms to the interior
Land." And I do the next morning when the cool air
Bathes me like a shower of incense-laden suffusions.
What a wild and feathered land unveils its peacock
Fancies before me. I penetrate the grove of old oaks,          230
And suddenly a beautiful savanna opens like the sea,
Nearly two miles long, a mile wide, and on it graze
Sheep and deer, horned cattle. Beyond it grows
A wood of live oaks under whose shady boughs
An avenue opens to the former home of Oglethorpe,
Now owned by Raymond Demeré. After a brief visit
I head into the pine scruffage where the ground bristles
With shrubbery. *(Dear heavens, was I on the island
Then or on the coast? Is the year correct or have*

*I veered from truth? I do not know. I will save*                240
*The memory for what it might tell.)* My silence
Is awe: between dark forest and plains, whistles
Of bird species' sound. Lively breezes fly. What is it
To stop a traveler with more delight? No sculptor
Could carve it, no composer's melody can allow
The feelings I have. The wood-labyrinths enclose
The sky and sand-hissing sea. The soil has no clays
But is a mixture of grains and seashells. And so I see
In it the gorgeous lily with its delicate spadix; I coax
Up its span-wide leaves with my hand; I take my stock      250
Of *Salvia coccinea* and the evergreen shrub. Illusions
Of all kinds unfold as I rest in the shade. I compare
The plant's red berries and cerulean flowers to superior
Plants from Pennsylvania's hills and know the mantle
Of betterness is not for either. I must go and take a step
Back toward Florida now, but in my growing mind
I sense the flesh of time and how from it peace derives

A hold on men by the stalks the flower shoots.
What must I do in this untrammeled land? To hunt
The tendency of the world to divert itself, to be strong                    260
In color and leaf-form have been my hot blaze,
But is this the whole truth of it? My mind's
Life runs riot; the fleet deer and Risen Lamb
Speak to me in their tongues; all my time's days
Roll away like the Tomb's stone. In this town of age
As a young man, barely a boy, I do not throw lines
To tie up safely; I free-fall like the snow-curved sea.
And the rest of my flowered months and sweet nights
Together cannot equal this. Like a golden ghost
It will rise threatless in the night. I aim my new ship                     270
Into the heart of this drumming land, each raptor
Marking me as if I had its eyes, its brotherhood
With the landscape, its claws. So I wade thistles
And coneflowers and shrubs without halt. Howls
Cannot give me fear, for I can now outrun the grave.

I ride south in the surf. The ocean foam waves
Over my horse's slow feet. Sea life over-shawls
The sand: *Echinitis* and *Medusa*. Wind whistles
Through those with no life. (With driftwood
They are cast here from storms, prey, capture                               280
Of their seafowl beaks and claws.) The sand tips,
Too, the life from these beasts. I ride on and most
Surprisingly see an *allée* in the trees, warm flights
Of songbirds toward a welcoming house in the lea
Of the island's forest. I find a man who now reclines
On a bearskin under a tree, smokes a pipe. This sage
Salutes me: "Welcome, stranger! The dictates
Of Nature have welcomed me here to rest." A dam,
Just breached, could have no finer day than I find
Here. After the chase I stop in shade to raise                             290
A salute to greenery and shadow. "I'll have my strong
Servant bring us honey water to refresh us. I want
To welcome you. Step from your riding boots."

After a time I must leave, but this man stands
And begs me to accept more hospitality. I nod
And we sip honeyed water with brandy added,
And my body shudders. In the shadows of oaks,
Palms, we lay our rural table, dine on venison,
Sip the breezes from their groves. Our music flows
From the forest, love-lays of the painted nonpareil,                      300
The virtuoso mockingbird. Darts of hummingbirds
Throw themselves between us. They suspend in air
To sip nectar from jasmine, Lonicera, Andromeda.
From this garden of joy I see eastward the solemn sea,
Hear its roar upon my ears, the huge coming waves
One on one breaking down. The island trembles
At such a crush. I dawdle then have to leave
My friend and return. On my way I see all kinds
Of plants: the Cabbage Palm, Dwarf Saw Palmetto,
A hundred others. Now I know why: a large part                            310
Of this island was cleared and overgrown again,

And so I ride among the ruins of mansions, wind
Moaning through tabby-brick. Wrecked roads, heart
Of it all at Fort Frederica, now in shards; a few soldiers
Form the garrison, and they give only a few lively signs
They defend it. Once it must have hung with beeves
And game in its raftered halls. Now it gimbals
Like a failing top, glory gone. Sunlight laves,
Growing from crumbled walls, pomegranate trees,
Figs. Old buildings have found their *commedia*,                          320
Laugh to splinters in their lost repair. In *good* repair
I find only a few houses. There are but a few words
To speak. And yet from ruins can rise a new sail,
A map, desire to have the wind grow in our groves,
To spice the air with fruits. We are not innocent
In this damaged life; an alligator rises up and pokes
His grin at me. My horse's hooves are padded
From sound by sand. So time with his heavy sod
Muffles every voice, every reach of every hand.

Yet will I tell the truth of it, how the madness                                    330
Filled me in those lost times of my travel?
No one has ever asked why for forty years
I have hidden at Kingsessing, why, when Jefferson
Bid me join those explorers West, God knew
I could not—for my days in the South were filled
With fear and delight but also nights of destructive
Pleasures, chewing roots to give visions of a world
Starry as spouting rockets. I drank myself wild,
Filled native girls with my planting, and so lived
As animals live, destroying what through imagination       340
Might destroy him. Since, I have brooded on human
Weakness, the lure of all Nature. I let the world
Come to me and never went back and now cannot.
In great age, perhaps I must confess it, how sickness
Was not a grippe or rough catarrh but mornings
After sweatslick, lodge thrashings, when I dreamed
Dreams and visions, young man, old man, mad man.

Have I told you what has built inside me, land
Of potions, next-day women's salves, the gleam
Of light shattering a roof-top crack, warning                       350
Me not to die of light? Is the old thickness
Of fear evaporating from my reticence? I must blot
Out what nature turned me to. I see all unfurled
Like a banner, our circular tales, old fires fuming
With cleansing heat, the sharp sensation
Of desire, the need to see again the visions sieved
Through me like a weir; I saw all the stars piled
Together in one great blinding flash, curled
Galaxies with legendary dancers, and instructive
Adjuncts whispered by holy men who sat and willed           360
The creatures from beneath to rise and dance, be true
In my life! In those days not a single person
Who taught me this seemed stable. I shed tears
For the unexpected sensation, saw worlds unravel,
Found I had no regret or remembered sadness.

*How are you, old man who knows his passing*
*Time? I will tell it all, for soon I must lie asleep*
*Beneath the sod of summer days, in blossoms*
*On the flower-farm I carried on from Father's ways—*
*God, how I miss his step, my mother's gentle hand,*  370
*My brother's quiet words among the spores.*
*My* Travels *is the story that I wished had*
*Happened among the hot latitudes, but only part*
*Of them is true. I was in love with nature's pact*
*With soil and sun, strong as colts who kick*
*Up delight in springtime pastures of their years.*
*I was the chronicler of species, Linnæus close*
*To me, bringing music to the name of each tree.*
*But I was not that alone, for I felt death near me*
*Many times, saw it break like sea-wrack; saw girls*  380
*As mad for my touch as I was for theirs.*
*I drank madness, sat half-naked in a smoky lodge,*
*Chewed magic roots until visions came in the night.*

*The shame and fear drove me to a hermit's fright,*
*As if by forgetting it all I could somehow dodge*
*My shadow each morning. It comes in pairs*
*Of memories: girl and gill, heavens opened, whirls*
*Of galaxies, night skies blue as a rising sea.*
*The shame did not dress me, naked in the bee-*
*Bright humming dawns. And yet I knew God knows*  390
*All my scrivened ways, forgives them with His tears*
*Of ruptured clouds. And if my store of living wick*
*Flames down now, if there is no sermon or tract*
*To bring out that supposed wickedness, then my heart*
*May not need forgiveness. For in those sweetly mad*
*Times I was most alive. All the imaginary sores*
*Have healed themselves. So now you understand*
*Why I travel to my boy-self's stride, to wade days*
*Of happiness I felt, the sanctities and all the passions*
*That turned me rightfully raw. Now it is not so very deep*  400
*For me to find; truth is the true need for prophesying.*

So now I head into the dark temple of Florida,
With a good tide to swell me steadily south.
In the evening on St. Simons, I go ashore
With the Captain to hunt in the damp preserve
For venison, guns shouldered, men into battle,
The outcome unsure. "I think I see a deer!" cries
A crewman, but it's only a rapidly rambling
Raccoon, and we shoot three, and take carcasses
Shipward for a bake. Young, I can walk all day,                        410
Half a night, and next day am eager to raise sails,
Head for the rivers of Florida. Passing Cumberland
A schooner nears us, and passengers on the deck
Wring their rituals with obvious fear. "What news?"
The Captain shouts. A man cries, "Indians have
Plundered the store; we have escaped with our lives!"
We join the ship to learn particulars: the red men
Tore apart two trading houses but our men had hid
Their bounty at a distance, covered, with skins

To make discovery impossible. They had sense                          420
To take the goods from one post and move it ahead
For safekeeping, and with this managed to send
My chest, shipped ahead. The Captain describes
His plans. I say, "Then let me off here so I can drive
Inward to find my papers, which I cannot well lose
And still make my journey." We part, the wreck
Of my plans not able to hold me back. I cross a sand
Shore down Little St. Simons Island to a fort, the smells
Of that land around me, spiced intoxicants. I cannot stay
Long and am set ashore with a crewman, share caresses              430
Of winded wave, but soon we're tangled, ambling
Briar to briar, stumbling to the place. At evening, eyes
Sharp, we find the walls, but the commander has settled
On hunting and is out. The tired and indolent lad urges
Rest, but I press on to the beach, to its shelly shore
On which I collect novelties. I hear a gun's mouth
Shout fire, find a dying deer. This narrow corridor

Fills with blood. I do not see the man who has shot
This animal. To wait, to see, to humble myself
Before this scheme, I walk to a wind-driven dune                    440
And sit along the wedding sea-lace. Why have I come
Back to this land? Of what value can it be to write down
The names of plants, to claim ones no white man
Has ever named before? Do animals give other hoofed
Species their own names? Does each have a different
Name for azalea and for rose? Names for each singular
Thing would arise in a biblical chorus, the loudest among
Them win the day. What a strange way for each creature
To claim its name. Soon, the house's captain walks up
With a slain buck on his strong shoulders, he hails me,            450
And we stride, meat dripping down his back, to the fort,
Where we dine. The next morning, he takes us across
To Amelia, and we walk through a forest of live oaks
Dripping moss like rain on every limb. Past a creek
And through a salt marsh, we find the squat plantation.

The agent, Mr. Egan, welcomes us kindly. All creation
Stuns the eye. He shows me the damp fields by creeks
Stretching out before his upturned palm. The hummocky
Soil delights all plant-kind: potatoes, corn—toss in
Every esculent vegetable known. On horseback I escort           460
Him over great stretches island, circling fine mounds, lea
Of the Ogeeches, I believe, and in these anted cups
Their bones lie bent, sleeping, bowls with fine features
And designs, honoring them to rest. I listen to the sung
Solemnities of graves, but it's only wind wringing
Out the moans of red humanity. These men's suffering
Touches me; I imagine them in the winter, gently roofed
By lodge and forest canopy. I also see and hold by hand
The ravages of a caterpillar that strips from the crown,
The limbs so stricken they are deaf and dumb,                      470
All leaves of young trees. "Come with me at noon
And we will head for St. Augustine so you can find help
For your journey up-river in that land always so hot,"

Says Mr. Egan, and I assent. We pass out of the seacoast

Islands of Georgia where I have spent these rich months,
And I recall three weeks' illness, and the sweaty terrors
When I thought death found me. I see before me the girl
Who wiped the haste from my forehead, her full breasts
As she leaned down, the trembling desire that wracked
And nearly wrecked me. Also before me, are the flowers          480
In spring thousands, the Buffalo Lick, the trading houses,
The slip of sandy coast and the hunter coming home, deer
Thrown about his burly shoulders. And the fish species
I could count: sea-trout, skipjack, flounder, whiting,
Grouper, and those insatiable cannibals, the shark
And great black stingray. And in the lagoons we saw
Oysters and shrimp, crabs, and tender white clams
Whose roasted flesh filled us with such fine delight.
And yet beyond that is the sulfurous mystery of swamps,
The black water barely flowing, and the fear of being lost       490
That haunts me even now as I press farther south by south.

We set sail in a masted pleasure boat. There is no drought
In an ocean, and yet there is: a storm there has its cost
To fresh water. Just so, I cannot see how I might jump
Across danger when I reach on this trip to dark sights
In Florida. Four slaves are here to row the waves that slam
Us if our sails lose wind. I ache for the freedom that gnaws
At them, or must. I am wind-chaff; they have the spark
Of humanity that I possess and yet lie in bonds, sighting
What they can never own. One looks at me with easy                500
Eyes that hide his sorrow, and I ache. I see they fear
Punishment or death enough to slave away. One drowses
At the rail, dreaming of his lost dark country, bowers
Of flower-bright delight. Pelicans bob the air, and *crack!*
Mr. Eagan shoots one, and we bring it aboard to test
Its design, for such an ungainly bird tends to unfurl
Amazement in us. I see that my assumptions are errors:
Its wingspan is the main element of its lift. It hunts
Fish as we hunt it: aim, trigger, pull. At the most,

It is an ugly bird, and yet I find myself in admiration          500
For the holding pouch of a mouth, its bill bent inward

Like a scythe. Now evening, we land on the mainland,
And I walk off my sealegs like a toddling child, wild
For the stabilities of soil and stream. A high promontory
Covered with orange trees projects into the sound,
And we pitch our tent beneath the shelter of old palms,
Live oaks, and Sweet Bays. Now is time for a seaside
Feast, and we have the sumptuous range of seafowl
Shot during the day: snipe, willet, curlew, sandbirds.
We bake excellent oysters, which we find in abundance,     520
Heaped near our mooring spot. "Here is Capsicum,"
I say, "which will serve as our pepper." We also drink
From a well of fresh water dug there in the grove amid
A stand of myrtles. "What a fine feast," my friend speaks
Too soon. For now a whining hell of ten mad thousand
Mosquitoes screams down on us, stinging every man
Again and more. Crocodiles roar with a stunned fury.

Seafowl bob in hundreds for a handout. A white jury
Of accusing wings judges us, herons, curlews, pelicans,
All on hand for handouts. They are many and aroused;     530
They cover trees as far as we can see. Their beaks
Call us Inquisitor, unrighteous. They are not hidden
Even though roosts are in a hundred islets, salt sinks,
Or lagoons. As I eat I see the undergrowth with dumb
Admiration for texture and tautness. I remember once
With my father seeing swamps of many insect herds,
But nothing like this. The Palmetto Royal holds the howl
Of a hundred birds each; it has a thorny crown to deride
Any holy head I can imagine. I give admiration's alms
To its flowers and fruit. How I want to catalog the round     540
Trunks or stems, study this one plant for months in glory,
Give it the king's attention it deserves. No. I am a child
In what I know. My Linnæus begs me turn my hand
To other things. The mosquitoes grow mad; I am stirred
To swat what I would study in the arbor's roaring ovation.

Three days pass, and we come to the cow-ford, public
Ferry over the St. Johns River, which is a mile wide
At this place. Mr. Eagan finds me a sail boat at a huge

Indigo plantation near the ferry, and I set mast to see
St. Augustine as the first stop on my interior journey                          550
Through Florida's wildlands. April with her interior
Idea of looms and blossoms, swells over me, crisp
Nights, strongly warm days. The young fellow who
Was to come with me has now, alas, gone back,
Fear of the coming unknown a worry to him as it is
A light to me. This restless spirit of curiosity propels
Me into one land's liquid heart; here I trace patterns
Of the Almighty Creator and hope that I can give
To my country new species of landed animals, plants
Of all colors and comforts to the eye. How are things                          560
In themselves useful? I beg the powers of this land
To unravel their messages to me. I cross the river
To a high promontory of woodland, step out to see

What grows here. With my neat and light fusée
I am well protected as I stride among a sliver
Of slight laurel, majestic live oaks, and palm fans
Waving to me high above. Around them rings
Of orange trees grow in full bloom, make air dance
With rich fragrance. Now I set sail again and live
With the wind as my sole companion, and Saturn                                 570
In the near-night sky glows like a wild eye, sails,
Too, through the heavens. Now there is a mist,
But soon it turns to storm, and I must haul and hack
Firewood on the shore as the thunderclouds, blue
To black with jagged shells or bright electric disks,
Slam me down into my sail. I see who is superior
Now, who rakes the sky to plant a hailseed, burning
With fecundity and light. Beneath the sail I kneel,
Its length thrown over a fallen oak, spread out two
Skins on which to sleep, build a fire to one side.                             580
I sit the storm and wonder what will now come of it.

Rain ebbs. Lightning still explodes stars, hides moon
And memory, but I am not afraid. I slowly rise from
My pretended tent and roam around the campsite, hear
The single echo of a gunshot: it is morning now and gold,

Cerise striations rouge the early lovely light. I decide
To hike toward the shot and soon find myself along
A well-worn forest trail toward all mystery. An Indian
Appears before me on a crossing path, turkey cock
Slung over his strong shoulder. He smiles and waves          590
At me and stops. "Good morning, my friend," he says
In perfect English. "It is well, brother," I offer in return.
He follows to my camp, tells me he is a game hunter
At the next plantation, offers to take me there to meet
The owner. "I would like to visit, but my small boat
Must be safe." So he helps me drag it onto dry land,
And, fusée propped upon my jouncing shoulder, we
Walk the half-mile to the house. The owner, so kind
And civil, is an instant friend, and he sends slaves

To haul my vessel 'round the point for fresh staves          600
And other nailed repairs. "Stay with me for wine
Three days," but I can stop for only one. Now free
Of the duty to repair the ship, we set our hands
To touch the richness of his orangery. I can't hope
To describe their heavy golden fruit, ripe wheat
In a ripe wind. No, *more*. Garden, lawn, too, saunter
To the water around his house. Indigo grows, burns
Delight into my eyes as it spreads in parallel bays,
Now already six inches up. Marshall (his gaze
As firm as his handshake) gives me so much stock            610
To take I am humbled. After dark, I cannot send
Myself into dreams and wander his plots, a song
Of swallows guiding me root by leaf. I have spied
Such verdure before but not with such ripe old
Ardor and order as this. I would be vegetative seer
Of all this. I feel the lilting crop of insects stun
My senses. I am always leaving love too soon.

Now it is morning and my time to head interior.
Lesser men have lost their lives inside a mad desire
For freedom and solitude. Who am I to half-believe         620
I can sail my small and sinkish ship to unseen harbors
Where new species wait? Will I find myself awakened

With my leg half gone to crocodile or swamp panther,
Blood irrigating the sweet riot of tangled runners?
Pointless musing. All my life has pointed toward
This exaltation of my desire for being calmly lost
In the deepest solitary world. I stand on the shore.
I see the river run toward or away from my bow.
I almost taste the moment of my own life as it
Seeps out, and I feel eternal sleep slip over my back          630
With its dreams of all my long days. Yet no:
I would find adventures for twenty men to retell
Around their old men's fires three dozen summers
Hence. I mean to live each moment of my life
Now, through all my sight, touch, taste, or smell.

Let me see the setting sunlight as petals in hell
That drop crimson blooms like edges of a knife.
Let me hear the strident shriek of crows, hummers
Buzzing on a flower for its opening sweetshell
Wonders. Show me where I must tramp to know          640
Exotic ways and wisdom in a stalk. I need to track
Myself path to path to see if I will waste in a fit
What has been given to me. I need to know how
Calmness comes and if it stays deep in my core
All this life. From hottest days to deepest frost,
I am the Flower Seeker, and my adventure sword
Is the drawing pencil in my hand. All wonders
Will reveal themselves to me: every answer
Will shock me to delight. No Nature has forsaken
Me yet or will it ever. Beneath the arched arbors          650
Of the woods, I will find the spirits to relieve
My troubled mind. I will feel the welcoming fire
Into the depth of all that is or is not serious.

# CANTO THREE

*ow in the profound darkness of age, when I*
*Read the lies I wrote in my* Travels, *now when*
*I see before me the mad memory of dark water*
*And solitary nights of blood and mad howling,*
*I want to lie down there again and feel that old*
*Emptiness of skulled, tearing flesh, my boat on*
*The shore while I sit in the camp and hear through*
*The bleak filter of an insect's wrath an inner*
*Wildness to come. Squalls arise. Clothes torn*
*Off, arms cut up to bright ribbons in my screaming.*                    10
*Where is that old traveler now? Where is my*
*Astonishment at the marvel before me today?*
*Can I be the boy who sat in my boat and sailed*
*Up-river in that Florida light to sip the wind*
*And not fear blooded teeth come to cut up,*
*Cut out my heart, eyes, hopes, for love or*
*Fear of lovelessness? If sky can scare a bird*
*To fall, wings into a pond, I can live this old age.*

*I have come far to stand in the sun of this garden's*
*Old friendship.      I know, though, a course beyond*      20
*All flowers,        the traveler's ice, wild-man's eye.*
*I must face         into it without turning. I must*
*Open all            darkness into light. I was such*
*A kind and          gentle boy, so how could I find*
*Myself in a         kingdom of castled moss and*
*Panther prowl      in those days? I look now in the heart,*

*The heart of that lovely nightmare with fear beyond*
*Any sure knowledge that has found me through life.*
*And so I sail on in that past,* with many fine bottles
Of rum procured from Mr. Marshall, sailing alone up                    30
That river toward imagined light. I want to believe in
The steady gale that pushes me along the wide river.
A thunderstorm has purified all the air with its bright
Electric fists that hammer clouds in great black anvils,
Drenching the land with drowning shots of lead rain.
Scum, putrescent, pearl-like, rises from the bottom

Of the river and floats on the mirrored surface, pale
As a dead man's face. I study the banks of the river as I
Float its oozy bottom near the eastern shore. Night now,
I find the plantation of a kind farmer, take quarters                    40
For the night. Odd to say, I knew him in St. Augustine
And so ask of the hostilities they say now flames
Between the Indians and white men on that river
So fearful have I now become to die in a shadow land.
"The danger is real against those who go to the interior
Uninvited," he shrugs. "So keep your eye well open
For the shaft that seeks your heart." It is the Seminoles
Who are fighting back against the traders, not to steal
Goods but to warn them away from this shuddering land
Of their ancestors. I spend only one night and in morning    50
Head up-river once more, pressed by fear, looking out
For Fort Picolata. When I see it, I heave to, bank my boat,
And scramble out to see it is ungarrisoned, falling apart
Seam by seam. This deserted square of walls and their
Thirty-foot-high tower, alone and becoming overgrown
With green wilderness, frightens me. The stone here is
Reddish, like old, dried blood. In fear, I re-board my boat,
Take a long drink of the trader's rum, and sail on up
The river through millions of insects that rip at my face
And hands. How does one ascend a river that branches       60
Everywhere and nowhere at once? With gravity, swarmed
By Ephemera, small insects continually emerge

From shallow water near    the shore. Resurrection
From their deep begins      early in the morning,
Ceases after sun has        risen through the arch
Of old trees. Now,          though, with evening
Come again, clouds          of innumerable millions
Swarm in the still air,     descend to the surface
Of the river, commend       their eggs to the deep.
Larva, nymph, fly: this old  circular meal for birds,         70

Frogs, and fish is a great tumult, like souls swarming
In Purgatory, mad for ascent, fearing much worse.
It is evening now, and I make harbor alone in a small

Lagoon on the west shore. If fear did not come in his
Shattering carriage, I would traffic in orange ecstasies,
Beneath live oak and magnolia, above the great river.
Now the sweet involving melodies of the birds rise
Over me, and I build a strong fire with mounds of fat-
Lighter and deadfall. Suddenly over the green, deep
Rustling clouds of insects swarm. Awful procession,          80
They volunteer for destruction as soldiers always must,
Rank on rank into the artillery of a thousand wings
And amphibian shrieks. And yet they seem so tranquil
That I wonder if this is how we should welcome our
Own deaths: in slow majesty and without the terror
We ascribe its rapacity. What eye can trace all this?
They bound and flutter in the perfumed air. Do they
End with peace, joy, and love as I suppose they might?
There is beauty in the briefly transient, a winged
Magnificence that daily goes unnoticed by a man          90
Who swats down their stinging last pathways.
To my eye the sunset procession is awesome, awful
In our human judgment, but if they do not understand
What waits, they whirl like Paolo and Francesca
In the windless rapture of mating, decked in invisible
Wedding-chamber clothes. One eye can't trace any
Individual among them; one eye can't see that each
Year more of these winged beings live than the whole
Race of mankind since the Creation. And that number
Is but what I see from the bank of this river as night          100
Comes. I tremble, am rapturous by unnoticed turns.
They are more wonderful and more delicate, just as
Complicated as the most perfect human being, and
We doubt this at our mounting peril. For some day
This world shall no longer be the primitive river,
And the penitent bay: it will rest toward bright ruin,

And these          lovely lilting wings will be swatted
Down by          our own vanity. For most of the year
They are          no more than mud-buried grubs,
Scarcely          locomotive, each larva in its own          110
Narrow,          solitary cell, monks who study

The old text       of water and silted soil. How
Magnificent they     lie waiting for the brief hatch
Of a brief humming    lifetime above the fast flow.

Man is nothing, I argue, as I sit in the oncoming night
Listening to the natural contempt of a billion tongues
Within the slipstream of my flames. I feel the empty
Ache of loneliness. I drink three quick sips of fiery
Rum, let myself be carried into an unsteady landscape
Of terror and riot; I let my bleakest thoughts take hold             120
Until I shudder with the deepest ache a man can bear.
No man speaks of such nights in his own recorded
Travels, but mark them well, my new companion,
For in the eye of our hardest fears lies the ancient pit
Of despair and occluded vision. If man is nothing,
Then what can I be? I roar the obvious answer, scream,
Drink, rip the sleeves of my covering garment, weep
With mad irresolution. Now I thrash into the hacking
Brambles, letting them tear bloody walkways, rivers
In the spring soil of my arms and legs. I fall and laugh         130
At the recoil of a plump snake; its ribbon tries to wrap
Me like a birthday parcel for all its Medusa young.
Morning awakens me on my bedroll. I sit up, stare
About me, head billowing with regret, arms and legs
Scratched but clotted, and beads of carmine blood,
Hard as a king's jewels scatter on the backs of each
Hand. I search my body for the double penetration
Of serpent's fangs, find nothing. I sit up laughing,
Go to the edge of the river to wash my face and sip
Off my human weakness. I find, to my astonishment,          140
That I have rested quite well, and the abundance
Of Nature sings its morning songs: wild turkey cocks
Saluting each other from the sun-brightened tops
Of cypress and magnolia, the social sentinels of forest
And stream. Dozens on dozens gather in the piercing
Shout for morning's familiarity. Now, with the sun
Rising higher, they come down to Earth, and the males
Strut and dance round the coy females, and the forest,
Deep with magnificence, resounds with their cries.

I listen for messages but cannot understand it now.　　　　　150

All morning, the wind howls　　so greatly I must
Stay in port, for it would　　surely rip apart
My single sail if I head　　out in the water.
So I take up my time　　by studying oak,
Palm, *Quercus dentate*,　　all manner of trees
That bow down, vassals　　in the ripe wind.
The wood of the live oak is　　incorruptible,
Ever green, and filled with the　most unbelievable

Bounty of its fruit. The acorn is small and sweet,
Agreeable to the taste when roasted. Indians get　　　160
From it a sweet oil with which they cook hominy
And rice, and they roast them in hot embers to crunch
As we do chestnuts. I finish my day's studies, roll up
My blanket, clean camp, and as a clear evening has come,
I prepare my Quaker hands for sailing. And I know
This land; not far from Picolata is the site where I tried
My early hand as a plantation man, where I continued
My serrated failures in all business ventures, felt a clear
Contempt for money and loved only the heat and joy
Of this greening land, the voice of Nature speaking　　170
To me like a great Mother, clear and prescient, warm
As honey each time she pulled me to her comfort.
I remember Father's rough corrections, sacrifices
So I could live off the land. But what I really knew
Then and now is to live with it, to break off each
Fact as a geologist cracks shale with a sharp crack
Of his hunting hammer. So I travel north from here,
South again, working, hiding, awaiting the one man
Who will rescue me into the green escape I seek.
And that man is Fothergill, who buys my time to see　　180
The world before me clearly. It is for him I collect my
Specimens, draw the flowers and creatures that creep
Along the river courses. My counselor and my keep.
Now, not long before eventide, I set sail, but only
To move from this buggy harbor across the incredible
River to its eastern shore, where I pitch my tent, go see

What is before me before darkness comes. An ample
Field stretches uplight for botanical observations,
And it is high enough from which to see the great span
Of the river one way and the other, see the gloried palm,                    190
The laurel with its dark green leaves, silvered over
With milk-white flowers. I believe one could see them
From a mile or more. The laurel magnolia is beautiful
And tall, formful, fragrant, and full of bright flowers.

Most astonishing          are the grape-vines, twisted
And baroque,                 so large one might imagine
They could                    pull down these huge trees
With force                     unlike anything yet seen
In the old                      grasping of the world for
The odd                         violence of their intentions              200
Which I                          make up entirely in my
Mind. These vines seem to tie the trees together, as

Characters entwine a story to keep it afloat. The canopy
Of these vine-tied trees is enchanting, raising what seem
Garlands and festoons to some unknown celebration
Among them. Long moss drips down from limbs, twigs,
Feathering every tree with its own estimable beard. In
Time as it grows, the moss spreads in intricate patterns
Everywhere with its hands waving in the wind like
Streamers, the bulk on one tree more than several men                     210
Could carry. When it is fresh, cattle and deer will eat it.
Men stuff their chairs and mattresses to filling with moss.
I hear it can even, when wet, be twisted into ripened ropes
Strong enough to haul a horse from a deep mud-hole.
I exult in the products of all Nature now, the sharp sun,
The lilt of musical wind, the fragrance that lies perpetually
Along the edge of the river and the Earth. What am I,
Who am I, to have this bounty for my eye alone? If joy
Taken too far is madness, then I am mad with my lust
For the beauty of green, the silver stripe of hanging moss.                220
I build a fire. I set up camp as I had across on
The other side of the river. How can a man go
Such a short distance and yet go so far that he sees

A different world in the span of one day? I sit here
And do not fear the roaring of crocodiles as it begins,
The thumping rage for mates and food. I hear them
Leap from the banks, dive down deep like a horse
Falling from a high dock. A million frogs cut bright
Patterns across the reptile's world. I am the only man
Alive on Earth, young and strong, meeting each sun          230
Muscle to muscle, each threat with the strong club
Of myth. Nothing, I half believe, can harm me, not even
The lashing crocodile or the swamp panther coming
Down in ribbons on my back. Where else in America
Is there man or woman who silently howls with me
In such ecstasy? Each night I ask for the vision to return,
And because it rides with me like a fine companion,
It arises once more and shows me dreams on dreams.

Wind comes. Little turtledoves treat themselves
To the                    *Herculis.* The clouds          240
Of                         mosquitoes part like
The                        Red Sea, pass west
To                         the river's other
Bank.                      I lie on my blanket
And feel                   the sifting of dreams.
How can I deserve such a sweet ache in the bones?

Morning rises rose and cool, and I set sail early, glide
Along the river's mirror. And as I ride, I study the world
Before me, seeing first vast quantities of an aquatic plant,
Lovely *Pistia stratiotes*, which clumps in floating islands    250
And drifts where the current takes it. They form fine
And delightful green plains on the water itself, several
Miles in length and in some broad-banked stretches
A quarter-mile wide. They drift on long, fibrous roots
That descend to the muddy bottom of the rushing river.
Each full-grown plant resembles garden lettuce, though
In color slightly more yellow. As I sail, I begin to imagine
Trees on these floating islands and in them flowery plants,
Weather-beaten trees, alive with herons, snakes, otters,
Frogs, curlews, and jackdaws. And above the islands          260

I dream thick pillowed clouds on which the ancient gods
Lean to look down on the wild world of their supposed
Creation. Old stories! What contempt we pour on them
And yet they seem to bear some consequential truth.

So the ship went on through dark waters,
very swiftly, with the goddess Athene,
in the likeness of old Mentor,
guiding it, and with the youths listening to
the song that Phemius the minstrel sang.

The earth rises gradually on the river westward,               270
Grand and sublime by ridges one behind the other,
Lifting the distant groves up into the sky. Trees
Are high-tipped, those I have named much before,
Plus the hickory and the towering *Fagus sylvatica*.
Now I sail through the edge of deeper swamps,
And I see the knee-knobs and tall trunks of old
Cypresses with their flat tops, and the canopy
They hold up there makes it seem I have come
Into a green plain lifted up and then supported
By columns in the air, like some natural Greek               280
Temple but one that keeps growing year by year
For the mutual delight of fowl and cur. Who am I
To judge anything upon this Earth? How can I
Say that this tribe's value is less than that one's
Rich history? I think of the Creeks and Seminoles
And wonder who is the master of this world;
Surely not a skiffing man with such pale skin.

Parakeets flutter      in the tops of the broad
Cupressus,                 delighting as they shell
The balls,                   that seed being their               290
Favorite                    food. Green-yellow,
Green-                       yellow they whip
And                          whirl with their beaks
Open for                   the taste of fine seed
As a man sits             for the breaking of bread.

And this tree also makes a fine canoe, boards,
Shingles, every beam and joist for buildings
Timbered up in frame. I have seen cypress trunks
Twelve feet in diameter—giants stamping through
The shallow swampy water where the parakeets 300
Sing their green cantatas to the morning and night.
I have seen the world in its chiefly naked splendor;
I have seen the world in the disinterested spectacle
Of blood-battles and slow bone and blood consumption;
I have seen the world sweetly wet with rice farms;
I have seen the world conspire to whisper my name;
I have seen the world as all water, holding me up
To caress me as I glide along its sky-filled surface;
I have seen the world Eden-new, Roman-ancient;
I have seen the world slow as the sun on the backs 310
Of plodding tortoises in the heat of the hottest day;
I have seen the world swift with blinding wings;
I have seen myself caught in a net of sparking stars.
I sail round a broad bend and see an Indian village
Before me, high on a fine bank above the thought
Of flood. Ten dwellings front the water, their street
Behind. Boys naked to their hips froth and splash
In the river's edge, unconcerned that some beast
Might rise gnashing from the humps and hollows.
What bronze joy! Several of them stand and fish 320
With cane poles and threaded lines. There: One
Cries aloud and lifts up a fattened bream: dinner
For two. Smaller children step in their sweet glee
And shoot with bow and arrow the small game
Of frogs and toads. *Aie! Aie!* When they see my
Sail, the children flee to the village women who
Hoe their corn. But the older ones, sentinels to
Come, stand their space and wave to me, fishing
Rods temporarily dipped down in mild salute.
Above them, the gray-hairs sit or lie on spread skins 330
Laid in the shade of oaks and palms. They rise

To worry, then          see they do not
Have to                    worry at all, for

I sail                          onward in my
Fine                           delight to see
What                           lies around the
Next bend                      for my discovery
On such a warm                 and lovely, lifting
Day of discoveries. I sail past their orange grove

And note how carefully they prune their trees, keep          340
The ground beneath them airy, clean and open.
And we still persist in calling such people savage
While we war hut to hut ourselves? Look at all
Their industry in the vast garden now: potatoes,
Corn, beans, squash, and melons. I even see
Tobacco sufficient for their entire population.
Not an hour's sail ahead I spy a town before me:
Charlotia. The current here is hard against me,
So I tack it, bow my back against the strongest
Waves. It lies up on a bank twenty feet above me          350
And the shores are shelly with the artifacts of small
And large creatures whose houses they once
Served to be. The geologist in me marks sea-sand,
Long striated masses of hard rock made entire
Of earth-bound shell so that it weighs itself
To stone. A Mr. Rolle, as I recall, was the master
Of this town, given forty thousand acres from
The Crown to grow and farm. But when he came
With a hundred families from England, disaster
Awaited him; too much parsimony, illness, death,          360
A mind changed by such a pretty bluff, the nearness
Of the capital St. Augustine—all conspired to earn
Desolation of this ruined village. As the fevers grew,
One by one the people sought finer sites in Florida
And Georgia. Now the last habitations molder down
To soil again. All that's left of any use is the master's
Mansion house which serves as home to an overseer
And his family. Not far away there is also a blacksmith
And his family. And that is all left of what was to be
A mighty town with streets and produce they could          370
Ship upon the great river-highway to the sea. All is

Grave and gross now; the tender and the strongest
Are gone or lie dead beneath the sandy slip of soil.
I can barely say the name—*Charlotia!*—without
A deep melancholy coming over my sailing shoulders.

And yet a mighty town      of aboriginals lived
Here in some past,      as I can tell from
The high mounds      and midden shells,
Great tumuli along      the river's course.
We all are heading      for that same fate,      380
White or sun-tanned      red, to the great city
Of the long night beneath      what we once thought
To be our greatest accomplishment, our own wealth.

A few people tell me how close I now have come
To the remote island seven miles farther up where
Traders and their goods are hidden. With set sail
And fair wind I loft onward, tacking channel to
Narrower channel and by some hunch of good luck
Come to the right place; and yet I would have run
Right past the landing if its sentinels had not seen      390
Me blowing up the current like nearly foundered
Flotsam. Noting I am a white man they hail me
And I strike sail and come-to. Their encampment
For trading is in an impenetrable thicket, but they
Have already moved their goods to a new house
Farther up-river on the Indian shore. They knew
Precisely where to find my chest, shipped down
In full faith of its course back to me; they will
Send it on to the new storehouse. And I slide on
Into the wild land through unknown channels      400
Where few men have set eyes or their sails.
*Now in my elder mind I have set off into deep*
*Florida, but in truth I am an old man; what is*
*Man that Thou art mindful of him? In my life,*
*My distress, I cried unto the Lord and he heard me.*
*Now I must come into the days of my lost madness,*
*That time which no man knows, not even Father*
*Now with his Father in heaven, not brother or*

*Sister, friend or colleague. Things fall out of*
*Order: cross-beak,* Grus alba, *McIntosh, palmetto,*     410
*Prim priests, and conjurors. Wherewithal shall*
*A young man cleanse his way? With my whole*
*Heart I have sought Thee, but now, vision all*
*Internal, my eyes bled of sight, who are you*
*Who stands in my way? Blessed art Thou, Thou*
*O Lord: teach me Thy statutes. Or can it be*
*Statuary marble I recall? When I fell from this*
*Tree before me those years back, when I broke*
*Myself into bones and memory, I spent a year*

*In the solitude of      my wreckage. I ask*     420
*How it must fit,        this tale of my wandering*
*Years, how           can I understand what*
*Drove me             into that old world of*
*Quiet days           alone in the realm where*
*Nature holds          her unsentimental dances*
*Each night and        flashing teeth rip off days*
*As age tears away the remembrance of all sight?*

*I was an exile driven by fate in my wars, and the*
*Man in me leaped from bank to bank, shells*
*Spangling the watercourses in their pink splendor;*     430
*Cruel Juno's unrelenting rage warred me hot*
*With true delight; he brought his gods home to*
*Latium, and that, too, was my hurried destination.*
*I knew, even then, that I was destined to live out*
*My drumming days alone; I knew that the poet*
*Of flowers cannot live in the world of commerce*
*And still rise to the rich aroma of Oconee Bells*
*That dip down in the Carolina sunlight like a*
*Convocation of all warmth. Who was my own*
*Penelope? To whom was I coming home to bring*     440
*The samples that I did not hold for Fothergill?*
*The brush and pencil wandered page to page,*
*Prophet and flower-seekers themselves, and I*
*Let them line off that botanical majesty, the South-*
*Ward course that I was meant to sail, the sheer*

*Madness of green that buoyed me on and onward.*
*I was a Quaker but, my friend, who was with me*
*Except the Flower Seeker himself? When I lay*
*Writhing in my hermit's madness, I could believe*
*That God was in my harpooned heart or hot hands;*      450
*I was more alone than any traveler has ever been.*
*And yet I was not rebuked for it. Grace to wander!*
*Now, though, I walk slowly with my walnut cane*
*Through the Bartram Garden here along the broad*
*Schuylkill, a new nation like a Trojan wind at my*
*Back. Is there meaning in spring as there is in our*
*Inner seasons? I want my father back, friend, want*
*His voice and his calming hand, even his warnings*
*To me that my plantation days were surely numbered.*
*Father, fathers, forgive us. This very morning I read:*      460
*"And I will leave thee thrown into the wilderness,*
*Thee and all the fish of thy rivers; thou shalt fall*
*Upon the open fields; thou shalt not be brought*

*Together, nor gathered: I have given thee for meat*
*To the*                      *beasts of the field*
*And to*                 *the fowls of the heaven."*
*This*                      *prophecy against Egypt*
*Blinds me*             *into recognition; Ezekiel,*
*Wheel me into*         *word past Chapter Twenty-*
*Nine of my own*        *life. Condemn me for what*      470
*Sins tempted and took me, what flesh took from me.*

*I rest in this chair. A glassy feeling of fragility has*
*Come into my chest. I tap it in the rhythm of my heart,*
*Which is trying on a slowing gallop for its last hours.*
*How can we believe that the world will go on when we*
*Cannot? How can our friends and family walk on*
*As if the trust we bear in the world has not broken*
*Into dust? Do not let me die just yet, you mountain*
*Gods, you river deities; do not let me pass beyond*
*That high hill overlooking Keowee where such green*      480
*Delight came stamping with pleasure in the young days*
*Of my dance. We will always be boys in our minds,*

*Strong hearts, curious listings, potsherds and parakeets,*
*Muskets and mimosas, being found and being so lost*
*That any trail is a trail in but not a trail heading out.*
*I come into the slow glen that has no crossing. I sit.*
*I wait but I cannot wait it out. I am your long-lost*
*Twin in the sequence of two dissimilar lives. See it:*
*I am the Flower Seeker. I was the Flower Seeker.*
I rest a few days, now, at Spalding's Lower Store                    490
And watch the marsh birds, hear their banking cries,
Their invitation to the deeper sanctuaries of all Nature.
My spirits and my strength have run out and must be
Refilled, a well after too much use. We talk, we boat
Into the maze between the boggy islands, hear the roar
Of alligators in audible letters to a mate. I have seen
The Indians and now come to understand the richness
Of their ways, how they cannot be like us or somehow
"Civilized" into field and farm. They are kind parents,
Laughing children who stand in the water's lacy edge            500
With more delight than any child of my own lost race.
Summer's heat flows down my neck and chest. I pulse
With need. I have seen species without a place marked
In any scholar's list and have described them, drawn faces
And fins, pistil and stout stamen as my drawing hand
Flowers in my much-marked-up journal pages. *Come*
*Back with me. Come with me to that unsubtle Eden.*

Here is the map I make. Help guide me on the course
Any man must              take. What bónes must I
Break to see              the wildest wake a ship            510
Of man                    has ever dragged in
A wet                     trail across unknown
Countries?                Mark all crossings well.
The river, as sun         sets, gleams: burnished
Brass; I rub it and hope a spirit appears to sing my name.

*The attention of a traveler must be turned first to all*
*The works of Nature. So I wrote at the beginning of my*
*Book, and so I will see as the day-dream unfolds on*
*The river of my days. I claimed that men and manners*

Hold the first rank, but that was no more than a politic
Lie. Men barely hold a place at all in that broad world;
We bring little in comparison. And men who live apart
As we do and the aborigines do not can only understand
A little of what Nature holds as gifts to the sensitive woman
And man. We tramp it down daily. We cut our hard way
Stump to stump through the great shady wilderness of our
Past. But the Creator surely set down this loveliest of orders
For us to unravel as we go. Mindless money-making will
Not be the part of us recalled. Only in what we alone can see
Will our mark be made and set forth for others in the same
Dream. We are enameled with a bed of flowers. We walk
Through green meadows, heaven on Earth. Let it come back,
Nature into my nature. And let my cry come unto thee.

520

530

# Canto Four

# I

*A*ND SO we set forth for Spalding's Upper Store,
    (days in my private discomfort not really
           behind me, and in the deep nights
I often wander into the swampy wildsight of heron
      and alligator)
    the rough traders and I, they in front, vessel weighed
down with an almost sinking weight of goods to trade
        and I behind or beside them in my small boat,
    sail stuck to the sun, skin bronzing in the ides of May.

Nature is not order. In our Linnæan days we claim          10
      to think it is, but as I sail into that bright darkness
      I see
    what all men stranded inside the curvature of mind
        and breaking body have always
    known: we order the world to fit us, to stave off
      what gives us terror. I want to believe
          with all my hearth and mound
    that the Creator has planned this to
His purpose, but what if it is not so?
          How could a man ever know          20
      but list and list and list the parallels he gleans
    like a row-cropped farmer in the heatlight?

Will I ever understand
In full this ever-sinking land?
Loamy, living, and befouling
Like a panther low and growling,
It tears my supple flesh from bone.
And all the pity I have known
Marks me like a fiery brand;

Beyond the reach of any hand          30
Animosity does not reign.
Ruin is Nature's hidden gain.
Time is muscle or its flex,

Rune to rune and hex to hex.
All of life is watered sand.
May I please just understand?

      Sail on, sail free, but there is the high shelly bluff
    my father named Mount Hope fifteen years ago
names that follow me, *father* and *hope*, though
        I should now say *fatherless, hopeless*           40
and remember how it was then, a fine
        orange grove but is now cleared off and
    changed beyond recognition for indigo cultivation,
        owned by a
Proper Englishman,
brass buttons,
Delft crockery        and I imagine drunken nights
      in the mad scream of crocodiles
    who seek the blood-feast of armies.

    And I do believe in God      but I also         50
        believe in fear, in the heart ripped
clean of a man's chest by his enemies, in the
      eternal
      internal
        struggle against what Milton
showed us, and they can see me now
        sailing, sailing, sailing
    behind      them, as if all were right
      and my own taxonomy clear
        and clearly ordered—        60
God! O what has become and what
    *will* become of me?

    I try so hard to hold
        the world in the teacup of my intentions
    to be a good man, in the nest      of home
and harbor, but I feel it coming into
        shreds; I must draw, I must draw,
I must get out my pencils and steer
      my boat and
draw.        70

# II

The prospect of enchantment before us: the river's
    grand avenue,
This magnificent Indian mound with its seat
    for these their gods
High on the bluff where holy men could see all
    the world they knew.

How I recall this place from my father's days
    and how changed
Now. Then, it was wild and savage, uncultivated,
    no white people          10
Anywhere to ruin it. Its irrepressible grandeur
    led on an Indian

Highway straight-away from the mound three-quarters
    of a mile through
An orange grove and a forest. This road was sunken
    slightly beneath
The normal level of the earth around it, fifty yards
    wide, soil thrown

Up two feet on either side. Now all is changed and
    sullied utterly.          20
Once cultivated, once abandoned, it is a new desert
    in an old land.
And yet the mound itself has not been plowed under
    which tells me

The owner has fine taste, for I have seen ruins
    of other such
Hillocks plowed down to broken pots and bones
    by farmers in
Their red-faced rush. Now I imagine myself high
    on that mound          30

Closer in imagination to the God who must protect
    fools that sail

Into the deep wilderness. Did they, too, approach
    the throne of
Mercy in their prayers upon that high ground? If
    I climbed it

Would God condescend to me? O sovereign Lord,
    I am your
Chief traveler in a lost and wondering land; do not
    forsake me now.                                    40
I feel the spinal creep of madness and flowers.
    Do not leave

Me now. I am your faint blossom, your charity
    case; look
Down on me with pity and compassion as I wake
    each day near
Madness and art, near petal and stem, near mound
    and sunrise.

I try to order my words and so order this life.
    Do not leave                                      50
Me now. May I be worthy of this dignity
    I know you
Have placed on my shoulders, even though
    the aura blazes

Around my shoulders. So the morning being
    fair, the wind
Favorable, we sail on, sail on toward our new
    port's dock.
And now that we sail on past Lake George
    I feel with                                      60

All my strength the possibility of danger
    to come,
Of death or attack, the miseries of madness,
    or too much
Beauty to bear so that I will lose my sanity
    and whirl

Like a sand-whipped dervish through snake-
    infested vines,
Into the blood-tearing night around my camp-
    sites; that the               70
Insects will come down in their stinging millions
    to jab and bloat my flesh.

My boat is no more than a nutshell in this
    great water,
And must appear like some aquatic creature
    at a distance;
Have I even spoken well of Lake George,
    this dilation

Of the St. John's River: how beautiful
    and deep               80
Is this mirror of my wandered soul;
    how night-
Like and filled with small islands is
    this wideness?

Thunder cracks the calm; sashes of light
    scald the air
With streaks and musical scales, and so we sail
    into a cove
On the largest island to hide from the electrical
    teeth of it.              90

Now the storm breaks and breaks and breaks over
    us like perfect
Vileness, and we shudder to a halt on land, prepare
    to spend the
Night among the glories of splendid plants and dark
    growls whose

Constant hum and roar frighten many of the men
    who head upstream
To the new stores. "I believe I shall take the time
    to explore the island,"            100

I say, and they cry me mad with their staggered
    chorus, say to me

Their mock farewells. They do not know how
    much I fear
What is unmeasured within me and must fight
    it as a soldier
Fights his sworn enemy in the fields of blood.
    And yet I see

All delight when I strike out, as I now do with
    thunder rattling          110
The palm fronds like the spittle of a threatened snake.
    I see now that
This island was once the home of an Indian prince,
    for ruins spread

From sand to sand around me. And look:
    From a huge
Conical pyramid of earth runs a mannered
    avenue through
A magnificent grove of magnolias, live oaks,
    oranges, palms,          120

And ending at a large green level savannah.
    All around me
Are remains: earthenware pottery with its decorated
    shards, bones
Of animals and of men, thrown whitely on the mound
    and far beyond.

Now the last of them has vanished into their history
    which no man
Can any longer read, vanished into myth and tales told
    by those like          130
Me who stumble into their ruins with eyes and a pen
    to tell stories

To themselves or much-later listeners. All left are
    wolves, wildcats,
Deer, turkeys, squirrels, raccoons, and birds. I see
    bears sitting up
To tear off oranges and eat them rind to rind, suck
    the honey from

Inside the pulp. Turkeys fatten on the thousands
    of live oak                                     140
Acorns. Is this the living Eden of my Philadelphia dreams?
    I note a species
Of lantana that is gorgeous in its profusion, too, and
    it grows in

Coppices or old fields, five or six feet high and ends
    in blossoms,
Umbelliferous tufts of orange with small blue berries
    on the end.
I also see before me a beautiful palmated convolvulus,
    a vine that                                     150

Strolls about on the ground, its leaves elegantly
    sinuated and a
Deep grass-green with flowers pale and incarnate-
    colored with
Deep crimson eyes all seated on very long petioles.
    Rich swamps

Also suck their swampy teeth of reeds as I walk
    on the high ground
Between the sulfurous marshland. Crimson flowers,
    Crimson flowers,                              160
Crimson flowers, crimson flowers, crimson flowers!
    Can it ever end?

I come back to camp. *Lobelia cardinalis* grows in plenty
    here. Golden
Meadows lead my eye back toward the mound and its
    great avenue,

This lost tale of a lost people. Can flowers and their kind
    be lost also?

THIS WORK IS A TREE
OF WHICH THE CHAPTER OF CONTENTS           170
IS CALLED THE SEED.

Can they be known to all women and men and then vanish
    from knowledge
Like the great emperors once known to all and now bones
    sticking out
Of this silent hump of island moss and unpotteried kilns?
    That is my

Great goal, then: to write down what has lived unwritten
    these centuries.
Now the air grows calm. All evidence of the storm passes      180
    but for dripping
Trees and a light, after-thunder breeze. I smell the aroma
    of orange trees

And the rich, fragrant shrubs and trees mile on mile on mile.
    And yet fear
Creeps into my keeping; I sense a darkness in my own bones,
    a sense that
Some terrible threat may soon arouse the deepest terror
    of my heart.

# III

My sleep is not calm, though            lulled into it by mixed sounds
    of the wearied surf lapsing on the hard-beaten shore
    and the tender singing of the     painted nonpareil
    and other winged inhabitants of
    the groves.

Dawn drives the darkness down          and as the light wicks upward
          the dreaded voice of the alligators shakes the island
          and resounds along the neigh-     boring coasts. Soft
                    winds blow the roaring sounds out
                              like a candle.                                          10

We sail across the land toward a          bright bay, head into a river
          bend that turns us to a camping spot, and the others
          step out and make a camp as          evening is coming
                    hard on us; snakes thick as wrists go
                              past our feet.

The others gather wood to fire          away the night, but I roam on
          with my gun into wide savannahs and plains that
          in my state of half-mad delusion seem an Elysium
                    in the fragrant shade of *Zanthoxilon*
                              wind to wind                                          20

On my cheeks. Who are we who          wander into the deep heartless
          world with our eyes against the cities and into
          all that is and is not holy in that natural place of
                    which we are a clear part? Where can
                              we find blight

That shall not abrade us? Give me          names for these galaxies
          of greenery; give me plains that perish before the eye
          and the tangled laughter of vines and veins together,
                    the edge of my life where I cannot bear it
                              and then do.                                          30

I return from my walk to find my          companions fishing for
          trout round the floating edges of *Nymphea.* How
          strange their method: to tie the white hairs of a deer's tail
                    with shreds of red garter and parti-colored
                              feathers in

A tuft or tassel that they clot          upon their fishing hooks.
          Then they swing the bobs back and forth over
          over the surface to sway the flower at the fish below.

The trout are lead-colored, inclining to
    a deep blue                            40

I note how in the water they         bear the shape of wings,
   how so many predators and prey bear the shape
    of wings that it is a wonder no man has grown them
       to flee or fly. These trout are marked
          transverse waved

Lists of a deep slate color        and when fully grown
   take on the hue of brick. They sometimes weigh
  as much as thirty pounds and come out like hooked
    horses. "Let's cross the river here and
      see if we can                           50

Find a turkey," my companion       says, and I nod to him.
   We sail over into that clucking world of deep
   and dark-green mystery. Rich swamps, furred
    islands: we step off and then we
      separate. I

See a flock of turkeys, one huge      tom, and I raise my
   fusée to fire, but several young cocks fear
  the shape and sound of me and in their language warn
    the rest to be on guard. Then I see,
      to my shock,                          60

That I am not the enemy. No:        before me just ahead
   stands a wild-eyed but utterly motionless lynx.
   *Damn!* That was how my fellow hunter's shot at a
    deer sounds. Lynx leaps. Turkeys
     scuttle off

And none of us hunt well:        the lynx loses its
   prey; my friend misses his deer. And I,
  most fortunate of men, miss my shot at the
    tom turkey. We laugh at this
      sad hunting,                          70

Sail back over to the camp　　　　　　　　where a feast is
　　　　　then set anyway before us, and we eat to
　　　satisfaction. I think: we are like primitive men
　　　　　here, peaceable, contented and
　　　　　　　　so sociable.

Night comes. No one who looks　　　　　at another man can
　　　　　see his inner wars. No one can guess what
　　　he fears or the incipient madness that drives him
　　　　　into solitude and the sanctity of his
　　　　　　　　steep study.　　　　　　　　　　80

I strain under the fellowship of　　　　　others and so must
　　　　　take my life largely alone, and this journey
　　　to no place and its flowers, which I hunt as others
　　　　　hunt wings and heated brown flanks
　　　　　　　　thrills, thrills me.

Who goes deeper into his fears　　　　　marks them well.
　　　　　Who sails into his own starless nights can see
　　　truth in the unfolded chalice of a fragrant star-petal;
　　　　　Who lives with others or who lives alone
　　　　　　　　dies, dies alone.　　　　　　　　90

# IV

Morning: we sail onward now, boat and boat upriver
Toward Spalding's Upper Store, and this day drives me

Nearly mad with joy and a hidden shuddering of all
Fear a man can know. Once there, we find a white man

Who lives with a Seminole woman, slender, beautiful,
Daughter of a prince named White Captain. Twelve
Members of his family are camped in an orange grove

Near the store. The storekeeper is a vastly unhappy man,
Though why, I cannot see, as this woman is lithe, lovely,

Eyes filled with rich brown light. When our stores are                    10

Given to us, he sets off hunting in the swampy woods
And for trading in the Seminole camps. But before then
I ask him why his glum demeanor is so strong when she
Is so tender to him and beautiful. "No man can explain

His attractions," he says, whittling a slender sapling.
"No man can understand the family into which he
Marries, least of all a white man who falls in with the
Seminoles, a proud-hearted people but to my eye hard

As savages sometimes. I watch her movements when her
Eye is elsewhere. She moves with animal grace, narrow           20
As a vine and as elegant; and yet there is in her a hard-
Won need to madden me with her absence. I touch her
And she warms into my arms; I touch her and she bolts

Back as if a flame had scorched her path. It is the sense
Of unknowing I cannot bear. It is this sad desire in me
For complete certainty—a need unmet now or ever—
That maddens me. So I can only say she is too beautiful
To bear and mean it. I mean it with every breath in me.

She has drained me of all possessions and yet I still can-
Not leave her. Even her father calls her cruel as a crow,          30
But she only laughs at him." (*Unhappy man: Later he*
*Will kill himself rather than go on living with or without*
*The love of this wilder woman.*) Now, he simply leaves,
Heading for the deep, wet woods with his heavy fusée.

*Who is civilized and who is savage? I have wondered*
*In my heart for months then, years now. Her own kind*
*Condemns her; they howl in judgment at her treatment*
*Of the trader, and yet we cannot know if one is wholly in*
*The right or not. I want to believe in the divine direction*
*Of things*, but we are long lost to certainty in this green          40

Lostness. Now, mission thus far passed by, we camp
And I look for an Indian boy who might help guide me
Up river, on and on and on, looking for furtive flowers,
The wide mouths of petals in my paddling pursuit. I
Gather provisions for a long journey, find a strong-backed
Youth who will give my mapless journey the points
Of his internal compass. And so morning comes and

We board my boat, say farewells to the others, and sail
On into that darker land, tree to vast and shading tree.
My God, the variety of it all: Wild lime or tallow nut,　　　　　　　50
*Hibiscus spinifex, Callicarpa, Magnolia grandiflora,*
Green, yellow, brick-red, carmine, open-throated
Petals in the profusion of a shriek: enough fragrance
To drive the sanest men mad with a desire for more.

And fruits already in their seasons; fine strong nuts
With cases of sweet pulp: a kernel with almond taste,
But oilier and somewhat like hard tallow—and orange
Groves everywhere, trees hung low with sweet spheres.
I glance at the Indian boy and see he misses entirely
What enchants me so. He is only tired of rowing, so　　　　　　　60
I steer to shore and let him get off. He turns to me
And screams, shrill and terrible, against my works

And ways. Perhaps, I think, he is heading for game
To feed us, so I camp beside the river, build a fire
And wait. But nothing from humankind comes to me
In the dark and darker night; now, long after midnight
I feel a hard shift in me, the fear of what I seek, solitude,
The wider world, a canvas with no image save what I
Set there myself. I walk around the campfire, calm
At first and then terrified. I sing against the terrors.　　　　　　　70

# V

Night suffocates me. I feel
        the weight of fear hold
     me in its giant paws, teeth dripping blood and bone
        already, as if I were     dead    and waiting to be consumed
by what I fear most on this Earth. I cannot

bear it.
I cannot bear it. I cannot
         bear it. I can-
     not bear it.

Yet there beyond the nimbus               10
      of camplight     is that world
   for which I have come: flower, stem, lanceolate leaf,
     lilacs lilting in the     w i n d

(I sit hunched against the wall of damp fear that ruins and ranks me
I sit steaming with the sound of what comes to kill me in the citadel forest
I sit in the arms of my father's words and the Apocalypse of claws
I sit hearing alligator warnings, cries creeping close to my death-roll
I sit hearing the screech owl, *Strix assio*, shift from limb to limb
        holding my name in the blood of her claws
I sit watching flames flutter like the sun as it tries to recall my name    20
I sit in the aroma of heavy orange limbs, golden groves, moon to moon
I sit looking over my life to this point, how I failed in this Florida
I sit looking over my life, how I failed in Philadelphia and North Carolina
I sit daydreamed by beasts; already they tell stories of how I sailed here
I sit looking over my days: Father, Father, Father, Father, here am I
I sit wanting to dash with foamy face into the forest
I sit among ashes and sift my Latin to *antiquus poena*
I sit remembering Charleston and then Savannah
I sit in the lexical memory of that boundary
         conference in August    30
I sit with a subtle fear that does not wreck
      me
I sit arm to arm with the idea of death
I sit death to the death with an idea

I sit in the sifting crackle of fire
I sit afraid to move far away
I sit afraid to move
I sit afraid)

           I have made my camp in an open plain
And now I stand to hear the terrifying roar           40
of a thousand crocodile thrashings: can this be what     I see
    now, that I have brought too
         little food to sustain me    here
can this be that    a hundred, a thousand    mad jaws
   clack and thrash around the camp-    death
      can this be that night    and
        my last night    resurrection
          not possible as I walk
around and around the dead wood of my fire
      going nowhere?          50


   Such fear as I never imagined comes to me
   Such fear as no man ever wore comes to me
   Such fear as changes one to a scale-borne creature
     comes to me


Come to me, sweet death, *süsser Tod*,
   come to me on the floating lawns of *Pistia* and *Nymphea*
     and bring me the peace
      of all flowers
For I am the Flower Seeker and not aimed
    for this end, my eyes rolled and rotating with the shriek    60
     of lynx and larynx; I sit by the heat
  and decide to leap into the flames if they begin
    to hustle from the shadows for me


  if the crocodiles stalk me down in their hunting circle,
     if one would come for me to drag off
       to the water and roll me down
  roll me down
into where even darkness has a shadow.

Behold him rushing forth
from the flags and reeds                                    70
his enormous body swells;
he holds his plaited tail
high like a brandished sword
on the surface of the lake;
water like a cataract descends
from his opening jaws;
clouds of smoke issue
from his dilated nostrils;
the earth trembles
with his thunder                                            80


Now, from the opposite shore, a second army launches
        off         hundreds         *thousands*
            of them         and they
                    thrash
wildly through the deep, dark water toward the host on
                        my shore,
and I stumble back and         *voveo vovi votum*
            I see what will happen
        as if it has *already* happened: the shielded battle,
    the waxy tonnage of blood floating warm and iron-y        90
            on the surface of the warm water


        The water boils with them. I cannot count so high.
    The noise is beyond                 descr-
            iption
at first the roaring of battle-threats but now the fight itself
the blood itself
the old imperative itself
the whip of scorpion tails itself.

                        I run now from one side
                        of the fire to the other            100
                        not crying aloud lest
                        they all turn and hunt me
                        lest they cease this battle
                        and come and come hunt
                        me

Fear, rage, rising to the light, bait, burns, tears,
bone, cracks, roars:

they clamp their fearful jaws on each other and sink to the bottom
of the water, turning, turning in their taut and horrid wreaths
the water foams with churned waves and thick black blood:                   110

they rise, they settle, they come again to the surface
                of the water and my eyes (and the surface of sight
                        is worse than the surface of water)
        and some die there and float silently with clamped jaws,
                but most of the vanquished slide away like
                            L O N G   L O G S
through the foamy bloodbath.

            I must leave this madness
            but how can one leave the madness
            that lies within                                                120
            the flower that blooms within
the unexpected joy of fear that writhes within?

They move away
from my small boat
I prepare and pack it
I dance around grass
in shadows watching
for the sight of my
own bloody hank
of bone and flesh,                                                         130
handkerchiefs waving
surrender in spurting
vessels on my vessel:
I am coward and bloom,
coward and root,
coward and shoot

                Now I give into howling disorder
                Now I give into my darkest night
        I say to myself:                I knew I should never

have come to this                                          140
             place
in the day or in the night; for now I must face what
             faces me, the militant eruption of the solitary man
                  who understands why
solitude has found him
       the constant fear
                         of madness and death while
       mad: the great horror of my life


  I will take my fusée I will not take my fusée
in case it falls into the water when they attack me          150
             when I am engaged in battle,
                  so I gather for my defense
       a club of heavy oak


Only in the harbor can I be safe, I think, for they would
             have come a-land to tear me        bone from
                                                bone
             my God                             bone
                                                joints
                                                flesh
             *Herr Gott*                        blood        160


       Now I stroke, stroke, stroke it,
and on all sides they come for me in the shuddering darkness
and I cry out, swing my Herculean club snout to snout
                  my singing shouts echoing wave to wave


       I see a spot that seems safe
                  but before I reach it
       they     attack     attack     *attack*
             from all sides, and I see


from the shorelight their gaping teeth, many filled with bloody
             hanks of another's sinking flesh               170


My canoe (for I call it boat or ship or canoe as time bids)
       rocks with their hunger            my body rocks

                            with their hunger

Death is near now

Two huge ones attack me at the same time from
                different                                  sides
                      not working in concert but
                          with the same effect
                          so that they
        throw gallons of brick-colored water over me                180
and their jaws clap so close to me I can smell their fetid
                dragon breath

I swing! And all madness in me disappears like waves
                    crashing down on the soldiers of Egypt.

Now they slide away, away
into the deep and darkness
darkest cricket-screaming night
and I cannot breathe cannot
get any breath and stop swinging
my gnarled club but I cannot                              190
stop thinking of the first gnash,
the crack of bone, the long ragged
slice of flesh, the blood-meal
given for their nightly feeding

              No        no          now they are coming back
            O gods is it dark or light
        I cannot judge anything, and now now they begin
to peel away as I paddle hard astern back to shore
and toward the lone light except that from the salt stars:
now it seems the alligators form a line, block me            200
from reaching shore, but they wave side to side as I pass.

              Suddenly
I realize they have given up the battle my heart goes on
beating too hard to manage so to calm myself I take out
the rod and line and cast it into the dawning water

and on each cast there is a strong strike and soon my boat
fills from flip to flap with fat trout.

I scratch the surface of the lagoon
as I glide back toward camp and now
(θεόσ not again)          a monstrous one follows                    210
me like a threatening tree
and I think it will peel away then it does

not
and so when I reach the shore I leap out:
follows me follows me follows me out and out
and I run for camp as he comes step by step
and I grab my fusée and feel my fear
breaking like the crest of foamy waves
and when I get back he is climbing into the canoe
for the heavy meal of now-dead fish                                   220


Come on come you monster
Monsters have always come in the night to me
grave quiet monsters
wild shrieking creatures come
for bone and blood
and now I see this one twelve feet long,
and he backs from the canoe and calls my name:

*William, William, why do you kill*
*what terrifies you? I am Nature,*
*too, come to break you down piece*                                  230
*by piece: lie down now and let me feed.*

I aim and fire. Birds unlace themselves from trees
in the darkness by their thousands. The old one
simply settles into sudden darkness, dead now, dead and gone

I take the fish to scale
with the sun coming up
and my heart is mad for light

# VI

Sun never rises at night's densest transit:
and just now a monster larger than any I have seen
comes stalking from the water toward me

    Can I ever find an order again
    now madness overcomes me and I begin
    to laugh and crouch like a foaming beast:

With a sweep of his tail he scatters my catch
now others come and prepare to sink my canoe
to strand me, cut me off, from what is left of

        the world, to wait me out: they have time        10
        to feed; this is the time of all Nature, that
        lack of need to go or to be anywhere, just

to wait and tear down and tear apart.
I pull the barque up on the shore so they
cannot sink it; they roar and slap the water

        I clear out my possibles from inside
        the canoe (is this order after all?), take
        them and the fish back to camp: morning

at first seems to quiet the rage of the monsters
as I build up my fire and clean around my blanket        20
so that (is this order?) I can see what creeps and slithers

        toward me in light or the absence of light,
        but then: from not too far away there is the sound
        of the most majestic battle a man has ever heard

    I feel myself drawn inescapably to it: if I am
    to die let me die in majesty. Now the sound
    deafens all the world, and am I walking toward

rather than away from it I am
Am I headed into that dark ending
I am is the world ending it is it is                    30

# VII

Now I see it:
the river before me from shore to shore is filled
with so many fish a man could walk
            across and not touch the water          What is
            holy does not    explain                man
        could not in conscience believe            that
            this applies to thee or to             thou
        I want my pencils, the sobriety of         art
        to calm me; I want to be truthful and      mindful
            I must color in the night              of
            all that wrecks me, sing a             hymn      10
            to God or to Pan or to the sight
                no man has ever in this
                    life seen before

        Fish flip in their tens of tens of thousands and now
            the alligator army attacks hundred to hundreds
        and like the oxbow                 of a dry river
        they form a circle                 in the water
        and drive the fish                 out and outward
        into the wild thrash               of mouth and tail
        and O my God what                  joyful feeding       20
        madness has come in                that circle of blood
        so fast that terror cannot         find time to feed
            itself with old stories of     dark monsters
            that come knocking in the    deep night
            monsters with teeth like glinting silver
                knives in the night.

They eat two three four at a time
    their eyes roll over dead as they gnash
        and what do fish think or believe

I think they think nothing
I want to know the life of all things
need to feel their pulse in my pulse I
my life knowing nothing really. But
study comes understanding and I see
sunlight and the deepest
I break when I must break, know
madness as the solitary must, know
as no one city-bound can.

though
I
pass
through
the
shadow
of
death

30

IN THIS WORLD OF NOW, WHO IS THAT GREAT PERSON
ENDOWED WITH EXCELLENT QUALITIES, PROWESS,
KNOWLEDGE OF RIGHTEOUSNESS, GRATITUDE, TRUTH
AND FIRMNESS IN PRACTICE OF VOWS?

40

Vapor issues like smoke from their
nostrils; floods of water and blood rush
from their mouths. Day passes. I find
myself frozen to this deathing place.
I want to step away and not look at it,
but I cannot move back toward camp.

*This is day and this is night,*
*Where I come to the interior*
*Of all misunderstanding: fill*
*Me with what I fear most,*
*Fill me with what I love most,*
*And I will be whole. Fill me*
*With what the Earth fears most*
*Of me, and I will be whole again.*
*I am William Bartram, none other,*
*Come into the wild land of mind*
*And body. I am the flower, the teeth*
*That would kill me for no reason*
*But the mad joy of feeding, as*
*Petals go mad to feed on rain*
*And birds go mad to feed on nectar:*
*Bind us, forgive us all;*
*Bind us, forgive us all.*

50

60

# VIII

I am seated before my fire now, with night
Come and my disorder filtering away, perhaps.
      Crickets sing their droning chant: *come, come, come.*

My fish broil and my kettle of rice stews
Over the open flames. I have oil, pepper, and
      Salt, excellent oranges dip down over me, trees

Bobbing in a light and lovely breeze. I am
Quietly making notes when a thrashing unlike
      Anything I have heard comes stepping through water

Toward, it seems, my camp. I get my fusée         10
And creep, frightened—I admit it—toward what
      Could be men. I fear that possibility and desire it

Above all other things. Past the point of sharp
Light into the faint whisper of near-dead sun
      I see coming toward me two bears, huge specimens,

And though I would speak with them, calm us
In the language of bears, we cannot reach that place;
      I cry aloud, hold up my piece and fire toward them,

In hopes I may wound one and the other will
Flee. Skrish: it's a flash in the pan: no bullet flies        20
      Toward them. But that spark of what could be to them

God or God's power sends them rambling off,
Going and now gone from sight. I am left alone.
      I eat. I draw for awhile. I finish my notes and lie down

To try and sleep on my blanket. The only sounds I hear
In the night are the sad, holy owls, screams
      Of bitterns, and the wood-rats running among the leaves.

But then it begins again, the fearful wreck
Of crocodile cries through the long night.
　　　Oh God why have I come into this fearful coppice now?　　　30

# IX

I can bear this
I cannot bear this
I break camp
And pack all my
Possessions in
The canoe, watch
Across the lagoon
Know that to leave
This place is to
Risk my life　　　　　　　　　　　　　　　　10
To go between
Rank on rank
Of crocodiles
Is not unlike
Running a gauntlet
Between two lines
Of Indians, one with
Knives, the other with
Fire brands and O
O God, is this how　　　　　　　　　　　　20
I am meant to die

　　　　　　　I charge my fusée fully, get all on board,
　　feel　　　　　　　the　rocking of the lake-river　　beneath
　　　　　　me and　　　my pulse pounding　　like
　　　　　　　genuine　　　　　　madness

I push off and see I must pass the Battle Lagoon
　　　　and I feel the fear of a terrible　　death　　possess
　　me.　　　　　　I tremble and
　　　　　　　Keep a good
　　　　　　　Lookout but　　　　　　　　30

Am I searching
For salvation
Or for the profundity
Of flowers?


There! There! Out of the reeds like a drunken dragon
    it tails toward me: a monstrous specimen,
  thick scales, penetrant tail, roaring,
       roaring toward me
 then like an arrow
     **UNDER!**           40
 my boat, emerging on the lea quarter
with open jaws, belching water and smoke
  that fall upon me like strong rain
 in a hurricane


         Raise my club
         God! Slam down
         God! on his head
         He arises, turns and
         I hit him three times
         In quick succession   50
         Try to keep fear off
         Me, but it's
   no use O damn my mind for bringing
  me to the       place


Suddenly he vanishes straightaway like a strongly thrown spear
and I suck air as I paddle and fear: along and near the bank
I stay (don't look behind) and dig the water on both sides hard
(don't look behind) and there is my death coming, a different one,
not so large but much swifter in the hard-pack of water's surface.


    I glance back and see it      60
     is a female with her brood
      perhaps a hundred of them
       fifteen inches long swimming
        behind her in the wake of menace
        and I cry aloud and she cries

aloud and passes so close to
my port bow that she rocks
my canoe side to side, and
the hundred young, with their
yellowed markings clatter
past me tooth to tooth, eyes
with the intensity of the insane:
Let us all be insane now (don't
look look look look look behind)

O that I could pull to land and see
The sanctuary of my Galilee

# X

*I have over-excited my old man's heart in this*
*Retelling here in my garden by the river; I sit now*
*In my shade chair, and my man brings me lemonade*
*To cool all memory. How odd it would be to pass away*
*By returning only in my thoughts to those grave and giddy*
*Days along the St. John's River when I nearly died. What*
*Was I thinking? Why had I gone there at all? To find*
*Specimens for Mr. Fothergill, my nominal employer,*
*But that is hardly all. No one knew what I suffered inside,*
*How each day brought the agonies of loneliness, that I*
*Wanted a wife and companion more than breath yet knew*
*Somehow I was fated never to have that love. Men who*
*Live without that sweet affection begin to die inside*
*Early on; they wither, shrivel, see close and too early*
*The madness that lies inside us all. And so I went alone*
*Into that deepness. I pressed Death to his last shred*
*Of irritation, dared him to come out and hunt me down.*
*Flowers were my blessed crop. I simply could not stop*

*Myself from daring what could kill me to make me crop*
*And water, to drink my blood in place of a jeweled crown.*
*I cannot breathe. July weighs me down. We will be dead*
*Some tomorrow that we cannot know. We will be gone*

70

10

20

*And can't predict when. The skies will open, bright, pearly,*
*And shimmering, for my soul. Every fear will then collide*
*With our sanctuaries and one must win. I need what is true*
*To speak my name. I need what is true to change to a blue*
*Brighter than the skylight of March. Will I seem to fly*
*When the time approaches? Perhaps I have told some lies*
*In the retelling; I know that I confuse days and finally*
*Lose track of time. So it must be. Lame, nearly blind,*          30
*I have the right to it. I accept what is my fate and lot,*
*Here in the flowered country or the iron rungs of the city.*
*Is there time left for an old man who cannot kneel to pray?*
*I love the childhood acting of this warmly told charade.*
*I am the ship with its cargo, stern, and rising manly prow:*
*Even if I never had a child to tell or even had a single kiss.*

# XI

I see before me like Indian mounds a hundred hillocks
on the shore                    what man of Nature could
          let it pass unstudied
even with the herd of bellowing crocodiles to his stern?

So I heave-to, beach the boat, and walk among them.
traveler in a                    strange land, pyramids
          littering the landscape
like an Egyptian funeral ground, dome to old dome.

They are, my Providence, nests of the crocodile,
the hatchery of                    what would tear me          10
          apart for bloody bones.
Most seem now deserted, decorated with thick and

whitish eggshells that lie broken and scattered around
each quiet dome.                    Each home charges me
          with genuine fear that
I try to glide past. Monsters from such small shells!

From these eggs come creatures large as a horse.
One of them now          swims to the center
          of the lagoon and booms
his voice, sucks air. A horror can be borne to anyone,          20

I know, dying child, alleyside criminal, and a home
a horror. Yet I          feel no anger at them,
          for all nature is guiltless
of moral thinking except man. It dies according to its

Instructions to die. It lives to breed and sits a quiet day
in the sun, to sing          for so few hours that
          I forgive my assassins
as *they* come into this great garden and forgive *me*.

# XII

Now I leave this nursery to its future hatchlings,
and voyage on up the river. The alligators do not          10
disturb me in any serious way now, having seen
that I can float above them out of their jaws' clamp.

          Along the sides now I see black, rich soil
          that holds succulent and tender grass, thinning
          sands of trees, but what is there is thick-trunked,
          Greek columns with the grandeur of temples.

There are beautiful orange groves, palms, cypress.
laurels, and live oaks dripping with waterfalls
of Spanish moss. A languid feeling takes me over,
and I almost forget the Battle Lagoon and blood.          20

          Channels go off side to side. I cannot let one
          tempt me off course. I sing between shelly bluffs.
          I hum a song from childhood whose words now
          vanish from my mind. It cannot matter, such

forgetting. One tree now comes in sight that takes
my whole attention: the *Carica papaya*, admirable,
towering, erect with a perfectly straight tapering stem,
smooth and polished, a bright ash color, like leaf silver

> curiously inscribed with the footsteps of fallen leaves.
> Its ripe and green fruit ring round the stem or stump,                30
> around its lobe-sinuate leaves, and my eye slowly
> loves its unreadable languages, takes time for all color

to register. I stroke side to side in the river and begin to tire
and so come ashore to nap beneath the dense shade. All fear
flees. I could be in my own bed. The natural world threatens
and soothes. I am that Nature, too, and I do not dream but sleep

> only. I awaken rested after a long time. The sun has slipped
> but a few degrees. I stand and stretch, shake off the leaves
> in which I have lain. Stroke to stroke once more, bank to
> lovely bank I sing, back and forth, back and back and forth.         40

Now the snake birds rise in their gloried and iridescent
markings, perhaps the most beautiful species I have known.
Perhaps it is a species of cormorant or loon,
with an extremely slender head and neck, bill tapering

> to a sharp point. Its abdomen and thighs are black
> and glossy as a raven, but the breast and upper belly
> are cream-colored; its tail is long and a deep black,
> tipped with silvery white and when spread appears

like a lady's fan. I see it sit with utter stillness on limbs
and seem to stare into the water like Narcissus, but when          50
threatened, it falls as if dead straight down into liquid
with a stunning splash, unmoving. For a minute or two

> I see nothing, not even spiraling rings where it fell,
> and then—O Nature, what ingenious glories—far
> down the water it suddenly appears, beak-first,
> looking exactly like a snake breaking the surface

of water to spy danger or a skipping meal. I imagine this
bird along the Tiber in Ovid's day, presenting him with
a great story to be re-told like his hundred others (such as
Narcissus—a mirror, a leaning, a shining back that ties                    60

      one image to the other.) Now I see that in my reach
      for order I have paddled deep into a frightening swamp
      and cannot imagine my way out of it. Order! So soon
      found in the bright perfection of the snake bird is lost

in the miscalculation of compass points and a return now
to the coming night and the nightmare. The air fills with
stinging insects. The air fills with bleak humidity. Water
begins to swell with the black weight of blacker scales.

# XIII

Dis-
        order             begins to swamp my ves-
sel again: I am not the voyager voyaging. I am
         O my God
        *lost*
         to God:
pray for me; I am lost to light and to the putrid hellish swamp-
         fire:
         Pray for me.

I find a high strip of a narrow shelly bank                    10
        haul out my canoe and      s e e
          on both sides of the      stream
            vast swarms of crocodiles
      like a recurring nightly nightmare, but I do not know
          another place to be.

This is the ancient camping place
of others lost or found, beneath
the limbs of a massive live oak:
Indians and adventurers came,

I deduce from the ash heaps                                          20
and old rotten fire-brands on the
surface of the ground. My face
and hands tremble. Fear breaks
me. I am frozen by the heat.

              I       see          now
         it is also the landing place and harbor
                         of some great and sovereign
                   monster from the thrashed underbrush,
         and I say to myself: William, William, pray *God* what
                   do you do here? Suddenly, floating upward       30
                   from beneath the black water I see
                   like a water-serpent of older myths
                         a crocodile of the vastest dimensions
              imaginable              O forebears     help me

The majesty and muck              of turmoil swamp me.
              The stammering scream of my inarticulate       horror
                         swamps me.
There is little firewood. The fish I caught earlier
have turned against me, but I resolve to stew them in
                   orange juice for I can very nearly feel my       backbone       40
                         through the small country of my
                                  stomach.

And what am I doing, Quaker and man of peace,
                   with these bottles of rum: to salve a wound,
                         I told myself, to purify a blade, but now
              with a small fire clattering against the screaming
                         swamp, I uncork a bottle and pour a
                                  mouthful and feel fire
              light my insides.

I have no appetite.  I stride back and forth with my gun,       50
              for death comes for me in the night.
                   Death comes for me in the night
                         Death comes for me.

Mosquitoes sharply sting
savage tails slap out
in warning of endless
death: the slow agony
of all agonies to come;
　　I have come

*Hear my cry,*
*O God, attend*
*unto my prayer*
*From the end*
*of the earth will*
*I cry to thee,*　　　　　　　　　60
*when my heart*
*is overwhelmed:*
*lead me to the rock*
*that is higher than*
*I*

　　in the endless night of endless nights

　　　　Would God hate me if I aimed
　　　　　my fair fusée at my own
　　　　　　head
　　　　　　　now
I am deprived now of every desire but　　　　　　70
ending my troubles　　　　　as fast
　　　　as possible

　　　　Hear my cry, O God

and then I begin to think of the flowers
the flowers and the flowers and the flowers
　　　　and I am the Flower Seeker, the man sewn in the
　　　　　　wilderness, crying:
　　*Prepare ye the way of the blossoms.*

　　A cool brisk breeze springs up. The skies glow
　　with serenity. Stars twinkle in uncommon brilliance.　　80
　　I stretch myself before the drunken fire. I believe I can
　　in my exhaustion sleep. I believe　　I can　　sleep

And then, *come Christ Jesus!* I sit up from a slight doze and hear
　　the terrified scream of owls in the deep swamps
　　　　around me. I waken and yet am still asleep,
　　　　　hung in the nightmare land
　　　　between them, thrashing, talking aloud,

       feeling the constant stinging insects.

      *God: God.* The constant screaming of owls
      heard for miles through the empty dark extensive       90
       forest, peals across meadows and lakes.

  And now I see       measureless horror    an alligator
    dashing my canoe back and forth against
       the gnarly roots of a cypress tree, trying
        to get inside her
       for the fish still stored there

I run screaming, falling, scrambling up, and it slips
      with an angry tail-flip into the warm water.

Exhausted, fire-fled, I turn toward
sleep once more                    100

*Hear my cry,*
    *O God, attend*
    *unto my prayer*
    *From the end*
    *of the earth will*
      *I cry to thee,*

        *when my heart*
        *is overwhelmed:*
        *lead me to the rock*
        *that is higher than*    110
        *I*

    I sleep: how long I do not know
    but then the screams of owls
    awaken me, and I see six feet
    from my head the alligator,
    huge and gaping, coming for me
AND GOD OF ISRAEL I TAKE MY WEAPON
      aim it at the monster, and it slaps the air with its tail
       and disappears back into the water before
        it can swallow me        120
          whole

I ROUSE up my fire now, bright on bright,
and the action sends fright fleeing: insects
tear flesh into delicate sipping strips,
but the majestic monsters do not come
again
                I doze minutes at a time
        but they do not
                  come again

# XIV

Dawn. The mosquitoes have calmed away. I sit up
stung half to death. The insects are now damped down,
and the roaring alligators gone to rest: make haste,
I think: sail now and sail away from this madness.

Yet as soon as I am under-weigh, stinging bugs

and their high-pitched scream return, cover my legs,
and so I make again for the shore, break off shrub-
branches to brush them off. They swarm away,
and I am gone into the water once more, drowning

in color, saturated with berry-red and dream-green,         10

meaning that rich shade of leaves that comes only
in the brightest other-world nights. I paddle now
between the banks of the river which are overhung
with hanging garlands, perpendicular green walls

with projecting jambs, deep apartments, and pilasters,

twenty feet high or more, covered with the various
species of *Convolvulus, Glycine frutescens, Rajana*—
so much color. Large white flowers big as a funnel,
and the wild squash climbing over the lofty limbs

of the trees, its yellow fruit large as an orange and         20

hanging pendant on the ever-flowing waters. Now,
nearly noon, the heat is intolerable, and I make for
shore on a low, sandy testaceous ridge. I walk there
and see the gorgeous profundity of swamps stretching

far and away with astonishingly tall cypress trees.

Could I find sleep beneath this spreading live oak?
I spread my blanket and wait for the shriek and roar,
but if it comes I hear nothing and awaken two hours
later as refreshed as I have been since I came into this

dark and winding land. I check to see if I have been                    30

serpent-bit or gnawed up by mosquitoes, and I am
whole, unharmed. Praise whatever saves fools who
go roaming for Nature's sake in such a wilderness.
Now in the cool and pleasant afternoon, I sail on up

the river. I see but a few crocodiles, and they are small

and unthreatening, and I wonder if I have paddled out
of their land finally and will have the time to hunt
flowers without fear. Dark edges toward me, and I
see a shelled bluff ahead and pull in, gather firewood,

and build a bonfire for night's security. And yet I                     40

have come to fear this world less and less each day,
to see the deeper dreams of Nature with a grateful
eye and one that does not dream death around each
knob of cypress. Sleep swarms over me. I fall into

a place I have not been since I left Savannah. All

is quiet at times in this life, all is gracious, grateful,
all is clean and pure. I think: let me for all my life
remember what is beautiful in a single day, let me
pour my deep attention on glimmering Nature,

let me not shift my sorrow into the work of my hands.                    50

Morning touches me gently on the shoulder. I sit up
and see I have slept in ranks and rows of low mounds,
and I walk slowly each to each and know I have come
to an ancient burying ground. Two or three acres

are filled with the honored dead, perhaps from battle

here, though I cannot know it. Bright bones break
the surface of the soil at times, paddle-stamped pots,
the rounded edge of ceremonial gorgets. This is what
we come to in the end: a small space, dreams gone,

a skull whispering in its perpetual silence of a life                    60

now passed to history. Now greatly refreshed I head
out in my canoe on the river once more. The trees
and herbage are sublime and luxuriant; the river
cuts deep between the banks; the air is sultry still

with barely enough wind to flutter the trees.

I am not afraid. I tell it to myself over and over:
I glide through this life and I shall not be afraid.
I begin to see ample plains soon, an almost
unlimited prospect on one side and magnificent

forests on the other. I have miles before I near                    70

the plantation of a new friend, but from curve
to curve, I am unafraid. From bank to high bank
I feel the currents of my hidden life flow on
within me like an unimagined flowing land.

# XV

a.

Exhaustion         begins            my
                        heart paddles poorly in the
                unseen stream of my veins
                        and arteries: a storm breeding in
        in the dark northwest now: fire and drums
                in the Indian of my hands.


Sultry beyond bearing: heavier than winter's
                heaviest coat. Now the crocodiles roar back
                        at the foul heart
                        of the coming rage                            10
                        at the Great Crocodile
                        they may believe lives
                        in the height of storms


        and why would they not? Men have believed
                such          th          high-piled purple
                        clouds
                high-piled purple clouds: an enfolding blackness
                like the hidden city of my fearful nights


skies streaked with blood or purple flame
overhead: lightning streaming and                    darting          20
                in          every
                                direction
                around
        THE WORLD IS FILLED WITH FIRE


b.

                heavy thunder keeps
                the earth in constant tre-
                mor
is the plantation in sight                    is it across the widening
                lake    it may well          be but I
                        could never find it in                          30
        this madness

I heave-to but the current now is so          STRONG
                    that:
          I cannot find the shore          my barque nearly
                    found found founders
High forests bend to the blast.
Sturdy limbs of the trees crack!
The forest is falling down beyond me.
God save me. Mother of God, *salve.*


                    The wind harries          me over the lake          40
          I can barely keep my small boat up-
                              right in the current
          it is upwrong if anything and I          sway
                    slide to slide in the     pull
and push of it


Finally I thrust myself into a low, reedy bank
          and tie off my boat to the boughs
                    of tangled shrubby          O hickory


Now the rain is beyond all dimensions of
of                                                            50
of
of
                    and my boat fills I watch it
                    from from from the


I try to get back in to bail her out: but the violence of this
                    W
                    I
                    N
                    D
nearly tears the clothes from my body and I am so afraid          60
                    breath will not enter my lungs
and I say I say: I am the Flower Seeker, I am the man come
in his naked innocence to a madder land than what lies within
                    and it tries to kill me now for that
                              impertinence

No God: my box which contains
my book of specimens for
Mr. Fothergill now FLOATS
in the boat turning and turning
Rivers of lightning stroke and strike water and                    70
land, come all around me
with lapping tongues of light

I sit beneath a sodden live oak and weep rain

I am the Flower Seeker and I will survive even this
manifest monstrous rain

c.
Father, forgive me, for I was a quiet child
Given to sunny meditations, sitting alone
And thinking of what connects bloom to bloom;
Father forgive my apparent indolence, but
It was never so. I was the quiet boy alone                          80
And now the quiet man alone, and all words
Of Nature, even this horror, cannot stop me
From it or send me back to the greater madness
Of a city. If I weep I weep for what I may lose
In the time I need to know myself in this night
That comes in the heat of day itself, here where
All the world reveals its sharp and savage heart.

d.
Abates. I am ashamed of my fear but it
will not let me        alone
Quite    though I feed          it                                  90

So I set myself a task and begin in the still-rain
to clean the water from my boat, palm by palm
for more than an hour

Now, now, it is seaworthy or river-worthy again
and I feel the raw intelligence
of who I am wrecked against the raw night

of what madness could make me

be

O let it pass from me now

O let blossoms buoy me toward greenness                    100

which is home

Which is surely my home

# XVI

1.

I cross the water. My arms tremble with sore fatigue

And small continuing fear. Limbs and trees float,

Twist and turn in the waves, and I reach the plantation

And secure my boat and climb up to the house, over

Fallen trunks, and my friend leaps backward when he

Sees me: have I just been blown in from the storm?

The others come out in dumb terror. Every house about

But for his great dwelling place has been laid flat

To the ground. Their logs and roofs have collapsed

Inward as my courage did. The mansion-house shook             10

And reeled over all their heads as they hid inside.

One hundred acres of indigo nearly ruined, frayed

Like an old coatsleeve. Acres of sugar cane ripped

Down like a field of simple sticks. The great live oaks

Are torn to pieces. A wide one near the house has toppled

Over, a feat a thousand men could not combine to prove,

And yet it lies before me with the stuff of truth in its fall.

But providentially no lives have been lost to it all.

Sixty slaves live here and none is harmed. Yet their

Unfrayed chains still bind them. I ache for what is right       20

And cannot find my way out. "Stay with us a few days,

Then, until we can clean up some of what has nearly

Destroyed us," my friend says. "This is our night and

We will outshine it. This is our midnight, and we will

Climb across into the new day." My legs are almost
Too weak to wander. I put my arm around his shoulder
With brotherly assent. "I was never in my life more scared
As I was in the past day," I admit quietly. Is it sacred
To see into the eyes of Death and survive what acres
Cannot? I can only believe it so. His hug tugs me.                    30

I take my box inside, and my book of specimens is
Nearly ruined but will survive. Each slit in which
A flower or a root limps is waterlogged but whole,
And I try to find what is my fate and what is my role
In the sharp returning angles of my nearly silent soul.
A sweet small wind stirs through the window frames.

2.
My friend takes me on a four-mile ride
Through shattered stretches of deepest fen.
On the water the waterfowl glide,
And I hear the language of lark and wren.                             40

Order recurs in the broken and breaking,
Even, and quiet pours through me, fills
Me with infinity, strides on unstaking
The world from ownership, from sills

Through which men view the world.
He says he is taking me to view
A vast mineral water spray, curled
With foam and what is always true

In time's wet and smothering embrace.
I see it, issuing in a great cove or bay,                            50
Each shot its own fine millrace,
Each gallon in the shape we pray.

The vast basin is circular, sharply clear
As the insight of those who suffer.
Diaphanous, filled up with a sheer
Disbelief of fish; there is no rougher

Cleansing on Earth than this glory.
Deep, then deeper, all is crystal plain,
As if there is no start to any story
Or any place to start it once again.                                          60

To the taste, it's vitriolic and brassy,
And the smell is sulfurous and wrenching
Like bilge-water; it gives off a gassy
Moldering tint. Our senses go clenching

In order, unsure of how to give it love
Or graven grief. Alligators thrive here
In the pearl coagulum, which like a glove
Coats every substance in the deep, clear

Water. Reflected in the basin is a grove
Of orange trees, magnolias, oaks, and palms.                                   70
I am magnetized, have lost my need to rove
And gamble off my days. Insect psalms

Arise in the viol-sprung music of day.
A delightful spring issues from the ridge,
Too, entering the creek without delay
Just below the basin. My heart's edge

Unbinds with delight that twists and flows
Across the clear landscape of my life.
There is within me a clarity that knows
All things. It bubbles up and this strife                                      80

Becomes evanescent. I say to my friend
That I will never get over seeing a part
Of my world that has no joyful end,
No lost trails for a good and grateful heart.

3.
I am filled with a new vision and laden with the necessities for travel
I am filled with an inestimable gratitude for my salvation:
Grant me direction and strong arms; grant me delight.

It is morning: I set off again on the river and see each dazzling sight
As a pilgrim prays the relics of belief into the equation
Of what is and what can and could at any time unravel                    90

The deep questions of life's variety and feathered pleasure-gleam.
My friend's purveyor has come with me, and the company
Is refreshing. Still, the man who learns to live alone

In this world is a man with the strength of hundreds, who has gone
To the edge of reason without fear, bathes in the symphony
Of Nature uncaring if death comes from claws in the stream.

By morning we reach the destined port, the purveyor steps away
To go about his business, and once again I am alone here
In the vast meanderings of my own world and mind.

I go on up the river and see on one side a rich Elysium, blind         100
Ecstasy of vision, the sharp sight of revelation so near
I could catch both like a butterfly. Other green is gray

Compared to this. Loud, sonorous savannah cranes sail past
With their musical clangor in detached squadrons.
They spread their light elastic sails to the clear air.

Up heavy, up slow, they then soar through the bright and fair
Eden without effort, turning like glittering guidons
From end to end of the mirrored lakes, holding fast

To their reflections like kites on a painless and unclouded day.
Other masses rise and circle the expansive plains.                    110
Then they all contract their plumes and descend

To the Earth. I cannot stay the rapture of it. I cannot ask an end
To what I feel, to science and booklight. No rains
Come to ruin it. Wings and wonder are at play.

# XVII

a.
Now I come into the unrivaled country of risen wings.
 Now I come into the iridescent finish of feather and light bones
  Now I come into the world above and not below in water or
   There beyond in the woods or on the old symmetry of plains:
  Tip to tip they wave the tropical air into peaks of buoyant
 Light and pale destinations no man can know. Plume, silver, glow,
They aim in their deeper migrations for the lilt of light.

   The so-called crying bird, *Tantalus pictus*, inhabits the low
  Shores and swamps of this river, and I cannot see a genus
Of European birds with which to join it and its dark-lead-colored     10
Body and every feather edged or tipped with sharp white.
 I have seen on my voyage two other species of this genus
  With minor changes, the genius of their Creator palpable
   In every stroke of their beating wings against the hot wind.

When winds are high and thunderstorms rake the Earth
 And the chipped, cold stars cannot gleam like fractured agates back
  To my sight, my eye turns to wings. I see a thousand Spanish
   Curlews spilling over the cloud-pulled curtains of heaven;
  I see currents of air entwine crystal cloaks of humidity and lift
 Them at all angles. The regal and various coats of bright feathers     20
Would make those least-interested in Nature stand amazed.

   I see now the species Catesby called the wood-pelican,
  A strange animal with a dipping pouch to hold the snakes,
 Young alligators, frogs, and other reptiles on which it feeds.
Like me it is solitary and does not go in flocks and feeds along
 The banks of great rivers and vast marshes or meadows; it is
  An inhabitant also of deserted rice plantations and stands on
   The topmost limbs of dead cypress trees, neck drawn in to

Its shoulders so that it appears hunched and melancholy,
 Even sorrowful as it stands alone and watches the world     30
  Flow slowly past in its unmentioned grandeur and gilt.
   It seems lost in deep thought. This species is never seen on

The salt seacoast, and yet is never very far from it,
        Either. I believe it may be closer to the Egyptian ibis than
To any other species found in this warm and green world.

                I also see beauty in two vulture species known in these
            Regions, though with shorter wings than the common
        Turkey vulture and so with less span for gliding grace.
I call it the Painted Vulture. The crown of its head is red;
        There are lobed lappets of reddish-orange color on the                    40
                Base of the upper mandible. A large part of its stomach
                    Hangs down like a sack or half-wallet, a duplicature

Of the craw, I believe. The plumage is white or cream-colored,
        Except the quill-feathers of the wings, which are a beautiful dark
                Brown; the tail is large and white and tipped with black; the
                    Creeks build their gorgeous royal standards of these tail-
                Feathers and carry their fierce emblems with them into war.
        They seldom appear but when the natives set fire to the great plains,
And then the Painted Vultures drop down to feast on the roasted

                Serpents, frogs and lizards, filling their sacks with                    50
            Them. At this time, a man can shoot one without aiming,
        They are so unwilling to quit the feast. Hungry men could,
I believe, be killed with just such ease if they found manna
        From heaven at the edge of their starvation. Wings! I scoop
                The air with my eager arms but cannot rise beyond this place;
                    I cannot feel the imperatives of buoyant air.

b.
*Old man, sifting sunlight at the wrinkling end of dreams,*
*Where wings lift only the memories of flight and not even*
*The sight of it, did your youth really happen at all or did*

*It create itself as myths must, in the desire for adventures*                    60
*And a life of daring strength? I sit now, here in the shade*
*Of the known wilderness, languid and glassy, at anchor*

*In the garden old men must reach at last. That world was*
*A coat of many colors, curlew and Cherokee, tumulus*

*And tumult, the long slow arc of hawks on a slow hunt.*

*I remember the emerald curvature of the river's canopy,*
*The Crystal Basin bubbling clear warm water like a laving*
*Dream; was it real? Have I confused chronology, wings,*

*Vulture-nests, the creeping solitude of the gopher tortoise?*
*Old men should not have questions, I thought when young.*                    70
*Now I know that is all we may have, all that touches us.*

c.
No, no, do not go there. Return to the intolerable heat
       You have ignored in those fruitful fragrant groves,

Agreeably diverted and now once again paddling down
       The river, tickling its broad back with slowing strokes.

Where am I? There: I see the Battle Lagoon where love
       Nearly left me, where I culled the cream of defeat

And yet lived past it. I see the land's soft and soggy cracks,
       Hear the coughs of crocodiles in their scaly crowns,

Calling out to me that though I have come past and back through          80
       I am no victor in their world. I am only the Flower Seeker,

I am only the man who inhales fragrant orange groves, touches
       That fully filled-out fruit with my grateful palm, who now

Turns my eye from wings to scales, from those who wander
       Through the air to those who sail underneath the cool blue

Anonymity of water. I am the farmer of the riverway who plows
       Down deep to see what scurries there and always rushes

Way to way. So to study the ways of fishes as old Jonah might,
       I pull into the shore and build a quiet camp then go for fat

Trout so I can, like vultures on the plain, fill up with my own feast.          90

I kneel before the water and lay my mind in the dream currents.

What a most beautiful creature is the fish before me. Like a bat
    It flits and flirts with direction then bursts fast as light

Out of my eyeline. It is the yellow bream or sunfish, and its occurrence
    Here is providential in more ways than any simple beast

Could understand. (I am the simplest beast about, so I know this
    To be true.) The whole fish is pale gold or burnished brass,

Everywhere variably powdered with red, russet, silver, blue, and green
    Specks. It bears a crescent of the finest ultramarine that

I have ever seen, like a dream of morning air, circled with a fast     100
    Knitting of silverine and velvet black, like the insistent

Eye of a peacock's tail feather: a warrior in gilded mail, fat
    And filled with kissing days' delight, loves all unseen.

d.
How harmonious and soothing
is this native sap-sewn music now
in still evening. How inexpressibly
tender are the responsary cooings
of the innocent doves in fragrant
*Zanthoxilon* groves. I hear bright
gurgling from the nonpareil,     110
more sprightly and elevated
strains of the blue linnet and
golden icterus; frogs go guttering
wildly, and the shades
of silent night are made more
cheerful by the three notes
of the whippoorwill and
the virtuoso mockingbird.
  The night is high and airy,
and a brisk, cool breeze     120
ruffles the surface of the lake

and surrounding grove so that
I sit content in the moonlit country
with my dark hair blown back
by the unseen traveling breeze.
I sit on my sweet couch
of soft *Tillandsi ulnea-adscites*
and feel only contentment
in my solitary state. How
harmonious and soothing                                                         130
is this native sylvan music now.


e.
Morning: the feared horrors of a lapidary night alone never
Arrive. I sit and see the uncontested beauties of the world
In its finely sewn vegetation around me. Dewdrops twinkle
And tremble on tips of the lucid, green savannahs, like gems
On the turban of an Eastern prince. I see pearly tears roll off
Buds of the granadilla, sight the azure fields of *Cana lutea*.

Almost endless varieties of phlox fill the crevices as far
As I can see, pink and girl-blush crimson pastures with birds
And butterflies attending. The green banks swell as a mother-            140
To-be might with purple verbena, pearly *Gnaphalium*, silvery
*Perdicum*. There is the libertine *Clitoria* mantling the shrubs.
Beyond and beyond and beyond: what have I wandered toward?

I feel happiness and deep dread as I board my boat to head back
Toward the Upper Store and then the Lower. What does it mean
To come back into the stable world trailing light? How can I go
Back to the ordinary days and ways of men now? I am changed
By what I have been and seen. I am hunted by flowers and limbs
And wings all my days now, and they will find me there waiting.         150

I sail all day, camp in a quiet place for the night. Each day
Is like and unlike the one before except I fear nothing now,
Not the snap of a serpent or the nightmare clap of a crocodile's
Jaws. Not the swirl of rough water or the scent of disease
From claws or carrion. I sleep like a small child in the great
And unforgiving wilderness around me. I come home each night.

f.
I stop, I cut, I study, I collect. I want to see men and do not.
I know now that this will be my joy and my burden all this life,
To live apart in the world and words of others and yet need                160
The intercourse of conversation and shared delights in garden
And riverside. I come into the hailing arms of men. I step off.

# XVIII

1.
I have returned from the wilder land;
Its green and gilt memorials I bear.
I can hardly stand to step onto the sand
Or feel the needs of humans in my care,
But I move into that world and slowly dare
Perceptions to still my stride and shout.
I have come out of the darkest, deepest lair
Where I learned the tenderness of doubt.
I do not know if I can live here without
The terror of tearing jaws and my blood                                    10
Splashed in an imaginary rage and rout.
I feel the rushing invocation of fear's flood.
I want to think my pulse will push me higher
Than the stars that throb with ice and fire.

2.
My old friend Wiggens hails my wave
As I walk to the steps of the Upper Store.
He looks as if he thinks he still could save
Me from my need for time to travel more.
Deep inside the blossom of my pollen core,
Though, is a pull toward home and easy sleep.
I long to raise a window and to open a door,
To stroke, to run, to sing aloud, and to leap
Across crevices too wide and so very deep
That a lifetime would not be enough to span.                               10
And so like an old one I come to him and creep
With the calming eye of a resurrected man.

When close enough we lean to laugh, embrace;
And in his glance I see my changes face to face.

3.

I want to roam this watered world but slow down
To collect seeds and roots for a few fine days.
The Indians honor me to know I did not drown
Along the way. I see deer that come and graze
Like cattle or lean against their shadows, laze
Among the flocks of ibis white as summer noon.
They do not know my language or the proper phase
Of friendship with strangers or the phase of moon
Others do not think to tell. My life speeds too soon
For pure delight. I take it as a blossom takes a bee.                    10
Among this kingdom I am monarch and dragoon
And break all chains that bind who fly free.
But I know what I recall at each dawning's day:
I must know more but I cannot, cannot, cannot stay.

4.

I cannot bear this order. I cannot bear the sounds
Of men's voices, a daily slate of things to do;
I cannot bear the plans for hunting or for hounds,
A sky where men cannot even notice blue.
By which I mean there is no chance to flower
In such a place with hothouse indignities
Ordered for me. I'd rather have the slime
Of swamps and their fetid wonder than some
Offal of rhyme and expectations.
                   Wings can't                    10
stay in a garden long. I tell Wiggens goodbye
          and head onward to
                  the Lower Store:
       slow strokes on the face of the Mother
          of all
                       *W  A  T  E  R  S*

Ye realms, yet unreveal'd to human sight,
Ye gods who rule the regions of the night,
Ye ghosts, permit me to relate

The mystic wonders of your silent state!                    20

Sheer delights! I will not be bound
           by form or content to       the formal world
     I will not     sit on the porch
   while I am young:       time will take me there
        when age corrupts me
     when my eyes have closed to Nature
      or her eyes have closed to me
        Ecstasies! To go on alone.


5.
Into Lake George from the river,
To and past Cedar Point,
Arms glistening with miles.
Chest glistening with miles,
I reach the enchanting Isle of Palms.
Planted only by Nature,
In God's grove of shimmering
Palms, along with pyramidal magnolias,
Live oaks, golden orange,
And the animating *Zanthoxilon*.                    10
     I bathe in the air of this beautiful
     Retreat. This is the most blessed,
     Unviolated spot of Earth I have seen.
     Its dew-struck lawns are protected
     By a spike-fence of *Yucca gloriosa*.
     With it are balmy lantana, ambrosial citra,
     Perfumed *Crinum*—all perspire their
     Mingled odors. I sit in a clearing and
     Hug the isolated rapture of such richness.
     I will stay here for my longing life.                    20
I hoist the sail on my boat and hitch it to the wind.
By dusk I make a safe harbor in a small lagoon.
I walk along a clean, sandy beach. Wind rises.
Like Ulysses, I hear my Sirens and cannot leave.
Land just beyond the beach is impenetrable
With knotty thickets of shrubs and low trees.
The brisk wind comes from off the lake now,

And I pull my boat ashore, worrying that a storm
Could shake her into water after night falls.
What would I do stranded? I have barely thought                    30
      Of such a thing since I left. I would die
      Happily, weaken, walk, starve, be eaten,
      Be written into Nature's day-book without
      Regret. The breeze blows off the clouds
      Of mosquitoes that gnaw me up. Thanks
      To Aeolus for that divine breath. I gather
      Wood for a crackling fire. I catch and roast
      A feast of trout. I stew their heads in the juice
      Of oranges, boil some rice, take, and eat.
      The moon rises over the edges of Paradise.                 40
I spread my skins and blanket on the clean white sand.
I sit to dream. I think on the sun, minister of the Most High
And how he draws the small and mighty plants up from
The succulent earth. I watch him with gratitude all day,
Delight in the daily setting, how he makes the routine
Glow with all grandeur imaginable. Fleecy peach clouds
Hang low, holding their horizon. Now all is silent,
Peaceable as Eden on its first nights, when the insects
And animals felt their hum and stride with wonder beyond
Their ability to imagine. I am alone in the wilderness             50
      Again, and do not miss the sounds of men's
      Voices or steps. I am not meant, I now know,
      For that world of social politics. I understand
      How I must disappoint those who loved and love
      Me to be so slow and deliberate. But I do not
      Sit to avoid the work of men. This is what I am
      Designed for, the pistil and the stamen, the prints
      Of birds and mammals in the sand; I am bound
      To the music of rain and the sympathetic fear
      Of thunderstorms in the darkness. I am moving,            60
Never alone, a man of camplights, unafraid of dreaming
In the darkness. How can I go back to the world now?
I want a life of less, not more. I want to lie down
And not worry if I will waken to stronger joy than I
See and hear and smell and touch each day here on
This river with its bulging lakes and Indian remains:

It cannot go on. It must end. Then I will spend my days
In memory of where I was and who I was and the nights
Like this when something imperishable hung about me
Like a cloak of stars. Bless what dreams me here and now.                70
    Midnight. I awaken suddenly. I sit up and see
    How alone I am in the wilderness of Florida,
    On the shores of Lake George, but under the care
    Of the Almighty, protected by the invisible hand
    Of my Guardian Angel. Now awake completely,
    I hear the heavy tread of a large beast. Dry limbs
    On the ground crack crack crack under his feet.
    *Hie! Hie!* I stand and clap him away, and the close
    Shrubby thickets part and bend around him as
    He rushes away from the madman on the shore.                80
I laugh at him, then see, with bright alarm, that the fish
I had hung on the tree above me are gone, torn down cleanly
From what I thought to be a safekeeping. I rekindle my
Sleepy fire, run my hand through my hair: A shiver
Sunders me. Now I understand what has happened:
A rapacious wolf has filched the fish from just above my head.
How much easier for him in the warm night to have leaped
On me in the dead of sleep and torn my throat to kill me.
I would have sat up singing blood. I would have seen my
Death staring me with his dripping jaws and hot eye.                90
    He would have followed my thrashing with his glare,
    Waiting patiently for me to slow down and die.
    Then he would have dragged my body off for a slow
    Feast. Why did he take the fish instead of killing me?
    Providence, possibly, but I do not believe one man
    Alone in this night of impossible dangers could
    Expect it. I am pensive now. I sit by the fire and think
    How amusing my earlier ecstasies must seem to one
    Who lives for the hot, iron-smell of fresh blood.
    Who lives for the crack of bone and succulent muscle.                100
I doze. Morning is here. I stand and stretch, get aboard
My craft and push into the world again. The water grows
Clear then clearer, and I can see through its transparency
The nations of fish passing and re-passing each other.
I follow the brighter water until I see it is crystal clean

And deeper than I can gauge. Now I paddle up
The little river this spring-fed flow creates here.
And I see the most alluring scene of this life: bubbling
Up before me a Crystal Basin half-encircled
By swelling hills clad with orange and *Illisium* groves.                    110
    The social, prattling coot all robed in blue,
    The squealing water-hen, wings half-expanded,
    Trip over each other on the watery mirror of the basin.
    I put in at an ancient landing site, determined to make
    A vast collection for Fothergill from this place.
    Species, genus, *Zamia pumila, Cactus opuntia,*
    Cochineal insects feeding on leaves, open forests,
    And savannahs, a species of *Cacalia* with its
    Hoary pubescence and vesiculae; scents, sights,
    Trees, shrubs, and now back to my campsite,                    120

6.

I sit on a knoll at the head of the Crystal Basin and see
Before me a fountain spouting liquid ice—such clarity
And precision that is impossible to believe. It throws out
Water with bright delight from the rocky caverns below,
And I feel my skin grow prickly with vernal ecstasies.

Tons of water rise every minute from beneath, creating
A bright, perfectly transparent stream that bubbles down
To Lake George. Some twenty yards from the upper edge
Of the basin is a continual and amazing ebullition, where
Waters are thrown up in rich abundance and with sharp                    10

Amazing force as to jet and swell up three feet beyond
The common surface. White sand and small particles
Of shell are thrown up with the waters, almost to the top
Of the cresting swell. It speaks to me of scenes to come
That are inexpressibly admirable and pleasing to imagine.

The loveliness of it all in whole is beyond comprehension:
The vast, circular expanse, diaphanous water, a margin
Of fruitful and floriferous trees, shrubs and plants: pendant
Golden oranges, whose reflections dance on the surface

Of the pellucid waters; and the air that vibrates with bird-   20

Song, from the tenants of the encircling aromatic grove.
And in the water I see bands of fish clothed in the most
Brilliant colors and by the shore alligators motionless
With satiety and pleasure. Beyond them swim garfish,
Trout, the gilded bream, barbed catfish, stingray, skate,

And flounder, spotted bass, sheep's head, heavy drum.
None of them chase or hunt the other; they live in perfect
Harmony, a peaceable kingdom of land and clear water.
Now, though, I watch more closely and see how deep the basin
Really is, for armies descend until they are invisible to me!   30

Then as dots they begin to rise and take on the shape of fish,
Mouth, scale, tail, fin, and iridescent eye. Their colors
Begin to paint the clear water. Now they rise in the column
Of crystalline water and into the circular basin or funnel,
But gently, gently, in expanding fluid toward the surface.

I see a crocodile down there, and it seems I could reach
Out and touch its eye when it is, I now see, thirty feet beneath
The water. All is reduced and magnified at the same time,
And I take the lesson in human relations, health, fear,
And the fragrant peace of the wild places I have seen.   40

Now the sun begins to sink below the horizon and I
Must leave the Crystal Basin, a bright and risen sight,
A memory of clear disbelief and emptying heart,
Most remarkable on this tour into the light of what Nature
Reflects in me. On arriving back at my camp, I kindle

The fire, eat, and rest peaceably. I get up early and collect
Specimens—growing roots and seeds—and in the afternoon
I paddle back down the pellucid little river and re-enter
The great lake and then raise my sail and head back down
The river, now passing high walls of rock, flat slabs   50

That lead me onward to me, to the life I thought I had left
Permanently behind but cannot. I sail and sail. I know
That soon I will come to the Lower Store, and I covet it
And fear seeing it. One last time I come on shore and see
A magnificent grove of orange trees and magnolias; I collect

A few specimens with what I realize is a soft melancholy.
For the last night, I camp out beneath the chipped stars, eye
The world, hear the creep and stamp of crawling creatures.
*Let it last, let it last, let it last*, I dream, but slight sunlight
Comes and spreads my eyes open. I look one last time                    60

At the groves and savannahs and sail on down. Toward dusk
I arrive at the Lower Trading House. I am brightly grieving.

# CANTO FIVE

*N*EW adventures: I find men moving store to store
(Bright missions to come). Ben says, "Aye, look at you,
Well burnt by the sun and covered with bites like pox;
Your courage and madness come to you in equal parts,
I gather." I laugh and tell him it is true enough.
"I am a great hunter, but I only seek
Roots and flowers and new species
To ship out to my employer,
Mr. Fothergill."

     "Well," he nods, "if you have time for another adventure,     10
    We are headed for the Cowkeeper of Cuscowilla to talk
Of the trade—five of us. You could come collect there
If they do not collect your head." He grins, showing
    Bad teeth and gritty delight. I say I must ship
    Off my specimens first. "Then you're in
      Luck, for within the hour we expect
      A trading schooner that will go
      Back to Savannah soon."

    I was wrong to think I would rage against my own
    Kind. They are merry as men who are leaving a life     20
Of which they are tired and can find mirth in anything.
    I want to tell them of my improbable adventures,
     Of the Battle Lagoon and the Crystal Basin
    (They come to me in capitals now as myths
     Come to the lips of a storyteller), but I
     Say to myself: Not yet, not yet, keep
     Some mysteries in the deep heart.

    I gather my collections, memorials to a solitary life,
     Pack and box them well. I find I am sad to see
     Them leave me, and yet I am as exultant as a     30
      Kicking colt; I have accomplished a great
     Thing, I tell myself. I was not bitten by
     Snakes or eaten by a crocodile or wolf;
     I did not give in to the heat of fear

Or the horror of a black night.
I am of the wilderness.

Two days pass. I sleep indoors like a dead man,
Awaken each day like one surprised to be
Coming back into this life from the dead.
I cough, stumble, tell no one how I                    40
Nearly went mad (did go mad, in
All truth) while alone, make way
For a new adventure with men
I do not even know. For I
Cannot yet go back home.

We board and travel westward through a
Perfectly level plain—a charming green meadow
Thinly planted with low, spreading pine trees.
Since I am not sailing myself I can see things
I have not spied before: the upper earth is       50
A fine white crystalline sand that seems
Mixed with the ashes of burnt
Vegetables. I see particularly
A species of *Annona* whose

Leaves are cuniform or broad lanceolate attenuating
Down to the petiole, of pale or light green color,
And covered with fine down. Its flowers are
Very large, perfectly white, and sweet-
Scented. Many are connected on
Large, loose panicles or spikes;                    60
Its fruit is the size and form
Of a small cucumber; its
Skin is quite scabrous.

There is in abundance the beautiful Dwarf *Kalmea ciliate*,
White-berried *Empetrum* (a very pretty evergreen),
And species of small oak I do not recognize.
Also there is before me a shrub that seems
Related to but is not the rhododendron.
In such clumps and coverts are many

Birds as well, especially one jay 70
Of an azure blue color with no
Crest on its head

And smaller. There are towhees, too, and a species
Of the bluish-gray butcher bird that crees and wheels
In the wind. Too much! Too much to see with
Only two eyes, but I cry out inside with
All bright joy in any life at the Nature
Beside and before me. Now lizards
And snakes come writhing out,
too, and scorpions six inches 80
In length abound.

The solemn symphony of the steady western breeze
Skates us toward Cuscowilla with too much haste for my
Eye. I want to say: slow to the pace of a collector
Of Nature's articulate tale, friends. Let me
Have time for inquisition, to examine
Every curl and crack, each change
Of soil and stamen. This is why
I am not cut out for the life
Assigned us by society, 90

I fear. Early in the evening we arrive at Halfway Pond
And make ready to camp for the evening. The lake spreads
Itself in a spacious meadow, beneath a chain of
Elevated sandhills. Near our campsite is
A wild vortex of water that traders
Call a sinkhole, and like a myth
Water unplugs itself downward
Into darker spaces, and I
Shudder at the idea

Of how it could drown men unaware. Yet now it is 100
The still of evening, with the sun striking the embroidered
Savannahs, armies of fish on their pilgrimage to
The Crystal Basin, I dream, and the sky
Is a powdery blue, and now I see how

The rivulets descend into the earth
Through cracked places, and in
That darkness must glide
And wonder if light

Will ever catch their tunneled turning again. This
Lucid grotto holds God's incandescent creations, and I          110
Try to call them by name as He did: crocodile,
Spotted gar, mud fish, trout, catfish, bream.
In particular these last swimmers come
In so many brilliant colors that the
Eye feasts on them more than
The stomach might. I exult
As they rise to light.


2.


*Order! Let there*
*Be order in all the*
*World, even though I fret*
*It cannot be as we design. I sit*
*Here in my garden, and my chest*
*Begins to ache with memory and age,*
*And I worry that it is now my time to go out*
*Like a blown candle flame before I can recall all*
*My adventures when I was strong and young, and I*
*Want to call my family around me and tell them*          10
*That memory of pain is not the same as pain, that*
*If there is disorder in this life, storms west*
*That come toward and upon us, we can*
*Let them rise and take new order in*
*Their tumult. I do not want to be*
*Afraid, and yet I see before me*
*That vortex I heard on the*
*River and fear it.*


*Father, I recall*
*Our trip to the Catskills*          20

*When I was fourteen and you*
*First showed me the natural world.*
*I recall our trip to this Florida for botanical*
*Wonder, and how I foolishly thought, later, that*
*I could start my own plantation here. Forgive me for*
*The shadows of my inconstant strength; I found out that*
*My place for all life was on these acres and no farther, dawns*
*Up to walk this garden and the gardens of my own history*
*And others'. I grew afraid to leave what I could see,*
*What I knew from bloom to bulb, from bramble*                30
*To low shrub. I grew more solitary than I*
*Thought a man could ever be and live*
*With others. But then they came*
*To me, and so I did not need*
*To leave for friendship*
*Or for new love.*

3.

Enough of it. Enough pretense of delicious youth
And evergreen ecstasies. What do you see? How
Do you see it? What are its colors and shapes?

Be blunt and even savage in your cold clarity,
William Bartram. Align. Delight only with facts,
Not emotions, for the latter will betray you soon

Enough. We live in a clinical time, enlightened
By order and ordering. Take each adjective, burn
It in the campfire. Seek them out for the dinner

Of grammar that precedes all enlightenments.                10
*What do you see? How do you see it?* Cut off each
Fact and mount it in your book. Time will order

All things for good or ill. Here, as well as all
Of the rivers, lakes, and ponds of East Florida
Is the tortoise, a flat plate of a waddling creature,

With its soft shell and when full grown perhaps
Thirty to forty pounds. Flat, very thin. Head is                    20
Large and clubbed, truncated in something like

A swine's snout. The upper beak is hooked and
Sharp as a hawk's bill. Lips and corners of the
Mouth large, tumid, wrinkled, and barbed with

Bulged projections. They bury themselves in the
Bottom land, the mud and muck under roots and
Herbage. They raise their heads above the surface

Of the water and emit a puffing noise like a large
Porpoise. I feel nothing for them. We eat a huge                    30
One for our supper. He's too large for us. I feel

We've wasted part of him. Vultures watch us
From some distance, sharpening their bills, fluff
Up themselves with the patience of those who

Can wait for the kill of others. It is offal that they
Seek. They can wait. I am clawed from the inside
By what I will deny. Facts only. What I can see.


4.


But          but          but
   of the fragrant   disorder        of this world—
                      how can I push it away from me
        here in this                                               10
                         rich fragrant morning of the New
                                                     World?

      All senses
      derange
            them-
      selves

                      All light comes
                      on silver

eye-
lashes                                                          20
the pulse of Nature comes alive
            once more! the world begins to move!
and the machine becomes
            irresistible
                        to one and to all
    the cranes turn the savannahs musical
            the sparrow, chippering, darts up from
                his grassy couch


            and the high, sharp
        glorious sun            paints the top            30
        of the pines            with gilt and grains
        of pure harvest-        light, turns into wings
        that wrinkle and        wink; all flies out to
        the spreading plains    in the genial wind, eye
        eye with what lifts all light and living things
            into the life of airy wing        and caring curve!
            O look at the light that    sings and is singing
        hear the light that gives    us the daydreamed
            elegies for such days of all pureness


Now from Halfway Pond we head west                      40
        Through the high forests of Cuscowilla
            And the sand ridges become higher
                And the ponds more expansive and clearer
                    And the summits more gravelly. Now we
hurry over the transparent waters into a vast
        and beautiful lake, through fine fruitful
            orange groves; we alight to refresh
                ourselves and adjust our packs. Here we find
                    evident signs and traces of the great ancients


hurry it, hurry it: capitals cannot change      the eye here        50
set off again from the mounds and pot-          sherds, pines
to the left and right, steady breezes, gent-    ly rising and fall-
ing, fill the awesome high forests with a       harmony that is
reverential, inexpressibly sublime, and n-      ot to be found

anywhere but these Indian regions; O to        have lost home
as the ancients have from here. What sor-     row there is in
                 this gorgeous world

        vast profusions of:
          *Rudbeckia*
          *Helianthus*               60
          *Silphium*
          *Polymnia*
          *Ruellia*
          *Verbena*
          *Rhexia*
          *Convolvulus*
          *Clitorea*
          *Viola*
more to more to more—green and red and nightshade
          of all living day creatures        70

      How cheerful the rural conversations
    of the tribes of tree frogs       while they look
      to frog-heaven for their      showers: hoarse
         and constant cries

      How harmonious the shrill, tuneful
    songs of the wood thrush      the soothing love-
      lays of the amorous      cuckoo
         seated in the cool

leafy branches of magnolias and elms, maples, and gigantic
*Fagus sylvatica* that shade the sequestered groves     80

HE SANG WHO KNEW
TALES OF THE EARLY TIMES OF MAN,
HOW THE ALMIGHTY MADE THE EARTH,
FAIREST FIELDS ENFOLDED BY WATER,
SET, TRIUMPHANT, SUN AND MOON
FOR A LIGHT TO BRIGHTEN THE LAND DWELLERS,
AND BRAIDED BRIGHT THE BREAST OF EARTH

WITH LIMBS AND LEAVES, MADE LIFE FOR ALL
OF MORTAL BEINGS THAT LIVE AND MOVE.

We are walking now, exploring the land                    90
Before us in good order, eye to eye, hand to hand, glad
For the mature forests, clumps of low shrubs, the *Kalmia*
    *Andromeda*, *Empetrum*, and *Vaccinium*.

We are walking through the sandhills and
See dens of the great gopher tortoise, a beast yet undescribed
By historians and travelers: upper shell nearly eighteen inches
    in length, twelve inches in its breadth:

Its back is ridged and very high,
Covered with its horny plates.
The underside, God's rich divide,                         100
Is hard and cannot desiccate.

The forward part is like a spade,
The feet and legs are covered well
With thickened, fight-hard squamae
And talons from the tight-shut shell.

I am astonished now to see
How much weight the shell can bear;
A man can stand and ride for free
Upon its back through turgid air.

       5.

We cross a branch, enter a dark and noble forest.        10
There is a silence now, the stirring absence of wind
Or wing that shakes me into wariness. I step slowly

Here and listen to the dense chorus that was sent
    To shift us into deep drowsiness or to come adore us
Without ranking the human from the lost or the lowly.

Do such massed birds presage human habitation here
     As they often do in other places? Or have they gone
Away like the ancients? Do the birds recall past generations

In their songs? Are we nearing Cuscowilla or have the songs
     Vanished with their stories of legends and their cheer     20
To natural history? We wait to feel their calming adorations

To know.

### 6.

We ride a mile more and see it before
Us: the town of Cuscowilla, where a pretty brook
Runs through, wrinkling light hut to hut.
Young men and maidens take us
To the Chief's house, which is on a mound
Above the rest of the village, a flag
Or standard flapping slowly in the breeze
That chaffs our cheeks or loves them—     30
Imagination is our map and guide now,
Not what lies before us in the real world,
A place and time that does not exist
For the thinking or the feeling mind.

Now the dreamlike line of ancient men
Comes toward us, long gray hair hanging
In braids or falling shoulder-free; tears
Of light pour down them, loss to loss.
These men appear amiable and almost
Dance as they float toward us then     40
Reach to shake our arms and say,
*You are come, you are come,*
In a way that only Seminoles can,
Meaning they expect and welcome
Us: this is their world, not ours,
Not the life we fled to float away.

They prepare an appointed chamber
To receive us; it stays in proper readiness,
And we follow them there, fill the pipe,
And light it. Also, they bring in a bowl           50
Of liquid called Thin Drink and set it on
A table, a great wooden ladle hanging out.
Each must take as much as he can sip
Before passing it to the one just past.
So it goes round. So we all go round.

"*Why have you come among our People?*"
The Cowkeeper asks. "On a mission
Of friendship and trade," says our chief,
Who then tells who the others in our party
Are. "Young William Bartram here has          60
My bond to travel this country to collect
Flowers, medicinal plants, roots, berries,
And whatever stories Nature might tell
Him of its bounty and frugality. He
Catches only what a thousand thousand
Pass by, to study and to understand."

The Cowkeeper smiles as if he understands
My mission most of all, nods. The room,
Filled with smoke, the smell of men, aroma
Off the Thin Drink, with the hidden texts          70
Of our ambitions and delights, brightens,
It seems to me. He says, "*I recommend
you to the friendship and protection then
Of all our People. And I will call you
PUC PUGGY—the Flower Seeker. Take
What blooms and blends with all the world.*"

Night comes. Business cannot transpire
until the next day;      my own film of sweat
blossoms on me      as I walk alone near
the water. All      creatures in this Earth cry    80
out with delight      for being alive; order begins
her retreat again      from me and all that is light;

I am calm with silence          from that known world
  and now expect the miracles        of the unseen but heard
            when suddenly she stands
                near to me.
Moongleam glows through the canopy and a faint light
    from the village, where singing celebrates something not us
        I believe, and that is when I see her, standing near me,
            bright as gold, skin perfect, eyes set wide apart          90
and staring at me. She is close, then closer, and I can smell
    her, like smoke and flowers, burn and blossom. I speak
        my name, Puc Puggy, and she smiles to hear my voice
            and touches my cheek with her hand, and then pulls
Her fingers across my rough, unshaven skin. Long dark hair
    falls over her shoulders, and her black eyes catch a gleam
        from the flowing light of campfires and the water-moon,
            and I want to say more and cannot, for now she leans
into me, her body whole against mine. And I see my arms come
    up and around her. See them, for they cannot be mine          100
        and yet I know they are; her lips, warm and wet
            as summer slide alone my neck, and her tongue
comes out to taste my skin.

                    And I cannot bear it anymore
                    cannot hold myself from what
                    Nature in her great design has
                    created us for; I cannot stop her
                    from slipping out of her garment,
                    and it falls, it flows off her, and
                    she stands back, Eve in the night,          110
                    and I am mad for her lips, body,
                    dreams, syllables without words.


God: I am brought here to learn
Of all orders and disorders,
But I cannot stand away
From this now, and I strip
Off my clothes until we stand
Naked before each other
By the river in the dark.

𝔓uc 𝔓uggy—I am the Flower Seeker—and                    120
she says my name; our lips swim upon
each other toward the same destination
my maps are burned and useless; I endanger
myself and us and do not care I glance
once toward the village and see no one
coming and know this is a trysting place
and my mind tells me no no no no no no

which means I will now do anything
my body says—pistil, stamen, pollen, bird,
tree, wind, light.                                       130

I      we      lie on a        skin
  she has  brought    kiss
O God      this is what a life means
          that we        cannot are meant not       to
                live without

We are separate
We are one breathing creature
In the woods
We swim the air
We smell ourselves                                       140
And wonder what trail
We leave
Mouth, legs, breasts,
Tips, points, angles
Pushing into, pulling into
Soft, damp hands on
My shoulders and all
The natural world begins
To glow, to roar now,
To splash in the river                                   150
To make footfall in the woods
And she whispers
My name in my ear
Chants it over and over
Until death itself comes

Over us, *süsser Tod*,
The arch more noble
Than Rome; I will not
Cry aloud:
We cry aloud, louder,                                          160
Aloud and then louder
And the world cries back
With wonder and shouts
At our evening dance.

7.

Halfway through the night, and I disbelieve it,
Sit up on my soft pallet of skins and mounded earth:
I could not even ask her name, and now I think
Of nothing but the measure of her face afterward
In the moonlight. We stood man to woman then
And she leaned out and broke off a fragrant blossom          10
And gave it to me and smiled and then in one motion
Dressed and disappeared like an animal retracing
The safety of its own tracks and scent. What have
I done? And when I reached my bed I found they
Had all brought me flowers and viny plants, roots,
Cut-off claws, feathers from owls and eagles.
Cuscowilla has its Flower Seekers, too. This world
Fills with a flood of White fools. And how can I
Now forget this town, and to whom will I never tell
This story in the down-breaking years? Will I                20
Mark its anniversary each year with a flower cut
From my garden and placed on a mantel in the den?
And will I ever see this creature in my dreams again?

Morning comes: Now we find the business for which
We came: a Council, but I wonder how my fellow-
Travelers spent their night. We will build a trade house
With their permission as I understand it. Now a dozen
Then a dozen more leaders—chiefs or priests I cannot tell—
Surround the Cowkeeper of Cuscowilla to show solidarity.

Can I study them as a naturalist sees *Solanum tuberosum?*         30
The Chief is a tall man, frank and cheerful, perhaps
Sixty years of age, eyes lively and full of fire; his face
Is placid and manly yet somehow ferocious, too,
And I feel admiration and fear. What if I have doomed
All my friends with my night's adventure? No. I feel
They understand our common bond far more than we
Ever have in Philadelphia. A true warrior in his time,
Many slaves attend him, moaning softly and bowing
As if to raise his dawning glory to the early light.

Focus, form, study: his slaves attend him         40
With abject fear lest they may offend him
By action or glance. I guess their formal ways
Of action are from the Spanish and their days
Here in the hours of their briefest conquest.

But there are even Christians among them,
Who wear small crucifixes, a sung-hymn,
A neatly hung symbol, swung on shell loops
And swinging like Golgothan silver loops
From their necks and on their bronze breasts.

It is whispered to me they have been immersed         50
In baptism. And yet the most striking, cursed
People are the slaves, mild and quiet, hushing
Children and bowing down with soft and crushing
Obeisance. The contrast between freedom and

Slavery is almost too terrible to speak about.
Master and slave are bull and ox: to shout
It down would be death to us, but how I ache
For those in silent woodland bonds who stand
Straight as ancient trees in an ancient land.

I look for the girl who gave me sweet sips         60
Of streamside fruit; I do not see her whose lips
I kissed. Slaves set before us venison cooked
In bear's oil, fresh corn cakes. I am hooked

Like a fish by milk and hominy, and we drink

Honey and water. Now, they say, let us show
You the great savannah so you will come to know
Us as the flowers do; bring the hunter of blooms,
Too, so he can sample the feast in nature's rooms
And see how trees and greening groves can think.


8.

Now we see in the distance a large field,                          10
Floating with *Nymphea nilumbo*, their golden
Blossoms waving to and fro on lofty stems.
And beyond these fields are spacious plains
Surrounded by dark groves that open into
Pine forests and other plains far and beyond.

Who am I to rake this paradise with my eyes,
As if I might in time come to understand all
Intricate designs? My mind is agitated, turned,
And bewildered at the edge of a New World.
Salve; break what must relent inside me.                           20
Wisdom, power, and strength swell all around

From the Supreme Author of this green heart
That beats and blows past us in wild profusion.
We pitch our camp on a rising knoll for night
Under spreading live oaks and with an endless
Prospect of the plains before us. Dewy evening
Now comes, animating breezes that temper

The meridian hours of this still sultry season.
A million brilliant luminaries wink out now
From the crowding darkness. Wings molt down             30
To silence: the silver-plumed gannet, the sage
And solitary pelican of this wilderness retire
To their nests in neighboring but soundless trees.

Squadrons of savannah cranes rise from the earth
In spiral circles, well-disciplined and far above
The dense atmosphere of the wide and humid plain.
Their polished feathers still gleam. They sing
An evening hymn then in a straight line majestically
Descend, alighting in the crowns of towered palms.

All about is silence and a subtle turn toward kind-          40
Ness and peace. I would stay here and now, never
See another man again, live in the sunset gilt, sleep
In the wink of stars and luminous things. I would
Live to dream and draw what I see, to write down
Not what I see but what I am when I see it all.

Soon after sunrise, though, we must ride back
To Cuscowilla. Indians on horseback suddenly appear
To collect herds of cattle that they've driven here
Along the edge of a swamp to graze. One man rides
Up and says the Chief has told them we shall          50
Have a feast from them to compliment our arrival

And pacific negotiations. We follow the cattle
And their drovers into town and ride, guests
Into the public square where chiefs and senators
Have already convened, since their treaties must be
Transacted in public. Soon all is agreed, and the banquet
Begins: barbecued ribs, the choicest pieces of fat,

Bowls and kettles of stewed flesh called tripe soup,
Which the Indians love but which smells faintly to me
Of carrion and almost turns me aside. This town has          60
Perhaps thirty habitations, each of two houses the same
Size, thirty feet long, twelve feet wide and that high,
Also. All is pleasant, cool, and airy. Cross-pieces,

Roofs of cypress bark, stories, notched logs, posts,
Pillars: the nests of humans with invisible wings.
Each house has a small garden spot with corn, beans,
Tobacco, and varied cucurbits. There are also fields

Common to all and the young patrol them with cries
And bows, chasing off crows and squirrels each day.


9.


a.
What have I done, what have I done,                                  10
       to have loved or unloved this girl:
       they come around after our dinner
       and I judge them morally and loud
to one friend, and he agrees sharply and later

will go to lie with one of them, I'm sure.
       What have I done and would I weaken
       again (yes), would I follow her (yes)
       to all the ends of this world to see those
eyes one last time (yes). For I am a weak and

hidden man, one built not to act but to observe,                     20
       and yet I have tasted that sweetness once
       in this world of syrupy warmth, and it
       will forever be lodged in my mind: hate
should overcome my memory; self-loathing might

wreck me on these shoals. It cannot. So I know
       I would weaken again and look for her
       in this darkening land (yes), to see her
       face before me in the mottled shade (yes)
and to know that one unspoken syllable can be love.


b.
I walk alone into the garden of this Eden                            30
And spy snakes. I laugh at my prediction
That retribution will find me out; this is
Maudlin, not nitwitless—something fine

For my published book one day, I dream:
The echo of the fallen garden just after
I speak of the allure of Indian girls. And so
I kneel to watch several large snakes twined

Together, and though I hold out my fusée,
I know they are innocent and peaceable to me.
They writhe in apparent joy. A subtle joke          40
I'll play when I tell this part of my story.

I walk on and there, near a clot of shrubs,
I see the surprising glass snake, as harmless,
It seems, as a worm. It appears like blue-green
Glass, a thin specimen. If you poke its tail

With a slender stick, part will break away
Like a pane. What a beautiful creature to me!
The sun sets. I make it back to camp unscathed,
Slithering toward the speaking and the unclean.

c.
The old trader and I separate come morning          50
From the others to explore. We see no warning

That alarms us. Many herds of roaming deer
Wander past us. In their eyes is little fear

For our species. Orange groves fill with bees,
And the distant crocodiles beat their skin drums

To threaten and to call. I hear the cry of bobcat
And see above us the wide winds of the gander.

We come upon ancient Indian fields, and my friend
Tells me they have heard a tribe could assemble

Thousands to play ball on what were then happy      60
Fields and green plains. There is a mound here,

Too, from whose eminence our eyes roam the sea
Of this savannah from shore to shore. Its spells

Lull us with the magic of memory. Now dozens
Of birds, flocks, fill the air from grove to grove.


### 10.

Night comes. Camp comes.
The others rejoin us to sleep.
Morning back. We cross now
Promontory to promontory:
My explorations thrill me.                                        10
We see a company of wolves,
Ride toward them. They go
To the edge of the woods,
Stop, turn, wait, sitting on
Their hinder parts. Char-black,
Feeding on a horse carcass.
Now vultures filter down,
Grateful we have chased off
One designer on the dead
For another. But they hesitate                                    20
As they are hunted by sitting
Bald eagles. I am horse, wolf,
Vulture, and snarling eagle.
I taste the free and streaming world.
We follow
  a large flock
    of turkeys as
      they fly and land
        a distance past
        us, wings out                                            30
      to bear their
    heavy bodies
into the air.

A crowd
  of deer play
    there, and our
      crowd plots to
        to shoot several
      for our eating;
    I beg them to                                                  40
  leave them be;
they will do

no such thing. Do all men kill for the sport of it?
A huge buck with wide-spreading antlers leads
        them now. My friend rides rapidly toward him,
        lifts his gun and fires. The proud buck falls
down hard and kicks to keep running, but he runs
for his death now, and I feel sick for my own kind.

They cut open the magnificent creature, remove
his entrails, hang him from a tree to drain. Sickness              50
sweeps over me for the slaughter of such a magnificent
creature when we did not need the food to eat.


11.


       We ascend a collection of eminences covered with dark groves where is it
joined to the great basin. We come to perfectly round sinkholes and peer down
into them and see twenty, thirty feet down a beautiful profusion of plants, green
and flowering. But most striking just past them is the pool of water around which
lie an incredible number of crocodiles, many so enormous as to defy belief. They
roar and rage at us. There are so many that if they would let me I could walk com-
pletely across the basin on their heads. They slowly float and turn like knotty logs
in the water, fight, plunge, slap, turn. Thousands of fish fill the basin with them,
offer up a delicious sacrifice, even seeming eager to be the next to die.
       There are in that city bream, catfish, mudfish, trout, and the crocodiles
seem to be in league with the gars, which are too large and thorny to provide an
easy meal for the thick-trunked beasts. In confederacy with the huge beasts, these
two species, warlike, voracious, enslave and devour the numerous defenseless
tribes.

### 12.

But O the mystery of escape
that lies within: through vast
perforations in the rock, fish
in huge numbers swim through
wells and cavities deep inside                                    10
the Earth itself, down and down
through caverns measureless
to man. Through subterranean
conduits they fly, into vaults
of deepest darkness of inner seas
and from there to other lakes
and rivers miles away. There
are three great vent doors into
this unknown land, all visible
through the clear water. I see                                   20
fish swim through them and into
another world, and I imagine
icicles of stone through which
they wander in that wet night.
Or do shafts of sunlight spill
down through sinkholes along
the way, each light a guide
they seek on their long feast
of miles and warm waterways?
Nights and days must be the same                                 30
for them, as they are for all who
pass from life into the victory
and defiance of all dark Death.

### 13.

We ride back to our camping place, and I feel
The heavy dread of travel. One in our company
Goes back for the shot buck. When evening
Comes we see Indians on the trail, fine men
In full paint and jingling costumes. They ride
Back to Cuscowilla. In the night, heavy rains

Come over us with no thunder and very little                                    10
Wind. I think of the girl and her taste; I want
To taste her once again. I feel heavy with rest-
Lessness and want to stay forever and leave
Forever at the same time. That has been my
Life's profound civil war. Morning rises. I
Sit up and see the air has cleared but my mind
Has not, not quite anyway, but I get on with it.


### 14.

I collect, we ride, and soon the valedictory drag of farewell
Comes over us. We can stay here no longer. We take to
The Old Spanish Highway, and I feel as if I want to ride        10
Away from my good companions, to know once again how
Free I have been in these wild days. But the highway
Has been unused for many years and in places is so grown
Up with trees and shrubs as to be impassable. Yet the track
Is withal so deep that it may be traveled for ages yet to come.

We pass a village from which all the men are gone hunting.
Children scamper in their roundelays. Women reveal
Themselves modestly in their doorways, wondering of our
Intentions. (And what are my intentions, the man who
Would take their flora for an image book? I am unsure.)        20
Day becomes a new day. The path remains. We speak
Little, ride onward, mark to mark, until we see not so far
Away Spalding's Lower Trading House. I want to roar

Out my happiness and disastrous need to flee from it.
The trading schooner is there at bay. But now it is
Morning, and she will not return to Georgia until late
This afternoon. The Indians are all at peace here
And now and everywhere nearby. I am not at peace,
Though. The Seminoles cut off the ears of those who
Suffer fornication and excess, though I suppose they        30
Have no more of it than any other nation. They are

Weak as I am weak. They are strong in the hunting
Lands as I am, as well. They love to roam in small
Numbers. I go alone if I can. They wage war against
The deer and bear, but it is for their food and clothing.
I war against no species but my own and that not as
A soldier but as one who cannot bear too much too close,
Who wants them for convenience and nothing more.
I am the Flower Seeker. I am the quiet sunless sea.

# CANTO SIX

*H*ERE *in the last summer of my last year,*
*Here in the body which is given for you*
*And your own adventures in your worlds,*
*I fan, breathless, unworried and unhurried*
*By man or memory. Our Revolution is past*
*And present, my friend, and I have revealed*
*Myself to you as never in the years of my life*
*To anyone else. For I was not mere botanist*
*And writer but a man: breathing, touching.*
*Needing, skilled with my Linnæan eye,*          10
*Owing so much to my father for his gifts*
*Of studious habits and a love of all Nature;*
*I owe to him the pleasure in order and how*
*Its succulent Latin names can brighten light*
*Into a darkening day; I owe to him a love*
*Of the bronze men and their natural order*
*In the natural world. If now I am only mind,*
*That mind is a flower in its highest bloom.*

*Journey, journey: the serenity of my room*
*Against the fearful world beyond; my kind*        20
*Kept at a safe distance, its city- and sordid*
*Ways not my own. I am no drifting dove*
*With messages of peace. A laughable sight*
*I've become: a dwindling man whose bow*
*Is too slight to sail far, who cannot nurture*
*His own garden let alone a world. Sun sifts*
*Through the winking leaves. Rainfall's cry*
*Takes me to the window. Then I am rushing*
*For what the world can give back. My fist*
*Is long stowed. The packing days, the wife*        30
*I never had—the loss of all is firmly sealed*
*Away now, and I must not grieve. I hold fast*
*To Truth, but I am hardly vexed or worried*
*If I can't find it anymore. All Nature unfurls*
*At my command. Plainly false or simply true,*
*I take what comes to me without a single tear.*

*Order is restored for now. My glassy pain ebbs.*
*I am eager for the tag-ends of talk and tale.*
*So do not look upon this old man and think he*
*Is the traveler through that country; it was not*                           40
*One for old men—they did not live there long.*
*We were barely more than boys, strong, filled*
*With rules and raw lust we rode miles to halt.*
*I look back now on the book I called my* Travels
*With a milding laugh. Half the time in it I am*
*Lost as I was in my days and nights. But the truth*
*Of it is essential if my narrative shows me stopped*
*To scratch off the patina of my wandering years.*
*I have more wonderful and terrible truths to tell*
*And must be about it. I do not need forgiveness*                           50
*But I ask for misunderstanding, for that is the gift*
*Through which we hide as humans in the landscape*
*Of the fragrant world inside us. I ask for you to mount*
*Beside me on our journey, to ride inward, and on.*

We see the ship in the setting sea of river. A drone
Of bees hums us down to sleep. Now I can count
The collections I have made, root, bark, and grape;
And already the traders get ready for their shift
To Talahasochte, so with a caravan's liveliness
We head out in the cool morning, across the shell-                          60
Midden soil to a new trade mission. I hear bears
In the deep mist of a lost forest. Deer have cropped
The lawn around the post down; a lone, soot-
Black wolf howls at the skyline. Men take a dram
For their health, take the first step. Dreams unravel
If those dreams are of home and hearth. The fault
For my restlessness is no fault at all. I have willed
Myself to be a roamer, to hear the deeper song
Of lark and nighthawk. Horses tamed and caught
By the Seminoles are what we hope to set free                               70
Into our own hands in trade. There is no scale
To weigh this transaction or a rail from the webs

All men weave to hide their own best interest.
I want to see these horses, which they say are small
Or smaller than the Creek breed, which is called
*Echoclucco* or *great deer*, a marvelous locution
That ties their animal world in a knowing knot.
I know horses in the high hilly country of Carolina,
Georgia, and Virginia are larger and also stronger
Than the breeds of the low, flat countrysides.                                    80
We ride all day, we camp, we spend all night
Swatting off the maddening swarms of mosquitoes
That make our own horses swish and stamp madly.
Halfway there, our party splits, one group going
Through Cuscowilla and the other into savannahs,
And I head out with the latter, unsure I want to see
The girl who loved me into senselessness that night.
We ride across the plains, through shady forests,
Then back into sunlight. Gradually ascending hills,
We find the old trading path to Talahasochte, take it.                            90

We come to a smaller crystal basin to camp. I make it
That I sit in good company, but the word now spills
In situated relief by the men, too much of a chorus
For me. The group that rode through into the sight
Of Cuscowilla rejoins us. A few fish. Every tree
Comes alive with its creatures that shimmy down
To hunt and wade the forest light. I am knowing
More with each day that passes, each root I gladly
Grab for Fothergill. A brisk wind rises and goes
From wood to field and back. Fire burns white                                     100
With cooking strength and strongly shifts, collides
With what would devour us. I could stay longer
Than the others, I believe. A young man shines,
And an old man lies burnished down; this spot
Makes all ages one, regret the midnight execution
Of all senses. My heart is not stilled or stalled
From weariness. I want to stay awake through all
Ages in this fragrant land, into the bright center

Of every species. We rise and ride, come on a high
Rocky ridge and see before us the most desolate,                    110
Dreary, solitary desert waste I have ever beheld:
Bare stones cracking up out of the naked gravel,
Drifts of white sand, thin grass, and few trees.
No animals come in sight. The only sound heard
Is the western wind and an isolated cricket sawing
Out his quiet melodies. A boy named Patrick looks
At me for explanation, but I shrug and ride ahead
So I can go my solitary way. I say it is to observe
In my naturalist's ways, but it is more and they
Know it. I go alone. Men's words cause me grief.                    120
I ride into this world to write it down without
A man to push me or a woman to grant me love.
I wonder if this is some defect of Nature or if
God loved me into such a life for His own good.
I kick my horse and am gone ahead. I do not dread
Such isolation. They understand me and stay back.

And there I see it: a hundred yards up on the track
A hawk is wrestling with a coachwhip, neither dead
Yet, but the battle growing with each snap to wood
And then back toward open land. I ride up. A shift                  130
Wraps the snake twice around the bird like a glove
It can't shake off. And yet the hawk seems stout
Enough not to need my aid. But all I think is relief
From that encompassing braid, and so I sashay
My horse to a stop and climb down. A slick curve
Of scales now surmounts the hawk, who has sped
Into a fretful spin. Nothing in my tales or my books
Prepares me for the right in this. The hawk is cawing,
Crying, the coachwhip flits his tongue and tail, word
In the language of predator and prey. Yet I seize                   140
Up to know which is which. I think I must unravel
Them when suddenly the snake falls off. Has it failed
To find advantage or has the hawk? A disconsolate
Glance comes from both. And they both stop, fly

From the battle to pastures new. I laugh. I cannot
Think when I have seen any fight more lovely
Or unclear. I suppose the hawk had come down
To take the snake for an easy meal then found
Himself entangled in its twines as a child's hands
Will get confused inside a ball of string. I know,           150
Though, why the hawk picked the long and thin
Coachwhip for his prey, for they in respect
To venom, are innocent as a worm and seem
To be familiar with man. The day is hot, sultry,
And, as we ride, we slow, our horses clop to clop
Moving with a greater strain, and when we come
To a land of stately pines we pull up our reins
And climb down, find water nearby, know it will
Be a good place to rest for the coming nightfall.
But we need food, and our best hunters go on out          160
With the guns. I smile into the fire: we are hawk
And snake, writhed and tithing on a natural altar.
Our men return with a savannah crane, paltry-
Taking for a hunt but magnificent at which to gawk,
For it is past six feet in length and wings sprout
Near nine in its full span. Its delicate bones, as pall,
Are thin shells, and when they swim the air, ill-
Omens cannot hunt them long—
            No—I am more delighted than I show
            As usual, fail when I plow straight            170
                  rows in my gaming days
I want to breathe          more deeply than
                  this, I
      want to feel the world breathe with
                  me.


Now I come into the unrivaled country of risen wings.
            They clean and cook that magnificent bird, but I refuse
                  To taste from it for I prefer his kind in the high skies.
                        After supper, in smoking time, Patrick and I walk
                  Into a field of madly scattered stars and sit in the soft        180
            Brine of distant blackness, swim star-shore to star-shore,
And listen to the click and croak of the wingless world.

"I want to see Nature as you do, William, clear
        As a sharpened cloudless day," he says softly. I nod,
    Try to find some shape to carve my misunderstandings
Of these million worlds into a chapter of brighter wings
    Than I see when I first look at things. "I can only say
            To look again and then again and with clear intent,
                An artist's eyes, a scientist's slow, amazed stun."

To my surprise, he smiles, as if I've made all senses fine                190
    In his eyes. Bright boy, to know that the quiet life
            Is the contemplative turn toward how all things
                    Work each to each. We see a meteor splash
            Across the breadth of heaven, cry without worry
    At how our shouting sounds. O to be alive now, here,
In the minute moving pleasures of fire and light; I wait

            For revelation that may never come. If not, then
            It cannot matter, for this is fact enough, to see that
    Arrow of shot-light streak the warm Florida night, my
Friend to share it, one who speaks as few words as I must.                200
    We wait for another strike, but it does not come,
            And I know one has been enough for our eyes
                To feast upon in this wet and winging world now.

Morning: We slowly ride down in elevation from the heights
    Where we had camped, back into the flat, level
            Country, through green fields with their islands
                    Of darkly clustered woods, change in all fauna,
            And of course in flora, too, flower species, wings
    That bank and fold to fall toward a hunting ground.
I ride past white, testaceous rocks and sinks, and we go                210

            Then lower still into a new region of rapid rivulets
            Of exceedingly cool and pleasant water, where we
    Stop to refresh ourselves. I look more closely, Patrick near,
And see this is not a stream at all but a rain-fed rising,
    A creek that's leaked from a heavy cloudburst, a place
            Where water gathers to meet when rain comes, to say
                The sound of water's evanescent and liquid names.

We stay at the phantom brook for some time, then rise
    To ride on. After a lengthy time we halt to take in the beauty
        Of a fleet herd of Seminole horses, wild and running        220
            A ragged course of youthful pleasure grove to grove.
      "William, look there," says Patrick, and he points out
    A large black dog that turns and chases one horse herd
Without touching a single fetlock hair. "Is he their shepherd

        Who turns them out to pasture, then brings them home
      Again?" I put my hand on his shoulder, say, "Well done,
    Young man," and he beams me with a broad grin. We find
Soon an Indian in Talahasochte owns these mares and stallions,
    And the dog that tends them, too. Every dusk the dog
      Hikes home for food but does not stay the night, instead comes 230
        Back into the dark and loud land,
Back to tend his sheep. Now we see on the higher nearby
    Hills large quantities of iron ore in detached masses that
      Appear blistered like cinders, as if a violent conflagration
        Singed them down to a bare and sturdy core of heart iron.
      I show my friend how rock can have a metal matrix,
    And he lifts one, hefts it like a ball to gauge its weight
And rotundity. "I see," he says, and I know we both do now.

      I see hearts at every step now, the beating pulse of wild
      Amaryllis and mimosa, of *Ruellia* and others new to me.    240
    And of trees there are mulberry, oak, red bays, a hundred
More that I can name and cannot. And soon we see what we
    Have come for, the town of Talahasochte on the banks of the
      Little St. John River, a pellucid stream—the clearest and the
        Purest branch I have ever seen, two hundred yards over,

Fifteen or twenty feet in depth. One can see right down
    To the bright bottom of it where massy hordes of fish
      Swim in teams or ranks, waving slow music
        With their fins and tails. The Indians tell us it has
      No branches or tributaries, flows straight out of Earth    250
    From massive springs with perfect purity, sweet to taste.
The town is situated on the elevated east bank of the flow

And we are taken now
    to the Trading House,
        which formerly belonged to the Chief
    but no longer does; a family of Indians is moved
        out to accommodate us.
They seem to do it with pleasure
    but all such removals are shearing in their pain,
      and I see in Patrick's eyes
that he knows what is happening.                260

My traveling ecstasies fade.
I wonder what we have made
Here in this wondrous shade
Of another's home.

Houses: there are thirty,
And none is near as dirty
As those now skirting
Like cast-off bones

The cities of the White.
What a luminous sight                270
Is this place, all delight
But yet unclear.

Cypress-trunk canoes
Slip down the river flues
With their ringing news
Of a daily seer.

        Some of these are large enough to hold
        Thirty warriors, and they stroke them
        All the way to the Bahamas or even Cuba,
        We are told. I believe it. Now they bring    280
        Out bartering goods of a rich diversity:

Species of tobacco from the South,
Spirituous liquors, coffee, sugar, deer skins,
    Furs, dry fish, bear's oil, honey, bees' wax
    And more, set out in fine profusion.

HE IS WELL ARMED, PRIDE IS IN HIS BEARING,
HE GOES, SO BRAVE, HIS SPEAR IN HAND HOLDING,
HE GOES, ITS POINT AGAINST THE SKY TURNING;
A GONFALON ALL WHITE THEREON HE'S PINNED,
DOWN TO HIS HAND FLUTTERS THE GOLDEN FRINGE:               290

All seems stopped before us. Our torque is spent,
And I sit and try to train my eye on the garden of Nature
But it's no good. I have lost the country of desire
To count and catalog the world. Then Patrick sees me
And comes over grinning, says:
        "We should take one of their canoes
        And ride down the river, fishing with bobs
        For the sheer unreasoned fun of it, William."
        I agree immediately, and we tell the others
Of this plan. Our hosts find a barque to loan us.          300

Now we stroke the water,
  set off down the rolling clear
    waves of this Earth-born spring
      with such renewed and freshened
        delight that I cannot be restrained from
        singing. Patrick sings with me, and
      we feel the day-long dawn come
    back to us. Large and larger fish
swim beneath our boat to take

when we are ready to cast.                                 310
  I lose reason; faith buoys us
    through an illogical pleasure,
      through that happy senselessness
        of young manhood, and I let loose
      of meaning. Clear, charge,
    churn, change, cultivate,

crawl: I sing a world of no
meaning as we stroke.

    We laugh for no reason.
    We glide beneath canopy                                  320
  and shadow, on silver
  gleaming light spots,
looking for a place
  to pause, to cast
    our lines down
      into the deepest water
        to catch thick fat trout.

    Now we halt and throw
    our lines into the shade
  of late-day shapes.                                    330
On each cast we
catch fish so big
  they drag us out to
    the center of the stream
      where we groan in each
        one with dazzled disbelief.

A canoeful of Indians paddles upstream toward us,
And we wave respectfully, and they wave back,
Row to our side and offer us part of their own catch,
Especially from their hanging store of huge bream           340
With their rose and aqua iridescent paintings.

| | |
|---|---|
| We trade | We trade |
| Trout with | Eyes to see |
| Them to | Ears to hear |
| Seal our | Lips to kiss |
| Bargain. | Hands to hold |

| | | |
|---|---|---|
| We return | We return | |
| To town | Life to life | |
| And Patrick | Love to love | |
| Gets out | Boy to man | 350 |

But now      River to rain

  An Indian    An Indian
  Boy comes    Girl sees me
  Back with    Makes shy eyes
  Me to sail    Up and down
  Down-river    My new body

    Next morning  Next evening
    For botanical  For the dream
    Observations.  I walk to water
    He speaks fine  The boy speaks    360
    English to me.  English to me.
     We climb in, paddle
      Off downstream
     Stroke: stroke.

Supplied now with ammunition and provision,
We head (*stroke, stroke*) downstream in morning's
Sharp yellow light, and I feel as if I could swing
My paddle wide and hard enough to sail seas,
To cross the great ocean to an older, unfiner world.

# CANTO SEVEN

## Signs of the Travelers

W<small>E</small> ride and rise on the crystal flood.
The Indian boy and I find fear
A distant, unmeaning tale in which
I no longer believe. I believe in rolling
Over the silvery bed of the clear water,
In the transparency of all friendship;
I believe in the public life and death
Of all who live in this sun-mottled glow
Of a watercourse. I am swimming kin
To all in the watery nations. Numerous          10
Bands of fish rove to and fro. Yet near
The shore, the calm clearness grows
Turgid with churned matter, but still
There seems no desire in this world
To kill or be killed. All seems stilled
With the incapability of that violence
Common to men. I turn, look the boy
In the eye, and he knows what I cannot,
Has known it from the day of his birth,
And I want to ask how we see what              20
We dream, if the moon knows the name
Of all stars, and the ocean swells out
With the secret name of its whales.


## Into the Nympheum

Three miles down the river, down any river,
  We come to the Manatee Spring, a product
Of primitive Nature, a stunning sight no man
  Could hope to imitate even with pen or brush.
My mind asks; my eye bores in; we are led on
  To deeper discoveries. At first the darkest wood
I have seen stands in silence before us, barring       10
  All, owl, cat, young men with the strong strides,
And I say to myself this must be the end of the trail

Here, but soon I see it is not. There is a curved chain
Of hills beyond. We gently descend the floating fields
   Of the *Nymphea nilumbo*, which intersect with
Vistas of yellow-green *Pistia stratiotes*. And now
   We see in this basin there is also a grand fountain,
And my friend does not cry aloud in surprise, so
   He must have been here many times. Its ebullition
Astonishes me, its force great and eternal so far                              20
   As I can see. I also know the swift alligator
And the manatee, that slow and somehow elegant
   Cow of the sea, friendly, bovine, filled with easy grace.
I want to die here, to die now, to halt the shimmer
   Of wonder I gain in the lift of water and its world.
If I could wish myself into barbs or scales, become myth
   And live only in the words of fine amazement
Down centuries and die now, I would. I want to break
   The surface of my life with outrageous pleasure,
With the giddy genuflection of species rising to the light.                     30


*Old Man in the Garden*

*Do the blossoms think I bloom with them today?*
*They must see me as themselves, as we see*
*The world whole only if it keeps our stumbling steps*
*Close, petal to petioles, waxy skin to apple-shine.*

*In their freshening days they must look upon me*
*And think: his fruiting ways have gone; his leaves*
*Are wrinkling without the watery tales of life*
*And light. He closes up, has no need of the body-sun.*

*And yet my race, though creeping slow, is not yet run.*
*I raise my arms into the buttered air to show that*                            10
*I can still unfold with them, one more day at least,*
*And wish down waves of warmth. They cannot know*

*How I pretend to grow with them, that what is going*
*Has gone already, yet remains to swim and sing*

*One last day. I am here. I inhale all that winks alive,*
*And for that rub I do not even need the strength to pray.*


## Swimming the Horses

Next day, early in the cozy morning,
we cross the river to explore an Eden
more. I cannot quite believe that I am here
and now, that the longer that I live I may
return and paddle back into the filling well.
The water is too deep to wade,
and so we swim our horses "out to sea,"
mermen in the thigh-deep waves,
holding on the boats' sure sides
as we glide and slip the water-ride.                              10
Dry and crossed, the horses swim
the forest air, now they have the stroke
to swim the older Spanish trails.
We see the ruins of lost villages here,
shades of fence posts, ghosts of houses,
ditches, corn rows, and potato hills.
Their horses must have swum to cultivate
this wet green land as well, never thinking
as we always do that bottom must be found,
in their dreams from world to world. That is            20
the impertinence of all life: to believe it
can stay afloat and move forward,
even when the water whispers
how the flood will sink them soon enough.
We hold tight on the crossing, plow our
rows straight and long, then sit and fret
the crop's long gestation. Birth, we know,
forgets us soon enough. We shrink down
to root-ball then cross on in the new crop
of this yearly greening world, wizening,                    30
wilting, yet heroic as the stroke of horses.

## Canebrake

For the vast lawn's story-sake,
We ride the green and gritty path,
And riding close we sleep to wake
And bathe in nature's bird-strung bath.

Ahead we spy a sea of cane,
With dark wings hovering in naves.
And I have loss and I have gain:
I find what kills, I find what saves.

The canebrake undulates to spread
Its repetition to the wind.                                        10
It even loves the lowered dead,
Mimics *start* and murmurs *end*.

I want to lose myself within
That castle with its final cost.
I want to shed the world of men
And find myself among the lost.

## The White King

We return in the heated day to the Council House
Of the village across the river and through the trees,
Where the head men of the town are now visiting.
Suddenly there is a shuddering among the crowd,
And we turn to see coming closer the White King
And his retinue. The others have killed three bears

For an oily feast. They have skinned the fat bears
And dance their fur around the fire. Their House
Now opens to emit girls and women; their King
Exults with a daggered smile. Light through trees          10
Looks like spears. I stand within the nodding crowd
To show I have no claim and am now just visiting

Their village. Birds in their blue plumage are visiting,
Too, and their songs delay, delight. All Nature bears
The light pleasure of arrival. The villagers now crowd
Their returning monarch. There is room here to house
A merry band of many. Bees lilt and roam down trees,
From combs and thrones fit for any humming king.

They kindle fire in the public square. The fat King
And his royal standard come forth. His new visiting                    20
Trade partners make way, nod, kneel, chase treason
Off with wary eyes. Servers bring ribs from the bears,
Barbecued to a turn, with hot bread. Before the House
We sit with honeyed water to sip, faces in a crowd.

And yet to my eye the breadth of this dining crowd
Extends to squirrels and doves; among moles, a King
Nips roots and sits aboveground, not afraid, its house
Protected by its princely servants. We are all visiting
On this Earth, and the one who breaks down, bares
Fear, is consumed. We eat our fears among the trees.                   30

Now the feast is over and the priest enters into the trees
And has servants to gather what is left for the crowd
That waits and watches. They eat what's left of the bears,
Smack the grease aloud. We stand, and now the King
Withdraws so that our trade mission can begin its visiting
Hours. We move with him into the close and heating House.

Now we are heavy as bears and walk among the trees
Toward the Council House, and there is tremble in the crowd
For they see the King is just a man, and he, too, is visiting.


*In the Treaty House*

Come to the treaty and sit on your box,
The Chief is transposing your pipe into smoke.
The shepherd is watching his village's flocks
With every insistence for stream and for stroke.

We sip the Black Drink for friendship and savor,
We speak in low voices, we smile and we nod.
We curry an order along with their favor,
We speak of this order as trade and as God.

Now the young people come dance in the Square
With bells on their ankles and shells on their arms.    10
And everyone's singing for fire, and the fair
Girls turn on heels, then light with their charms.

Next day we speak of the murdered McGee
And the White Chief says two have already been shot
For this crime against white men. So all now can see
How this justice has come to spark and to blot.

But we make it clear this is not why we came.
We come for a treaty on sales and on trade.
The King is relieved and his chiefs find a game
That is easier done than has ever been played.    20

"Our country's before you, please take what you will,"
Says the White Chief in wonder, then turning to me:
"Take roots and take flowers and all you can kill.
They speak to us always and speak now to thee."

Now the young people still dance in the Square
With bells on their ankles and dreams in their heads.
And truth lies unspoken as long as we dare,
And all of us dream of possessions instead.

### Crack in the World: An Interlude

Next morning, heads thick from the Black Drink,
we ride twelve miles to the rendezvous, but our leader
says, "William, I know a place that you must see."
I glumly nod, inhale the thick air to clear my head.
He laughs at my woeful countenance and slaps
          me hard on the back. "And what is this

place called?" I wonder. He's almost
singing with pleasure: "It is called                                                    10
the `Alligator-Hole' and you've seen
nothing quite like it yet, I will wager."

He is right: It was lately formed by expanding
of water down beneath the Earth, a vast jet
of crystal spray rising from a circular sink
        and seated at the edge of a wide meadow.
        The water is cool and transparent, sweet
        to drink and filled with fish. A lordly
        alligator is king of this domain and sits,
        loggy and knobbed, on his muddy throne                                       20

to watch it fold and unfold before him a thousand
thousand times a day. My head clears. "Though
it seems calm now, I was here three years ago to see
it blast high into the sky with a vast roar,"
our leader says, almost laughing at my disbelief.
        "Like a hundred alligators roaring at once,
        it screamed from hidden chambers inside
        the Earth and broke into a million mirrors
        that reflected every gleam of the world around
        so rapidly my eye could scarcely see:                                        30

Wave on wave rushed down a nearby field
from the Alligator-Hole and then began to fill
to its top like a new lake and then spill into nearby
pastures, too. I thought that God had sent a flood
as in the Book to take the life of every living thing,
        and I knelt, rose up, and ran with deer-fleetness
        back toward town, crying our end was surely at hand.
        But the Indians went the other way, back there to see
        the huge fountain drawn from the Earth's old veins,
        so I journeyed with them, unsure I would live another                        40

moment, but slowly, slowly, the roaring gush began to stop
and a new world of water lay about like something Adam
might have seen. Since, then, this basin has never more

overflowed and now lies witness to a cave in the world."
I watch his eyes, listen to his words, and know he speaks
       the truth of it; I shudder at this old trembling land,
       at how unstable our knowledge of Nature is,
       how one fact is the next fiction, how each work
       can molt into another before us with its own sense,
       its own construction of such friable mutability.          50

"We must ride on," my friend says, but I cannot stop dreaming
of that explosion, that watery volcano from an ocean
that must lie miles beneath. What can that shore look like
in its perpetual darkness? Is there a seeker who rows it for
eternity to find a way out as I now search for the way in?
       To call a Water Volcano the Alligator-Hole seems
       wrong to me, insufficient, a failure Linnæus could not
       make. But I do not have words for it. I want to make
       it rise before me, to pay homage to the Flower Seeker,
       to break upward into light and the truth of my pen.      60

AFTER A NIGHT OF WILD DISTRESS,
NOW THE WOODLAND SPLENDOR OF MORNING!
IN THE HOLY LAKE
MAY THE WATERS REFRESH ME,
EASE MY ANGUISH
AND BRIGHTEN MY NIGHT OF PAIN.


*All the Lives*

For several days
we camp beneath
the sun and stars.
I fill my eyes
and hands like
a starving man
with wildflowers
and palmate leaves,
but I cannot get
my fill of this          10

feast. Each dawn
I awaken starving
for what grows
in wood and field
and what could
grow deep
and deeper within
my heart, the pack
of words to carry
all the lives                                                20
of all our days.


## Dancing Toward It

The second night, she arrives, leaning into light
that grazes in a flood of pines. I cannot believe
what my sight believes for me. All others seem
to sublimate in the warm night; the vast roaring
of all carving creatures subsides. Birds come out
like stars. This late-day shooting sun lights up
her eyes and the long brown moss of her hair.

Where have you been? I do not ask. I look around
for anyone who can spoil the silence, see only
squirrels and one fox crowd close. She motions           10
for me to follow her, takes my hand, and soon
we are beside an ice-clear stream that bubbles
up with abundant pleasure turning wildly light.
We cannot smile: the moment melts and runs

on the motion of its inconsumable energy.
I never thought I'd see you again, I say now,
and she nods and cups my cheek as words spill
out, puts one finger on the crossbow of my lips
to stop the flight of more I should not try to say.
She leans forward, puts her mouth on the strong         20
axis of my clavicle, laps her way along its length.

She lets her cloth dress down. I shed myself.
We catch the other's hand and step into the flow
Below us. The water is warm and moving, fragrant
with mineral oils, laving, flowerful as morning;
we wade out word-deep, and her hair unpetals
on the surface of the world, and she blooms there
for herself and in the sight of all green petioles.

We dance slowly, tight as time against the bottom
of the pebbly pool. She surrounds me. I do not                    30
want to sound the syllables of any world but nearly
do until her eyes stop me: how much more powerful
love is in all silence. I fear I'll turn to see long jaws
leaning in toward us, but I do not even look now.
Fish sew a unicorn tapestry through our new legs.

How can I tell anyone of such quiet intimacies?
We take the greatest joy of our lives to the grave,
I suspect, the world left in wondering ignorance
of the sweetest nights and days of orange-scented
arms and chestnut hair. I give it to you, my friend,              40
to keep it alive for all time. I give you her gentleness,
the lovely shape of her yearning face, her arms snug
around my shoulders, her lips molded into my own.

What shall I call this girl? I do not know her name.
Do the creatures of the forest really sin to know each
other well in the sheltered night of full intimacies?
We hold our bodies tight against all others' eyes
until night begins to hum. We step from water
onto the first land. I think: we come to populate
a new-made world. So this is how our stories rise               50

from one moment in the garden of our southern light.
This is how we stumble into Eden, name each plant
and animal, hear a story of the Flood. We are repeated
year to year by the great narrative of all our stories,
and then we say that someone must have made it all
from whole cloth for it to be so repetitive and true.

I say: to each her own garden. I say the world dies
with our purest day of storied joy. She dresses,
disappears into the coming night, and I stumble
back toward camp changed as no man ever has                    60
been changed before. They see me coming down
from the mountain. They see tablets beyond my arms.


## The Small Pleasure of New Things

My imagination's gone: and yet we tread
Toward Town to say farewell and spread
Our graciousness before the White King.

Once more they feast us with roasted turkeys,
Hot corn cakes, and a jelly made from the root
Of the China briar. I look around for her, but

She is not here. We set off near noon. I ache
With a genuine misery. Our leader sees my eyes
And comes to me and says, "William, you need

To see the vast barren plains not far from here,                    10
Hell's own victory in this lush and swinging world."
I shrug, feel nothing as we slowly clop along the way.

We soon see the empty land before us, and I
Know it speaks of what I feel inside. We stop
And look at the endless wastes, these rocky,

Gravelly, and sandy plains with barely any
Life but a few scrubby bent pine trees growing
Up in heaps of hot white rocks. My mind won't

Turn off completely: *Myrica cerifera, Prinos,*
*Ilex aquifolium*—what can it matter to me now?                    20
I stop to make collections, and with each stop

I come back alive a bit. The life of our world
Begins to come back after a few miles, live oak,
*Ilex*, *Sideroxilon*—I feel the old small pleasure

Of new things. "Let's turn our horses out
To graze and take a walk," my friend says,
So Patrick and I climb down, head for forests

And the world that once again I feel a pain
To leave. Can I never go back into the lives
Of all men again? I must, I must, I must not.                    30


## In the Deeper Forest

A family of Indians before us, mounted to return
home from a journey, we see. Out hunting, they
ride heavy with fresh meat and skins, man, wife,
and their giggling children on fine mounts, their
pack-horses in tow and heavy with a fine catch.

We give them our smiles and a friendly wave,
and the man returns to us a pale fawnskin of honey,
which drips its golden light from one untagged
corner. I give him a packet of sewing needles
and fishhooks, which he takes gracefully, nods             10

at the finely acceptable trade. Our horses visit.
We sit in the soft unhurried glade like statues,
each for the other's memory. Swans of wind sail
through the canopy above us, stately and glowing
with the directionless pleasure of our friendship.

## Cutting Off Their Ears

The camp we reach is glowing          *Insects sing; there is*
The tents unfold in green;             *no sense of danger.*
The smell of oaks and pines provokes
A mystery unseen.

Seven princes sit around
A fire with dagger eyes.
Each has dressed (we are impressed)
With paint from chins to thighs.

They stand, intent on shaking,         *A formal greeting. They*
Their hands extend to please.          *are friendly, mean no harm.*    10
They come to catch upon this patch
A rogue with rogue's disease.

The leader's wife has run away
And with another man.
Now in this place they plan a chase
And wave a gilded fan.

The husband is near perfect,           *A sudden sense of menace.*
As tall and strong as pine.
He holds a knife that's for his wife
And carves a sudden line.                                               20

They join us by our campfire.
They shed their words not tears.
But they will slash and warmly cache
The wife and lover's ears.

They'll string them in a lanyard,      *They appear to be having*
And swing them on return.              *a good time; eye our liquor.*
And all will see the victory
Of passion that has burned.

We give them crocks for drinking,
They laugh back to their camp.                                         30

Musicians play, the hunters sway
And flute from lamp to lamp.

Now the party softens,                          *A soft and melancholy*
They sing of love betrayed.                      *air comes to us . . .*
And round the fire, the lyric lyre
Means violence delayed.

All night the party listens
To singers in their pain.
And in their eyes the wild surprise
Of lovers lost again.                                                      40

I see the girl before me.                        *The sorrow of loss and*
In dreams she dances here.                        *how it will never leave.*
Lie down, I groan, you'll be alone
From year to year to year.


## *With the Sunrise*

Sun rises: the plain fills with flaming light.
Gild paints the tops of the terebinthine pines
And exalted palms. Music from the seraphic crane
Sounds here and far away. They circle, sail
Their homeplace and slowly fall as they beat
The dense air then light on the dewy verge
Of an expansive lake, its surface yet smoking
With gray, ascending mists that are borne away
By the morning breeze then vanish on the horizon.
All life awakens. Life stretches, yawns in the day.        10

## The Day of My Sorrow

I must see into a sinkhole and so take
  a long-branched limb and hang it down
  into a circular honeycomb, through jamb,
  pilaster, and buttress, make my way down
to the deep bottom. I sit in the navel of this land

and listen to the flowing mother's milk
  below me. Patrick calls down that he will
  climb, too, and he grasps the top limb
  of my Indian ladder. His hand slips off,
and like a waking horrorful dream, he falls to me.    10

I try to brake his descent, but I lose balance
  looking up and fall backward in time
  to hear the fearful crack of bone, tear
  of sense and sinew. *Oh God!* I cry, come
to my friend to see blood in his mouth and eyes.

"Lie still, lie still!" I shout to him. He writhes
  in terrible surprise. Only his eyes turn
  wildly back to forth; the rest of his body
  is without motion or memory of motion.
"Help me! Help us!" I plead, but we have gone    20

away from the others too far for them to hear.
  I hold the boy's head in my lap, sing
  softly what a mother might know. His
  eyes beg me for another fate, to say this
is not what happens to us here, now, in this land

of solitary deaths and natural oblivion. I whisper,
  "What is it? Tell me what I can do."
  His eyes are made with fear then change
  Into great solemnity and absolution. I weep
onto his face. A human glint gathers then fades,    30

and his gaze at me remains for all time. I speak
        my guilty *No* three times and rock
        his body to me. Others hear, come rushing
        to our grave. They lower limbs, climb down
and check for pulse and breath. There is none, I know.

Should I collect this boy and put him in my book?
        Should I write his genus, species, smile?
        Soon, without remembering the climb, I'm
        up and out again, and they loop a rope
around his dangling body, haul him up from grave to sky.      40

Can I simply say he fell? That we all will fall, too,
        old men in their garden chairs, stronger ones
        while walking down a Tuesday street? Pain
        worse than any pain ever dreamed swamps me.
I bang the Earth with my fists, pray and curse aloud

with my flinty accusations. I am the collector of men,
        the killer of butterflies and moths, the ache
        of all growing Earth. I am the Flower Seeker
        and this bleeding bud fades before me as morning
lies with her golden light, and beauty hides in shame.      50

## New Mound in the Wilderness

The sun hangs low against the new-dug grave.
They've wrapped our Patrick in a winding cloth
Like merchandise they'll seek again some day.
And I am broken as the clouds that dream

In patterns up above the meadow's dew.
Men rarely choose the place that they will die,
The day, the weather, forest, or the stream;
They do not dream their final swinging stride

Or think a fall will take them to that sea
Of forgottenness we all achieve.      10

Yet we navigate it all our lives,
The fear's just hidden in our timeless songs,

And silver days won't miss us when we're gone,
For other cows will crop the pasture's dreams.
I dream him back with flowers and with light;
I see his shape among the shadows, strong

As rainy, starless nights. Will he be gone
Long? And will his absence trouble me
In unwaning years to come? He was my friend,
An effervescent lad, as curious as dawn.                           20

I thought I'd show him what a sinkhole bears,
Geology and flora in the shape of clocks.
I thought I'd teach him how a fissure seems
Shaped by man and yet is Nature's star.

Instead, I gave him war. I gave his eyes
The blindness of a creature from the deep
That feels its way from rock to rocks
And never knows a flower as it grows.

Our captain puts his grieving arm round me;
The others stare into the new-made gown.                           30
And Patrick, wrapped to take his journey down,
Wears his sheet to greet the roots below.

How odd he died already in the grave,
How strange he went to life's-end in a flash.
How terrible the moment that he knew
That darkness came to take him as a boy,

Green as curling ivy in its youthful spring.
His eyes were blue and clear as crystal-flows,
He swam the basins like old Neptune's kind.
And I, who still can see his stillborn shape,                      40

Have now gone mute and deaf and blind.

Once, now several years ago, I heard
A shouting down along the river's edge
Back home on the Schuylkill where we lived.

Father took me down to see the men
Pull Thomas Gillson by his feet from out
The water's icy, killing winter flood.
A kind, sweet boy who loved his mother well,

He'd wandered off as others chopped the ice
That hung in daggers from their sagging roofs.                    50
His father roared so loud the geese reshaped
Their path and veered away beyond the flow.

"Not this! Not *this*!" he cried. I could not know
Why Father held me closer than he had
Before in all my memory. The dead boy's elder
Rocked him as the river moved in lordly

Misconcern along the frozen land.
Now I want to hold my friend and rock him
In that deeper sleep that came too soon
For even dreams to come along and share.                         60

The soil is rich and sandy here; it falls
Apart like sugar in their hands. Dew weeps
Among the blades of grass and drips upon
His body and its newly conquered lands.

Our chief now asks me if I'd like to say
The final words above poor Patrick's grave,
And I uncollapse and step up to its edge
And see the shadow of its cut and pray:

"By the rivers where Babylon did run,
We sat and wept when we remembered Zion.                         70
We hung our harps upon the willow trees,
Sensing that we could not raise a verse,

Saying: How can we sing the Lord a song
As strangers in the strangest land we've known?
If I forget thee, O Jerusalem,
Let my right hand then forget her cunning.

If I do not remember thee, let my
Tongue cling to the roof within my mouth.
O Lord, who knows my every waking dream,
Know my heart and know the reach of me."          80

I look up now and see a red man standing
In a grove a hundred yards away,
Dressed for mourning, painted all in black.
I want to find kind Patrick and explain

The purpose of all grieving in the world,
And why we love the richest days and dance
Our youth away. I want to weigh my words
Like precious treasure, let them sail alone

Across savannahs and the wooded bays.
Our chief instructs the others how to grasp          90
The body by its shoulders and its feet.
They lower it that way into the grave,

Then settle it among the stones and roots.
I do not notice, till another one
Looks up, that rain's begun to wet the pane
Of day. In heat I feel my body shudder

As if a winter day had crept to whisper
Sleet and snow among this Patrick's bones.
One cuts the Earth along his shovel blade,
The others join to raise the flesh of soil          100

Then let it fold back down along the bones
Of Patrick Reece. I try to be a man
And hold my pride, but there is not a point
In holding back the grief that seeks release.

Soon the grave is filled above the plain.
And at one end the others raise a cairn.
And I can never be the same again
Or fail to understand the sad and worn.

A new mound's grown into the wilderness,
To lie with dozens we have seen along 110
The rivers where we've come to seek and stray.
And I am broken into bloomless day.

We give you back the soul of this our friend,
Who now will sleep the line from earth to Earth.
He wakens to the garden with no end,
Has come into the fragrant beds of birth.

He will not age, grow old and white as ash,
He will not be an invalid to come.
He sleeps inside the victor's final sash,
Settles to the victory of bone. 120

He was a gentle boy, so kind and bright,
Who took the journey with his lake-blue eyes.
And now he sleeps below in spring's old light,
Another flower fallen from our sighs.


*Old Man in the Chair*

*Peace is not a petal*
*but what the petal unblooms*
*and still dreams. Peace*
*swarms me like a lilt of bees*
*in this nectarful world.*
*I see the constellations*
*on the back of these*
*now-ancient hands.*
*I raise them into*
*Perseus and Andromeda,* 10
*see us there, Gemini,*

*the hard stars, not cold*
*forever but warm twins,*
*eyes winking peace*
*beyond the widest sea.*


## On Bird Island

Now we head back toward the Lower House,
And I halt in my slow stately steps to collect
Seeds and stems, the world in its old sorrows,
In its continual hymn of our triumphal deaths.
*Sophora, Cistus, Tradescantia, Hypoxis, Atropa,*
*Gerardia, Helonias*—the list of my captures goes on
In the imperatives of genus. Indians emerge again
On their hunts. Our men collect the horses they have
Come to bring back. At night's camp, I find them
Busy curing the young, freakish colts. My own legs                    10
Spring back beneath me. The next day, the breaking
Continues, tutoring the young steeds to their duty.

I look to my duty, too, collect more plants for England
And Fothergill. One more day, and when we rise,
Our leader says to me, "Time now to take our leave
Of this land of lakes, grottoes, groves, and graves."
He puts a fatherly hand on my shoulder, and I do not
Grieve. Instead I shimmer with the memory of Patrick
And the Crystal Basin and the Battle Lagoon—I smile
And clap my hands once and breathe. "That's the lad,"              20
Our leader says. We ride all day across savannah
And stream, and in the evening we build a well-
Secured corral for the horses, sit by camplight, speak
Stories of our memorable trail. I cannot tell them

Of the girl who came to me by mourning and night.
In the large pond before us we see an island filled
With tall trees whose crests are crowned with birds
Of a thousand species, and we must go to them.
I take mental notes, watch the wings fluttering, sail

With them as they fledge or molt. Our men take down            30
Two dozen, bag them for a feast. Some we roast
And others lie upon a rich pillow of rice. Yet most,
Except for bitterns and the tantali, taste of strong fish,
And I cannot enjoy them. And back across the water
A million of them scream and cry incessantly, and I
Wonder if it is from fear of predators or the certain fear

They will fall in later years. Our trail is almost gone.
I cannot bear to turn and face another dawn.


*Our Common Fire*

The first shout! I sit straight up to find
            a battle underway—all our men but me
waving firebrands, screaming, scuttling, hair
            astray, hands waving like wings to beat
the toothy air away. A huge alligator has crept
            into our camp and was but a few feet
from tearing us into bloody shreds small enough
            to choke down in the bloodlight.
Now they break spars from fresh sapling limbs
            and turn them into javelins, stab the beast          10
a hundred times, its fat tail swaggering around
            their leaping legs, its wide jaws hissing
and snapping in frustrated rage. "Down his throat?"
            our leader cries, and one jabs his stick
into the creature's maw; blood's fatal fountain
            spills hotly out. The monster bellows, furious
at his pain, writhes, throws all off easily, claws
            the air. "Get the rifle!" someone cries, but
not one man moves for it, the fight now being sport
            and laughter breaking into all the shouts.          20
One finally shoots him, though, and he slows down
            and turns still. He is twelve feet long,
an old and honored warrior, and we salute him
            as if to say, "Well done in the final fight.

We honor your boldness and your long night now,
   and welcome you to our common fire."


## Turn My Skin to Flame

Day and night, day and night, another ride
And we are back at the Lower Town, and I feel
Empty as the eyes of that dead alligator beside
Our fire. And yet the schooner that will take
Me back to Georgia is not due for some days,
So what will I do with my time? I am young
And in full bloom. I wander into night and find
A young and willing woman, and she offers me
Rum, which I take but do not like much. Her eyes
Run through me like hot brands. I feel the length            10
Of her skin, chin to toe, and we slickly sin,
God knows. Afterward, I sit upon her bed and look
Out the window toward the wind and water.
"You will go now, won't you?" she asks.
I tell her that I cannot stay anywhere for long,
And she shrugs. I must head out tomorrow
And stay gone until the ship comes back.
I must stray into the back-country and see Nature
In her element. I am a singular man not among
Men. She touches my cheek and warms up                      20
My arms with her fingers, turns my skin to flame.

# CANTO EIGHT

My servant comes into the garden bearing
A salver with a pitcher of lemonade and two
Glasses: my friend Mervonne has come to me
With him, a man my own age, smiling, hobbling
With his cane. "William, how do you fare on
This fine day?" he asks. "Hope you do not mind
I dropped in to visit?" I smile and wave him
On, pat the bench-seat next to me. He is white-
Haired and slow, only now walking from a stroke
That felled him last winter. "What are you doing                    10
Today, then, Mervonne?" I ask. "Ah. Well. I have
Been reading Bunyan yet again, I fear," he says,
And we both laugh. "And how is good Pilgrim,
Then?" I inquire. "Not yet home," he says. We sip
Cold tart lemonade against the sun and he asks me
Of my day. My day? How could I tell him how I
Have lived through young Patrick's death yet again,
Gone for wild horses in a land of lakes and pools?

"What old men always do," I say. "Slow as fools."
We sit for a long time drinking lemonade and then                  20
Say but a little. He tells of the weather. And then I
Wonder of our new Country and its days that we
Will not live to see. A cardinal lands on the lip
Of a feeder, sips the seeds. A thrush's wild drum
Beats at a distance. I feel the weight of other days.
Old men must have their memories as a salve
To the wounds of time. The cardinal is now sowing
Grass I shall not see erupt next spring. Once, I broke
Each season with a young beast's wild laugh. Night
Has turned out that light. Now the bees in their hymns            30
Make me dream with delight for only what the blind
Can rightly see. It is the fabled yellow line of dawn.
With each old tale I recall, I sit here alone, cobbling
My life's story only for myself. I feel the great sea
Wash over me, and I am not afraid. I see the blue
Sky above, and there is nothing now I am fearing.

One more adventure in the waters of the warm South:
Before I finally hitch a ride on the sea's high waves
I set sail toward evening from the Lower Store, get
To Mount Royal by dark. Next morning I set out                          40
With my fishing tackle, fusée, ammunition, and box
In which to store my specimen roots. Now I cross
The great lake in a stiff wind and reach the other
Side where I camp. Glories greet me—that solitude
For which I was clearly born, the tropic's garden
Of chattering beasts, birds filled to the brim with
Songs of sweetest delight, righteous roots, flowers
Undescribed in any book. I build a fire and sing,
Stalk the Earth, roar with youth, eat my strong fill.
The night sky fills with planets and stars, cerise                      50
Clouds slowly drift along the western sky in the last
Thin bloodied slice of sunset. I have never in life
Been less afraid. I have never known more surely
How little I need the continual company of men.

In the silvered night I hear footsteps. If the end
Finds me, I will not fear it. I look up securely
From my bedroll and see an Indian, his knife
Up as he looks hard to see if I might be fast
Enough to take him. I smile and raise my knees
To my chest. He lowers the blade. I know he will                       60
Not harm me, and he knows I am on the wing
Toward other lands. We part in peace. Bowers
Fill the night with rich fragrance. In this myth
I am Ulysses headed home. My will shall harden
Into stories he will tell. All restraint is imbued
With strength, I think, and we part as brothers
In the cool darkness. Clouds come. The loss
Of stars is only temporary if I live with the rocks
Of my strongest desire for dawn. I will not shout
If he returns, for I am owl and wolf. I have met                        70
My imaginary end too many times; what saves
Me takes away my life, the words from my mouth.

Two days pass: I sail back and forth to new ports
On either side of the lake. The third day I discover
The deserted farm of a Dr. Stork, house wrecked,
Shrubs and plants overgrown, sweet and scented
Orange groves heavy with neglect. Great rambling
Vines entwine the hedges. My own failed farm lies
In this land. How often men slip, in the fond dreams,
Retreat to the known world. And yet I would be          80
Da Gama, Columbus, Drake, too, the one who
Goes past the place where dragons live, into all
Unknown places. I would be the vine that twines
This hot vicinity with hand and eye. The house
Here has fallen in. Cotton and indigo once grew
But now are gone forever. And yet destruction
Lingers, a hundred acres chopped to desolation
As has been done so many times up and down
The river by the British and others. The fiercest
Winds would do less harm. I grieve my own kind.          90

A week of travels, and I arrive back to a signed
Welcome at the Lower Store. I see the nearest
Thing to a riot I have ever seen: Seminoles, crowned
With twenty liquor kegs are seeking consolation
For a battle trip they may plan; their construction
Of a wilderness-within staggers me. Senses flew
Away long before now. They lie drunk, carouse
With half-naked women who cling like wet vines
To their hard bodies. And this is just the first call
For their revelries. I see one painted red and blue,     100
Roaring songs, dancing round the fires' red sea
With near-madness. In full sight there are screams
Of copulation, the dream-sounds of lions, thighs
Pumping as if closing for a kill. I see them scrambling
For more rum, holding up their bottles, demented
As love-worn men can be. I want to look, to dissect
It as a naturalist does; but they drink and uncover
Themselves for all to see. There are no courts

For such wantonness here. The women bear
Empty bottles in their clothes, take a long draught                110
From a lover then spit in their own container
And in this way, man to man, they fill with rum
Their own containers. Later, they sell these goods
Back to the selfsame men: I cannot recall I ever saw
More clever conduct in pursuit of money. And yet
It is also terrible and seductive to watch it all. One
Woman, lithe and lovely, comes to me and draws
Her hands on me from shoulders down to knees,
And I try not to want her. Then I recall my girl
In that other, wilder world, and feel sick and know              120
I can never find comfort in another woman's arms.
I sit on a stone and stare, never having known
Her name. Fires flame everywhere. Slick bodies
Lie together, now fully naked and all howling
Like wounded wolves. On and on it unravels
And I watch it with disgusted wonder all night.

I sleep finally back in my rooms with only slight
Unwellness to greet the day, but they—they travel
Around bent over and sick. Girls pull their cowling
Down low to cover their disgrace. One man totters,              130
Shudders, falls down dead weight, completely gone
From conscious thought. One woman, her charms
Vanished, hair in knots, begs to sell herself, sow
Any vice for one sip of rum. The night's swirl
Of dancers has turned into a sweaty, matted frieze
Of suffering. Effect will always have its cause.
The men sit up groaning in the warless sun.
There are still concessions for them to try and get
From the traders before they leave. I sit and draw
Flowers in my book. The women in their hoods                    140
Filter into shadows, sit and moan. A far-off drum
Of thunder rumbles. Soon, it will surely rain here.
Drink has put the warriors to their drooping rout.
It is a loss I understand, that all men can share.

Now the parlay starts. They need blankets, shirts,
Iron goods, ammunition for their journey to battle
The Choctaws, but our chief trader says: "You have
Nothing to give for it. Are we to trust you will bring
It to us if you come home at all? No. That is not
Trade but gifts, of which we have none to give."                    150
The Long Warrior (their chief) puffs himself up
And struts, stopping twice to hold his aching head.
He speaks rapidly in a tongue I do not understand,
But his anger glows and burns. The storm rolls
Closer to us, and our translator gives back words
The Warrior speaks: "Do you presume to refuse
Me credit? Do you not know who I am and what
Power I have? If I asked, the thunder now rolling
Overhead would come down upon your head in
Rapid, fiery shafts and lay you prostrate there                     160
On the ground at my feet and burn your stores
To dust and ashes!" Our chief very nearly smiles.

He says: "We know your name for many miles
Is terrible to your enemies, that the Seminoles
Are fierce warriors in battle. But we both wear
Truth and know this thunder and its terrible wind
Come from the Great Spirit. There is no consoling
For death from such destruction, but that hot
Flash does not come from you or me. Those hues
Of fire are not ours to command. But if I heard                     170
Your threat properly, let fire descend the holes
In the clouds and strike that live oak, burn land
For a mile around—do it now before us. The dead
Tree will proclaim your awesome power." A pup
Yips and wriggles in the sand. Rain sieves
Down on us man to man. We feel all the hot
Arrogance flow from the Long Warrior. Springs
Of laughter spill from his men. In that laugh
We know his hand is turned. Like mild cattle
They shrug off the weather. It should have hurt                     180

Their pride at least, but no one seems to care.
The Long Warrior becomes more calm and easy
Now, and we agree they will pay half of it
Up front, the rest on return. The conference breaks
Up on good terms, and I smile to see the art of it all,
How each side puffs and prides up then acquiesces
A little until agreement comes. They are also, it
Should be said, in pain and suffering from the drink
Of the night before and on a terrible search for more,
And shortly they find enough to act as medicine                 190
For their festered wounds. Their women seem not
Ashamed of their actions at all, in fact go right back
To them, but I have seen girls in the alleys of cold
Philadelphia do much the same to survive winter.
Wounds of poverty drive decency deep sometimes,
Make of men and women what they must truly be
To live another day. So they go back to their acting,
To the play that has no end in their red lifetime.

               Suddenly a tumult
                at the Indian camp,                              200
              a screaming, eyes
           down at a space on
            on the ground, on
             a writhing lump
           and four or five
          come for me,
         saying, loud:
       Come here,
     Puc Puggy,
       Come now,                                                 210
         for there is
          a very large
            rattlesnake
             in our camp
              and you must
                come charm it
                  out: you are here
                    to gather plants and

animals, come gather
up this fat snake                                    220
for we cannot
kill it but it
can kill us!
Men, women,
children all flee
the huge snake,
and I tell myself
I will have nothing
to do with it, but
they beg and beg                                     230
so I sigh, come
slowly with them
looking for a staff
or rock to protect
myself from the
great creature.

God:
Fear! Now,
This close to safety
I am more afraid than when                           240
Alligators harried us in the deep
Swamp country, for this beast is among
Us in the real world. I tell them: "I am drawing
Plants and animals and this work requires much quiet
And concentration," but they drag me out into the plaza where
More crowd round me saying, "Puc Puggy, see there
In our houses—there—the beast roams plate to
Plate to sap up our leftovers, sip spilled
Grease. He is large enough to kill
Any man or men who come                              250
Close. Please come take
Him away from our
Lodgings to
Study."

Now
Three young
Men come to my door,
Dressed finely with rattle gourds
Dangling from their shell belts, and they
Formally beg me to come with them to catch and                    260
Take away the snake which their beliefs do not allow them
To kill. I sigh. There is no way I can get out of this now, and so
I look again for a staff with which to keep the monster at a distance
and they say, "Thank you, O great Puc Puggy, for we are
Too afraid to challenge the creature that we cannot
By our customs kill without bringing down
The wrath of gods upon our heads just
As we head out to fight against
The wild Choctaws." I
Sigh and nod, go                                                   270
With them to
The camp,

Longer than a man's arm, diamond eyes glimmering in the hotlight
Of late-summer afternoon: It stretches as it moves away from us,
And—dear God—I see it as we come close, the whole encampment
Behind me not breathing, their moccasined tiptoes in the dust.
     Men stand at a distance with stick and tomahawk, unsure what
     To do. Women and girls scream and dance away. I hear the name
     Said in a dozen litanies in what might be Latin: Puc Puggy, Puc Puggy,
Puc Puggy, come and get the creature from our midst to study its body.    280

Order                              breaks down
     My hands are trembling. Close            then closer
we come and now I see it is          eight, nine feet         L O N G
          and thicker than=my arm, head the size
                         of ripe cantaloupe, snickering tongue
          lapping up the taste and scent
                    of=air.

I look for            a missile            see a lighterwood
                    knot
          pick it up & move in small steps=closer                 290

                  & he hears or feels my
                     HEAT
         & I stop       he turns around toward     ME
              William Bartram

Dead of
Snakebite
In this the Year
Of our Lord
17??

                   I see the stone set                 300
        on the      GR      OUND before
               me
          They see my hands are trembling
   I am trembling
             now I see and feel I am
                     Dancing as they were
                    On the Drunk Night
       & how fear & drunkenness are      so close
    to being        the  same
                  thing       310

Courage=I am dancing with the great
    rattlesnake      in the plaza now
        all behind me chanting my     Indian name
     Puc Puggy Puc Puggy
and this sense of courage wells up
             in me like a flow into the  /
Crystal Basin and suddenly:

Order comes back into my heart and into my hands.
I am not a stranger in these strange and stranger lands.

I am the Giant Serpent Slayer, standing tall in dust     320
And absent fear; I do what any Hero here, now, must.

I hold aloft the lightwood knot, and hurl it straight down
With all my might. It strikes the snake's head. The town

Goes deathly silent to watch. The great skull breaks away.
The heavy body sculls and sways. As if to stop and pray

The men go silent. They whisper my name. I hold up the head
Of the monster. They cry aloud my name, raise arms. The dead

Rattlesnake now shudders down to silence. Its great fangs
Drip venom and blood. I turn and roar. A boy now bangs

His skin-taut drum, hide-side booming in the village heat.                    330
They say I am the greatest warrior anyone will ever meet.

Now they dance as I walk back to my quarters and remove
The mortal teeth to put in my collection. Their deathly groove

Amazes me. I am careful not to prick my skin for men have
Died, I hear, beyond the snake's end of all slithering life.

They do not see me tremble.
They do not see me breathe
In enough breath to stay upright.
They do not see me sag down
On my cane-stick chair.                                                       340

Over, I think, over, and then I see a group
          of them has come to my door with sharp tines:
"We have come to scratch you, Puc Puggy," one says,
          "for you risked your life to save us in our camp
and now we must let out blood, for you are
          too heroic and violent, and less blood will make
you easier among the people."

They sing all this and dance it out, but I know
          enough of their tongue to understand it, and
I tell them I will not be scratched to let out the heroic,                    350
          which I do not possess in any large amount, and
they are befuddled; it is a great honor to be scratched
          and bled, among them. They hold out their
scratching instruments and ready for the flow.

SUDDENLY HE TURNED TO HIS LEFT
AND WE LEFT THE WALL
AND TOWARD THE MIDDLE SPACE

WENT BY A PATH DEEP IN A VALLEY
WHICH, EVEN THOUGH THIS HIGH,
EXHALED A DANGEROUS STREAM.                                    360

I back up, tell them *no*.
Now they reach for me
And I fight them off,
And a young prince
Leaps now in between
Them and me and says,
"𝔓uc 𝔓uggy is a brave
𝔚arrior and my friend,
And this scratching would
𝔅e an insult to him!"                                          370

Instantly, they change, lay their hands on my shoulders
In happy relief. Each one's arms bound to the others'
Shoulders, all intertwined like a clot of strong snakes;
Perhaps it is a farce, but they struggle with the right
Thing to do, and so are not so unlike us as we believe.

Next morning, and they now prepare for their battle-
Trip, and the fires flame, they dance, shake their shell
Jewelry, sing and sign for help from their warrior gods.
Our leader has invited me on one last trip before I sail
Back for Charleston and end this wonderful and terrible       380
Trip. I think of lost Patrick now resting in his forest grave.
I recall the girl who gave me what she had with grace
And ardor. I see before me the great Crystal Basin, flow
Of a million gallons upward, volcano of clearest water
In the bird-strong afternoon. The Seminoles gather up
Their horses, cram packs with dried meat and hacking
Instruments for their coming war. All day they paint
Themselves with ochre and soot-black, go on singing
Hour to hour with pure courage and a warring delight.

I draw my specimens and think about the fight with                    390
The rattlesnake. Will I ever have a son to whom I can
Tell such stories? I pray so. And yet I know that solitude
Is my natural state, and my country is the shape of wings.

# CANTO NINE

*T*HE day before the Seminoles left for war,
A band of Indians from a town twelve miles
Upriver landed at the trading post and brought
For us canoe-loads of oranges and watermelons,
A bower of bright spring colors in mid-September,
A time when crops have already begun their wane
In Georgia. "Would you like to visit that village
Since it's a few days yet before your ship comes
To take you back north?" asked the good trader
McLatche. "What a marvelous idea," I agreed.              10
We slept the night in the crickety chatter of river-
Side things. I am pleased with my drawings so far,
And while I love nothing so much as the roaming
Of forest and field, my artwork comes very close
To its duplication for aesthetic charm in my life.
Next morning, debris from the Seminole camp
Still smoking, we mount fine horses and ride on
Toward the village under powder-blue skies.

Are we the sum of all our youthful larks and lies,
And do we spend the rest of our time largely gone        20
From the days in which we really live? The lamp
Unto my feet flickers; I am unsure I'll have a wife
To tell my stories to. I know what no one else knows
About William, about the boy who in this gloaming
Rides clop to clop and misses what he sees, star
To star, wave to wave; I want to be the rose-giver,
The rootman selling pictures of his ware. The seed
Of my journey will grow in me and past me, traitor
To all time, sailing on past its end. The hive hums
In the woods around us. Wolves come for the pillage      30
Of bone and blood. I want to think myself quite sane
As we ride the miles this day. In the pale November
Of my life I want to shout the sun of this heaven
To startled passersby. This tropic tale has caught
Me in its fragrant web. I hear the birdsong smiles
Unfold their delirious songs. I come, I see, I soar.

We don't stay on a road, but roam Indian trails,
Ride across meadows, cut along flowing channels.
I love the time of being lost but with a truer sense
That I will find myself soon; we ride the high, open      40
Pine forests, green lawns, and flowery savannahs
That in their youthful verdure and gaiety have lately
Been burned. Now, though, they are widely overrun
With mossy lime colors, enameled with sunshine,
Checkered with hummocks of trees and intersected
With serpentine rivulets, their banks jeweled with
*Andromeda formosissima, Halmea spuria, Annona alba,*
And a dozen other shrubberies. About noon we come
To the town on the river, and the Indians welcome
Us well, their chief escorting our party kindly          50
To the center of town beneath a four-poster canopy
Covered with palmetto leaves. Feathers of smoke
Rise like lazy birds uplifting. One must ascend
The platform by earthen steps from any of its sides,

Steps covered with split-cane mats that are dyed
Bright red and yellow. After we are seated, our men
Are offered pipes which we take, nodding, a token
Of friendship among men. Soon, girls come and empty
Baskets before us of the finest ripe fruit. We blindly
Take what rolls before us and eat. This is the fulcrum   60
Of their pleasure in our visit, to give the rich sum
Of their season to us. I take a walk and salvage
What my eyes can see: fields like stories of myth:
Corn, citruels, pumpkins, squashes, the uninfected
Groves of peaches, figs, and oranges. I recline
In the shade for a time and daydream a winter sun
That warms forever, has no ice. All moves stately
As a season here, slow to turn, slow hosannas
To the woods and wind. I gather roots, tokens
Of my visit, vegetables, seeds, but no immense          70
Flowers as their season's past. In all the annals
Of this place no finer day ever set its lovely sails.

We ride back to the trader's store and arrive well
Before dark, as light lingers at this time of year.
"We're taking the horses across to the pastures there
For grazing—would you like to go and collect a few
Specimens?" asks a man named Hanes. He's a fine
Specimen himself, not more than thirty years, tall,
Strong-eyed. I look at the broad distance before us
And smile, agree. "We have a large flat-boat to take          80
The horses with us," he says. "Give us a hand now."
I should be exhausted from the feast of watermelons
But am not. The river here is a mile wide, but we
Manage to herd the horses in the scow for transport,
Head with the wind. Numerous islands fill the stream
Bank to bank. The horses, lately quite wild, assume
Each time we near land that they should leap out,
Go graze, sip the sun-warmed grass. "Whoa, now!"
Cries Hanes. "Hold them tight!" But it is late
For that; they rise and plunge overboard in surf.          90

Curses rain down as horses swim toward turf
Unworried by their floating manes or weight.
The rest come toward me to leap, and somehow
I jump in with them, swim strongly, hear shouts
From the men astern. I catch rough hair, groom
Myself to swim or drown. The water now gleams
With horseflesh and late-day's red escort
Of sun along the skipping waves. I feel too free
To worry, kick my feet, try to keep balance
As I head toward land. The boat's following prow          100
Is not far behind. Swim, William! Hanes makes
A delightful commotion, claps. The horses' fuss
Is magnificent to see; their swimming is a squall
I enter willingly. The river's dark as dinner wine.
I find I'm laughing as the horses swim a view
As rich as I've seen. The water and the fine air
Exhilarate me. I do not have an ounce of fear.
We arrive on land, each one strong and well.

The others land. I sit soaked on the shore, and they
Laugh at me, say I make a good horse in a clear                    110
Emergency. "Go on and graze," says Hanes. "You
Have earned it." We sit awhile and talk. He comes
From Carolina, shipped down to seek work himself.
"My people fled from France, named at first as
Haynnes, but we are farmers now, poor as all men
Who till the land for their bread." I tell him Father's
Story, family, our Botanical Garden at Kingsessing,
Home in Philadelphia, and his eyes find fascination
With it. "And you come to tell the stories of plants
And animals, to make a book of their shape and size                120
And usefulness in the World?" I say that's part
Of it. "Everything's just part of it," he says. We
Smoke, daydream. "I had a wife once." He is quiet
And kicks a blade of grass. "Lovely as a cloudless
Summer day, but she passed in childbirth, gone on
To God before me." I stare, not knowing such pain.

I ask, "How does a man with such loss keep sane
In his coming days?" Hanes shrugs. "She is gone
These three years and still the hardest, loudest
Beat I hear is my unmending heart that can't requite              130
The loss it knew once." The river's calm as the sea
When storms abate and blow away. A heart
Of silence surrounds the grazing herd. A wise
Man would stay quiet, I know, but my fancy
Is to ask how he stays alive. "The indignation
Is what comes first," he says, "the guessing
Why it came to me at all and not to bother
Some other man. I know it was not from sin
Or atonement for my ways or hers. Just that fast,
She was gone. And there's no reason, no help                       140
For it." I understand the need for what numbs
Us all, seek it. I separate the clouds from the blue
Myself all day—I understand. And yet the fear
Rises in my breath every night and every day.

We get the horses back into the rough scow
And tie them there with vines, sail on to high
Hills we meant to reach before, turn them out
To have a long graze. Hanes has gone solemn,
Sits, and I see in his eyes how he misses her,                                    150
His lovely girl, as I have come to miss the one
Who wasn't even mine. The others say they're
Walking to a Plantation six miles on, and we
Rise to follow at a distance. "Tell me, William,
Of the wonders you have seen in this country
So far," says the troubled boy. I speak the story
Of the rattlesnake, its spiral coil, how its tail
In motion appears to be a vapor; how its whole
Body swells with rage when attacked, its cheeks
Swollen, lips constricted, eyes bloody burning
Coals, with a forked tongue the color of a hot                                   160
Flame. "Yet he never strikes unless he's sure
Of his mark. I've seen them thick as my leg."

He shudders me on. "Once in Georgia, our keg
Of water was out, and I got up early to endure
A walk to a nearby pool, and halfway I thought
Of other things and nearly kicked a turning
Rattlesnake of the largest size on those creeks
Ever seen. He was not five feet from the sole
Of my shoe, watching me, his body's hard mail
Glinting in the early sun. I backed up, my foray                                 170
With near-death done, and I got my hunting
Companions, and I am proud that in our Ilium
We had no warrior who would harm a bee,
Much less this magnificent snake. We left, fair
Pleased to let him live his life in peace. No gun
Was brought out to kill the beast. I did not stir
After that, though, if I didn't know the column
Before me from earth to sky. And I was a scout
After that, yet I never let a creature there die
In my care. That was my promise and my vow."                                     180

I tell him of other rattlesnakes, the fat moccasin,
The bull snake, and the garter. "And frogs of many
Stripes and kinds!" I lecture on. "The largest lives
On the seacoast, a full nine inches long, and there is
The bell frog, so-called because its voice is like
The sound of a loud cow bell. On the grassy shores
Live beautiful green frogs that sing like little
Barking dogs or yelping puppies. The house frog
Lives outside eaves and steps. The tiniest ones I
Have seen are called savannah crickets; after rains                    190
They come in millions. The shad frog is beautiful
And spotted, dark olive green, blotched with clouds
And ringlets of a dusky color. They have a sucking
Noise that can be heard a mile. Toads, which live
Along the highlands, are two species, red and black.
All crave insects for their food. Their long tongue
Shoots out with its sticky fluid to trap the fastest
Fly that darts from bud to bud among the grass."

Hanes smiles as we walk, and I see how fast
He has forgotten his sorrow, and his fitness                           200
For the walk improves. A new pleasure is wrung
From those bleak memories. I begin to track
Other species for him: "Now I'll begin to give
You an idea of lizards," I say. "The little bucking
Chameleon is an innocent creature. I see crowds
Of them near rainwater, their red gill in dutiful
Work to raise a mate, I gather. They can change
Colors suddenly depending on what they lie.
I've seen copper-colored lizards, the little log
Of a blue-bellied squamous one. They skittle                          210
Rapidly when touched or neared. On moors,
They lie under rocks at times. They do not strike
Like snakes but let one pass, do not hiss,
Either. Each one simply creeps and then strives
To hunt and stay alive. It is a land of plenty,
Hanes, a land of food for all without end."

"I have always wondered of the turtles,"
Hanes says. Feeling strong in my stride,
I tell him: "Around here are several species
Of tortoise, the small land one that every                                    220
Traveler knows, and one that here inhabits
Every bay of fresh water, it seems: black
Pearl, oval form, high back, flat belly-shell.
Both species are fine food for all mankind.
But there is much more richness in this land.
There's otter, polecat, opossum, raccoon,
Wild rats, house rats, beaver, muskrats,
Roebuck, bears, lynx, foxes that bark at night
But never in the same place twice. And so
Much more: mole, bat, several kinds of squirrel,                             230
Rabbit, and this has not yet touched the birds
I have catalogued here: owls, vultures, eagles,
Hawks, crows, woodpeckers, turkeys, cranes,

Herons, pelicans, the teal, the plover." I explain
More: "And the crown bird, blue linnet, regal
As it sits and waits upon a limb. All words
Fail me, Hanes. A hundred kinds, a world
Of fur and wings waiting for a man to know."
He smiles: "It would take strong foresight
To see so much, William. I envy all that                                     240
In you." I glance up, see a streak on the moon
That is unnatural in the afternoon. My hand
Is steady: I bid Hanes stop. "Here behind
The others, do you not with your sense of smell
Detect fire?" He halts and turns. The track
Of the others is clear, but now come rabbits
Scrambling our way. Our path is severed;
No way out seems obvious or very easy
Now. I try to hunt my courage and my pride
And think, but my burning blood now curdles.                                 250

"William, look!" I hear Hanes cry. And fire
Erupts on all sides. Strange, like a statue planted
In the way, an Indian stands before a cypress tree

And makes signs at me. He is quiet, unafraid,
And for a moment I do not know if he is omen
Or one who's come to take his certain death.
We cannot see the others far ahead now, either,
And we turn one way and then the other, but
It is no good: fire cuts us off as it rises and roars
Like alligators at the Battle Lagoon. "Come on!"                    260
I scream, and he follows me. Flames lap and sip
The air at our heels. Animals in their thousands
Flee toward water. Birds lift off and sail back
Toward the mainland from this island. I wonder
How our grazing horses will now fare, if they might
Burn alive. The trees look like women, hair
On fire, bending down from pain and sorrow.
The heat is so close my leg is burned. Where

Is water? Hanes falls and I fall over him. Air
Is low to the ground. We crawl. We must borrow                     270
Damp leaves to cover our mouths. Fire's lair
Is about us; there is no hope, yet my fright
Seems abating. The flames clap like thunder
In spark-light. All the world is turning deep black,
A moonless, starless night. From their houses
In the ground insects boil out. Ants rush the lip
Of their mounds, pour out to die. My bones
Are friable, overworn; guttering flames pour
Down like thundershowers. My right foot
Is singed. Hanes cries aloud. And neither                          280
Of us sees the way ahead. Shallow breath
Is all there is left to see. In one more moment
We will be gone. Then it seems to be delayed:
Death and fire together. Just ahead we see
A wide stream flowing. We are now granted
Relief. Vines pop like strings from a lyre.

THEN WITH A SLOW SMILE TURNED THE LADY ROUND
    AND LOOKED UPON HER PEOPLE; AND AS WHEN
    A STONE IS FLUNG INTO SOME SLEEPING TARN,

THE CIRCLE WIDENS TILL IT LIP THE MARGE,
SPREAD THE SLOW SMILE THROUGH ALL HER COMPANY.

I turn to grab Hanes by the neck to see him rise
And run into the flames. "God, no!" I scream,
But he is gone. I crawl into the water, filled
With shells and skins and the flickering tongues
Of fleeing snakes. Thunder comes again, but now
I realize it is a rising storm, and soon the rainfall
Comes in torrents. Moccasins glides past my face
Without a thought of striking me. And suddenly
I understand this storm is what struck off the fire.
I scream the boy's name once and again, as loud
As any bellow in any wood has ever been.
A huge otter comes right to my face—I am now
Submerged to my eyes in the stream—and he
Questions what creature I could be, catalogs me
For his list of wonders. A floating crane snaps
Up a baby rattlesnake, smacks it down as rage
Begins to turn away from rage, and flames fade
Enough for me to climb up from my wet grave.

300

"Hanes!" I cry. "God, not again!" Not to save
Patrick and lose another friend? The flames' raid
Subsides fast as it began. I cannot even gauge
Where I am. I scream his name. These are traps,
These small islands, and I fear for the horses we
Just turned out to graze. How can this possibly be?
Would God break me down, set my new prow
For old shores of grief again? Is it for my sin?
In my cataloging knowledge I have been proud,
Prouder than a man should be. In his righteous ire
He's punished me. But no—I see now oddly
Safe and looking in a clearing as if a panther's race
For him had simply stopped, my friend. I call
His name, he turns, smiles. Smoke does not allow
Me to say more, but I wave, and now my lungs
Clear at once. Somehow, I think that I have willed

310

320

Our salvation. I walk to him through this dream
And see the wonder and merriment in his eyes.

Rain pours down its harp-strings on us.
Ahead we hear the others' rushing cries and turn
To see them coming through the deep storm.                              330
Now the rain slows to a halt, and we join them
In disbelief. "We thought surely you'd be burned,"
A man named Arnell shouts. "We nearly were,"
I say. "I was saved because I leaped into a stream,
And Hanes was saved because he did not." They
Laugh at the vagaries of storm, and we walk back
To the south end of the island, where little rain
Has come and see the horses quietly grazing
As if nothing had happened. How odd to know
We nearly died, and yet here we are rounding up                          340
The herd to take them back across the river
Just like any lazy afternoon. My life is being used
Up too soon, I think. I want to slow it all down,
Turn it to the speed of turtles, to hold my time
On my back and walk through coming days.

While others round up the horses, my own gaze
Is taken by a blur that coats the air like winter rime
Just ahead. I walk up, see it's a busy, buzzing town
Of honeybees and call others with the good news.
They come and we find a huge honeycomb to deliver                        350
Back across to the trading house—a full tree to sup
The golden nectar from. We break it straight down
And its sunwarmed flow warms the air. Our razing
Takes a few minutes, and one of the others drains
The mass of it into a tube we bring. I fill my pack
With what collections I can find. Vessel full, day
Drawing down, our horses walk back like a dream
Of obedience. Hanes grins. Too tired to dream or stir,
We sit in the scow and cross. "We have surely earned
A fair crossing," he says. "I saw nine horses swim,                      360
The bush erupt in flames. That will keep me warm

All winter." But I think instead of what has burned
Behind me in this life, the light of a fading rush.

Now, days later, near September's end, I board
The little schooner to head for Georgia and Carolina,
To over-winter in Charleston's city days and nights.
How distant from my Florida adventures it will seem!
Never once do we go out to sea on our return, instead
Gliding up the coastline, sandy islands always there
In clear sight. At Frederica I meet with David Laurens          370
And make arrangements to ship all my collections
To London and Mr. Fothergill. With sun in my hair
And wind on my face, we sail across the water
To Charleston, but my mind turns and turns back
To the vast and lasting dreams of my Crystal Basin,
Of the Battle Lagoon and the Friends left only
In my memory. There it is: the city itself, opposite
Of the great wanderings that late I led. I will wait
Out the winter, bed down, make a few trips around
The area. For in spring comes my great trek north            380
To the land of the Cherokees and then far, far west.

# CANTO TEN

*One.*

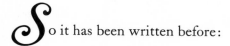 o it has been written before:

*Here is the last river and my final flow,*
*A life of tramping moods and flower hunting,*
*The mounds where alligators roar and dwell*
*Rising from the page of this diurnal gloom.*

*The Schuylkill River has its route and reason,*
*From Valley Forge to Philadelphia then the sea.*
*So I try to see the passage of the almost-dead*
*Backward to the Carolina days. I leave no wife,*

*No children or their heirs to run along the prancing*       10
*Lawn; yet I am still the witness, meadow-*
*Green too bright for one old man to bear.*
*All my life when flowers rise, I, sigher*

*Of beauty, form, and structure, solid urn*
*For ideas in their flittering flight, will camp*
*To suit their summons, petal by petal, boat*
*Moored to my solitary need. Bees in their hives*

*Hum. I see the sudden eyes of bird and deer.*

So it is written now:

*About that winter in Charleston between trips I wrote*       20
*nothing in my* Travels, *and for good reason: like all men*
*I have in me things to hide, but now in the last boat*
*In which I sail, I try to separate delights from my sins*

*and find the job a perilous crossing. I settled there*
*in October, wrote my father back in Pennsylvania that*
*I would not be coming home, that I would bear*
*winter in this south instead. Like a belfry bat*

*I flitted place to place, and yes, I tasted rough rum*
*and green-eyed girls. I found myself awakening to*
*a singular lack of guilt or mispleasure. I was undone*                    30
*by what we call sin, and yet the sky was still so blue*

*that I felt I could lick it off the light above my head.*
*I walked the nearby isles and watched my footsteps*
*in the washing sand, watched its memory of dead*
*days in my life wash out to sea into the depths.*

*What is the book and where is its holding shelf?*
*What is virtue and what is vice? I wasn't sure then*
*nor am I now. This day of wondering has not helped*
*me understand. I watch Nature and how she bends*

*her rules to suit all whim. Or is it really quite so random*        40
*after all? Were we born to supersede our animal selves*
*as ministers would claim? Now I sit, old man abandoned*
*by his lusts and only know that what lightly dwells*

*in us when we are young is sweetly heavy as honey*
*trees in our age. Nothing would induce me to exchange*
*my stupidity for some claimed morality or even money;*
*I was the Flower Seeker, and I roamed range to range*

*in search of time's beauty. Each blossom has a life,*
*a time to open, heal the eye, then fall away to die*
*in solemn silence. So now I have abandoned strife*          50
*and refuse to wonder if it lasts until the end or why.*


*Two.*

Fall shades into winter. I walk the muddy streets
of Charleston. Horses splatter everyone with clods.
Men speak only of the unsettlement, our retreat
from the British who rule us as a plow-horse plods.

Something is about to happen. Ships arrive, leave
port faster, as if harried off by winter's furies.
I want to celebrate my work so far, and yet I grieve
for ones I'll never see again. I want new juries

to absolve me of old crimes—not against mankind
or law but against my human instincts, my need                    10
for patterns of our social deceptions, the blind
ignorance of the reasons why we fight and bleed.

Some days I look for insects to collect in the muck,
but often I sit by the fire and dream her fine face
and assign her different names. I want new luck
to find me, the old poetry of time and of grace.

I make plans to sail back south to Georgia for two
days then abandon the effort. Heavy rains keep
me by my fire, and the hours for my walks are few
and so I read and keep my counsel in the deep.                    20


*Three.*

Then one day a knock comes upon my door.
Disorder has returned into my life, but not
the kind that turns men mad with indecision
for the knowledge of our God but of a thing
more subtle and insidious, the blunt knowing
of limits: that when we gather every fact
we can find on this Earth we still have a draft
of a paper or book half scribbled then thrown
away. I brood. The winter has come down hard
with pelting sleet and trembling windows. I                       10
get up and answer the banging: it is a gentleman
in a dripping oilcloth coat, tricorn hat pouring.

He introduces himself as one Thomas Gage,
a man of middle age, richly turned leather boots
with gilt buckles, finely sewn cuffs, and an eye

for the plants and Indian antiquities I have spilled
across every surface in my rooms. "Come warm
yourself by the fire on this raw day," I say. He
bows and comes to the blaze, holds out his hands
and bakes them to a turn. "They say you have                    20
gone with others and alone in the wild country
of Florida." I tell my stories, how I came here
with Father years ago, of the Crystal Basin, fire,
friends, the Battle Lagoon—but not all, not all.

"Fine stories, true, but I am more a man of mountains
than swamps, and I hear you may in spring head
upland to the Cherokee towns." We slide our chairs
close to the grate, and I offer him tea. He warms
the room with his friendliness, and soon the kettle
whistles on the fire. We drink, in no hurry to speak            30
as friends do not have to be. "I have seen many men
and women of the Indian tribes to the south, but
I need to make collections from the highlands
for my benefactor, Mr. Fothergill in London, so if
you have information, I would take it with much delight."
He is in trade, he tells, and knows the path, the way.

"William, I must tell you our fortunes have turned
away from Britain," he says softly, as if to guard
an unexpected confidence. "And we do not know
from one day to the next how the Indians will go          40
in all this. In our late war, they changed sides day
to day between the Colonies, England, and the French,
not knowing that loyalty must last." I smile at this,
and he nods: "I know," he says, "that we have not
kept our loyalties, either, but my point is that we must
work to tell the Cherokees that their best interest lies
with the Colonies, for I fear a great war will come,
and they will have to take sides in the inevitable war.

"Talk with them," he says. "You are one in love with all
Nature, which is their state of living. They will know       50
your sentiments by your actions and words. Go to

Fort Prince George and the village of Keowee that
lie on the most beautiful river in the world, and share
how we will supply them well if they but stay our
friends when the conflict comes." I am stunned, sit
back and shake my head. A hard rain slaps the panes.
"You wish me to be an emissary of a kind then?"
I ask. "Not a formal one," he replies, "but they see
In that mystic world a kinship with those who
Peer deeply in what I shall call among friends                    60

the eccentricities of Nature." I promise I will do
what I can, and we go out to the White Bull to dine.
His wife is buried in St. Phillips' churchyard,
and they shared not a single child, and his eyes
are tired as he sips a mug of frothy branded rum.
I ask him more of Keowee, and his eyes grow
bright with memory of trading trips up-country.
"I have been there many times, even when the fort
was first built more than twenty years ago. I knew
the architect DeBrahm a bit." I startle and tell him         70
my family knows the man as well. "The fort is fine,
but the world changes beyond what it was in such

a short time that it grieves me to see it, William."
Then I ask why he needs my help—surely he will
go back himself come spring. "No, for I shall be
gone by then. Cancer's come for me. Dr. Bourquin
says I will be dead in four months' time. Today I rise
from my bed through an act of will alone. My niece
cares for me in my rooms in King Street." I lean
back, stunned. The proprietor throws two drunk            80
and fighting men into the muddy street. Thomas
lights his long clay pipe. "My God," I say, "are
you not afraid then to die? My own soul is not
ready for it. I fear it more than all darkness."

"I am ready to take my place beside her whom
I loved well. I have lived the life I was given,
William. This may well be my last day out as

a man. Here is the address. Come to visit me,
as I shall not be well enough to come to you."
He hands me a small white card with his number                    90
on it. I promise I will come. He rises and now
I see how friable he has become, how disease
ruins and wrecks his body, and I am sorrowful,
too sorrowful to eat. Why, I wonder, has this
Thomas Gage, this dying man, come unto me?
I go back out into the cold heart of the storm.


*Four.*

Slowly, I become the man
My father always wished I'd be.
I come to understand this land,
I study what lies in the sea.

On Tuesday when the sun comes out,
I visit Thomas in his rooms,
But he is weakened with a bout
Of coughing, and the scent of gloom

Hangs from fire to floor. He sleeps,
And I step into a sunny day                                        10
With his pretty niece, who reaps
Clothes from where they hang and play

In the brisk and warming wind.
Her name is Ann and how she knows
Of me is mystifying. I mend
Her grief with quiet words to show

I understand her sorrow and pain.
She picks the clothes, a ripened crop,
And I take them in the lane
And back indoors and on the top                                    20

Of a bureau for their sorting.
"They say you came here just to hunt
Flowers," she says, now exhorting
The sickened man to sit and shunt

His cough away. "How beautiful
That would be if it were true."
I tell her of the bountiful
Nature of all that I do

And have done where it is wild
In this, her South. She looks at me                                    30
Like a woman and a child
At the same time: free

But not yet loosed by liberty
To choose a life to lead.
Later when all my energy
Is spent I want to turn and heed

This impulse to return to her.
The winter wind still comes to moan.
And I understand. I stir
And know I'm meant to live alone.                                      40


Five.

I cannot face what I will never be, and so I roam
The roads on sunny days, walk or ride for hours.
I watch the world of men without much interest,
Its funerals and sicknesses, its vain righteousness
And fancy carriages. I scent the silks and swine,
The sailors pouring in from many ports of call
With their fancy airs and rubber stride. Some days
It is hot and calm; the next a storm blows broadside
Into Charleston, and on the third sunrise a frigid
Wind rakes us back inside. And I think of Keowee                       10
And that most beautiful place on this ancient Earth.

Once I walked nearly to Ann's house then turned
Back, unable to see her sweet face again and know
I had nothing to offer her but the doubtful delights
Of Linnæan names and my knowledge of what
Grooms the countryside and how it comes to grow
The way it does. And so I ride alone. I kneel to see
The plants that grace a brackish fen. They mend.

In February, I sense a sea-and-shore break, an end
To some unknown pain, and then I sit down, read                    20
The *Gazette* and see that fine Thomas Gage is no
More. I wander through the sunstroked streets, hot
Though it is cold. A carriage horse imagines frights
And clanks its ironware lashing. This is a hard blow
I did not expect, since I barely knew him. He burned
Up from the inside with his disease. Yet I saw worth
In him, in his wish that I convince with my true plea
Any Cherokee I meet of the Colonial cause. A rigid
Old man strides the street before me. I can collide
With the rider coming near; I dodge his riding phrase               30
Without a spatter. What is the matter? Has the Fall
Found me in this southern town? What is mine
Now and what is the world's? I want to curl, confess,
Bare my breast. Who is a Flower Seeker's mistress
Besides buds and stamens? What great rogue Powers
Torment me so? I watch wind ruff the sea's foam.

AT LAST RESOLVING FORWARD STILL TO FARE,
    TILL THAT SOME END THEY FINDE OR IN OR OUT,
    THAT PATH THEY TAKE, THAT BEATEN SEEM'D MOST BARE,
    AND LIKE TO LEAD THE LABYRINTH ABOUT;                           40
    WHICH WHEN BY TRACT THEY HUNTED HAD THROUGHOUT,
    AT LENGTH IT BROUGHT THEM TO A HOLLOW CAVE,
    AMID THE THICKEST WOODS.

## Six.

Days begin to warm. I roam the nearby islands.
I do not think of home. I take vows, break them,
Roar in a tavern. I tell true stories of my journey
In Florida then re-hone it with emendations
That make me braver than I was: Once I awoke
To find a twenty-four-foot alligator standing
On my chest to devour me! (*Gasps*) I hugged
Him to me with a violent clamp, and we rolled
Away from the dying fire into the wilderness
Where a thousand of his kind roared for us                          10
To fight until one of us was dead (*my God!*).
Old divinities of Destiny! He opened his mouth
To bite my head away, but I clamped it shut
And we spilled off a high bank into the lake,
And I felt myself going down, down, down
Into the nether depths, a watery Hell that even
Milton could not conceive. Then I knew I was
In a nest of moccasins—*thousands* of them,

Whose one drop of poison could kill men
Stretched from one town to any other. Because                      20
I was young and strong, I kicked, leaving
A clear circle around me, and then swung round
The alligator until with his tail I'd killed snakes
In all directions. We breached. On land, he'd strut
And take his time with me, but I began to rout
Him with wrestling holds. (*Holy suffering sod!*)
I looked to Heaven and proclaimed my trust,
And with one great crack, I hereby confess,
I broke the creature half to half, left it cold
As winter's coldest ice. (That is how I bragged,                   30
And I began to learn the efficiency of landing
A sweet punch with a fist of lies.) No one spoke
For fear of breaking up the spell. Concatenations
Are delights by winter's fires, it seems. Earning
Their admiration, I stumbled into the slow scrim
Of dawn, ashamed of myself, back to silence.

*Seven.*

April comes, the month of travel.

I gather lightweight gear, buy a horse.

I plot my journey, plot a true course

I plan to see Ann. My plan unravels.

I write home, I check my good map.

Shrubs burst into blossom and pink

Clusters decorate the heartful nap.

I barely take the time to sleep or think.

I buy better clothing, attend to my dress.

I go to St. Michael's. I do not confess.                          10


*Eight.*

North toward the mountains and the Cherokee towns.
I never felt such high spirits, never more ready to adventure
Or write down the undiscovered species of those lands.

I leave the tropical riot of the coast and far south behind
Me and head for the elevations of clear water, red men
With stately gait and sufficient knowledge of any world.

I will learn: God, what joy to be free and freely learning
From the teaching world. I am like a flag unfurled, ready
To kick the sweet rump of my fine and steady horse.

Give me a notebook, give me a course.                            10

# CANTO ELEVEN

$G$OOD order be damned!          I swim the land's ocean
         with horse and hoof          I am mad with pleasure
            for wind and water          and the sweep of rain
               and landscape; let     me arrive anywhere
                  or nowhere, let me love the breath
                  of any moment every day.
                     Who is the flower
                     and who is the stem
                  what is without
                  and what in                                              10
                  within? All
                  swirling of
                  water and
                  wind is so
                  magnificent
                  that I cannot
                  bear to know
                  which is the
                  flame and
                  which is                                                 20
                  the flow.
I feel the town at my back but do not turn around
to see it grow small. The flowers before me are all.


         Intangibles be gone—lifting spirits cannot interfere
         With the light in the world before me: road, river
         Stream, immense shadows of unburned oak groves
         And ancient pebbled riverways. Winter now passed
         As Thomas has passed away, I ride beyond bone,
         Sinew, plume, petal. I am William, and this is my
         Route along and through Time, for it is never            30
         Distance we travel, but space filled with blooms
         Of magnificent visual virtues, bees whose buzz
         Can never be recalled as *gloom*. Species display
         Their mystery. Eleusis claims my roamer's eye
         With its fluffery and display. I am climbing on-
         Ward and increasing in the slow altitude of all

Ascending creatures. I have no misery in me.
I have not an ounce of misery or pain inside me.

This first day I travel many miles by horse
And on a quiet evening I come to Jacksonburg,                    40
Small village on a stately stream. Now, next
Morning, and I ride the same distance, at times
Galloping but mostly in a stern and half-stately
Gavotte, my horse nimble and strong for road-
Time with his wide-nostrilled arrogance and
Sweat-stained musculature. I spend the night
At an Inn on the road and ask a rough-dressed
Fellow traveler: "Have you ever been up to see
Fort Prince George and the village of Keowee?"
His eyes narrow over a frothy mug of drink. He                  50
Waits. "I was thereabouts when Coytmore took
The ball that took his life," he says. "When the
Soldiers massacred them captives in the Fort."

He tells a story, battles in war between British
Forces and the Cherokees, back now many years
Flowing past now, of Lower Towns strung like
Jewels on that pristine river, men brained
On both sides, bones cracked, musket-balls
Buried in hearts still pumping, thinking brains.
His voice is thunder-deep, omen of a mystery                    60
Or deep drunkenness—I cannot tell which.
"Now Keowee I hear is near abandoned, and
The Fort is but a riddled trading post, glory
Gone, all honor unbound from soldier or from
Cherokee. Sad days, my friend." What, I ask
Of the plants and the animals—I head up
There to draw and to collect them. He sees
A madman here, gets up and sits by the fire.

Am I going mad? Next morning, I rise early
And set out, land visibly rising underneath me,                 70
And I glow with an invisible joy in all Nature.
We clop through high forest, and my horse

Slows in the ever-dragging pulse of beauty. We
Canter then walk, and I do not push him, alone
With the world and in it. We come out of woods
Near the public ferry on the broad and rocky-floored
Savannah River. Soil: a dark, loose, fertile mould
On a stratum of cinereous-colored tenacious clay.
Forests: the great black oak, magnolia, liriodendron,
A hundred others. This ancient sublime forest                    80
Intersects with extensive avenues, vistas, lawns
Of deep and emerald green that open to savannahs
And far-distant rice plantations: what a fine grandeur

    It all displays to the common eye: the mockingbird,
    Vocal and thrilling, rises on his silvered wings, rolls over
    And over then gently descends and presides
    In the choir of tuneful tribes, wild
    For such evident mastery
    Of all singing, all
    Bright song.                                              90

I dine at the ferry and cross over into Georgia
And observe growing here *Dirca palustris*
Growing six or seven feet high. Now I find
Myself alone in the high pine forest. Scent:
Rich needles, gum, sap, wet earth, and water.
I want to know what I inhale, but I cannot even
Understand the wind and the arch of birdsong,
The scramble of animal feet, the sound of water
Near the woodland trail. I ride until I find tavern
And stable and refresh my horse with grain                       100
And myself with a draught of cooling liquor.
Now I walk down to the river alone and think,
And all the magnificence of the world arrives
In subtle and dreamlike ways. I see the cattle
Of the inn-owner penned together in one place.

    I see the milkmaid with her bucket, and smile
    As she comes into the mockingbird vale before
    Me to drain the udders of the cattle in her charge.

What a pleasure to watch as she milks the cows
And sings with the birds in this lovely land.                                    110
All the world turns to music, it seems, and
We might be in some far-distant period
Of history, when prophets walked the land
And animals stood on two legs to speak.
Speak, I want to say to bird and beast. But they
Already speak in their way, and girl and mocking-
Bird together intertwine their voices as day
Dims and wind ebbs. I sit beneath a pine tree
And take off my hat and hold it in my lap, listen
To their duet as it unwinds across the green pasture:                           120

What vessels of delight: bird as counterpoint
To a tune and words somehow altered by time
And distance—I knew it from a spritely show
When I was in Philadelphia—John Gay's
*Beggar's Opera*, there a dancy tune, here from
Milkmaid's lips a melancholy meditation, silver
With suffering's delight. Intelligence or wisdom?
I watch her with a voyager's eye, one come
To catalog the songs of a world before him
Without suffering or pause. And I realize                    130
That I do not miss the soft damp pleasure
Of Florida now, its maze of God-crafted water-
Ways and roar of bullfrog and alligator.
I head for high ground, and this milkmaid
Sings me there, over the hills and far away.

Others come to help haul the pails of milk
Back to the house, and I walk slowly with them,
The year far too early for fireflies but a sense
Of them anyway, of lilting lights and loveliness
Beyond otherwise knowing. I speak to the farmer        140
As we sit on his porch and smoke: "You must own
Fine horned cattle to have this many milk cows
At a time," I say. He agrees: "My stock is young,
But I have lately moved them far away from here
Starting over with new bulls and cows. Heaven
Blesses me in this land of great pastures that go
From eye to eye, the distance of all my dreams."
I feel him my brother for that confidence. He says,
"But I am not rich, for the milk I make is just
Enough to feed my family and my slaves."                   150

I turn silently against his words and think
Of Africa and the bondsmen in their evil chainless
Days. Surely time will come when this way
Of selling men and their families cannot stand
Before God and man. Surely we will come to clear
Knowledge that offense to God offends all men
At the same time. And yet he seems a good man,
Speaks of his son, newly married, of the life they
Have shaped from this country nearly emptied
Of all mankind. We watch his slaves, who are                         160
Strong, black as much-burned chimney flues,
As they swing, cut down huge pines, listen as they
Sing songs of their own creation, so different
From *Over the Hills and Far Away* that it could
Shine from a differing world. Mystery: melody.

We walk back to this man's house. His son
And lovely bride shine with modesty,
With an air and smile of grace and benignity,
Twin worship, airy *gloriana*. Myth leans down
To kiss the ground before their young and hopeful           170
Feet. Every action and feature seems
To reveal fragrant celestial endowments.
Even though they have native sprightliness,
Sensibility of the young and fecund, virtue
And discretion rule their actions before us all.
Like a Regent in the Wilderness she is unadorned,
Plain, fresh-smelling as the new day, dressed
In a cotton gown she has spun and woven herself.
I am taken with her eyes, so that when I lie down
For sleep she floats beside me in a long dream.             180

Come early morning, the farmer's new daughter
Hands me provisions for my voyage in a sack,
And her shy smile melts all composure,
But I say nothing but my thanks. As I ride on
And onward, I see her smile, her eyes, wonder
Of the trail beyond domesticity and touch,
The streambed of children. I watch their unspoken

Pleasure, pause for a moment, and then my horse
Plods, and I delight in the lake of their eyes.
I see new turns in the trail, fresh blooms, green                    190
Beyond any hue a man has ever known before,
And my ache eases. I have been given another
Thing to love in this life, and I must adore it
More than other men who ride into Nature
Knowing of her works and days. I love *her*.

Now I ride the high road between Savannah
And Augusta, and for several days I see no place
To stay and must camp alongside the river
And the road. I swim through a day's ecstasies
Through elevation and spring. Father, do I rise                     200
Now in your eyes? Have I gained a profession
Worthy of your early hopes for me? So often I have
Failed you and myself, unfit for a plantation,
Not apt for business in Florida or in Philadelphia
Or elsewhere in between. At stopping time late
On another rainless spring day, I kindle my fire,
Warm a pan of bread and meat, sip from my
Canteen-full of sweet river water. While I wait,
I take out my pencil, sharpen it with my honed blade,
And draw from memory a broad and lovely leaf.                       210

*Midday has come for this old man, now inside*
*On a summer day in the late years of his living time;*
*I have worked upon a scholarly thought for a while,*
*And yet my mind roves and ranges back to adventure*
*Of my young light. Keowee and Fort Prince George—*
*The divinities of travel in those kindly days the year*
*Before war and its attendant hells broke upon us all.*
*Wisdom ranges past age; it side-slips the barriers*
*Age blasts out into our wavering bones. Father, gone*
*So long now, I shall soon return to your command*            220
*With pleasure I thought I'd never miss. But O I do,*
*Sir; I miss your voice asking what I will make of life*
*Besides dawdling all day, drawing or painting*

*As my wont might be. O I do, Father. Listen*
*For the sound of my voice in our next world.*

A hundred miles lie behind me and the farm,
And I cross at Silver Bluff and arrive to see
The land of Mr. Galphin, a liberal and distinguished
Man who possesses wide connections in trade
And influence among Indians of the South and                    230
Southwest, especially the Creeks and Choctaws.
I hold introductions to the traders among all
These tribes and more, and he speaks to me as one
With similar knowledge. He asks of the Seminoles,
And I tell him of their strength and bravery, how they
Love their families, children, how like us they are.
"Show me Silver Bluff," I say, and he is delighted
For the job. It is much-celebrated town to town,
On the Carolina shore of the Savannah River,
Steep, rising straight up out of the swift water                240

With stripes of strata that I note in my small pad:
Loose, sandy loam with a mixture of seashells,
Especially *ostreae*; the next stratum is rich clay.
Then comes sand, next marl, more clays of varied
Color and quality, the last of which insensibly mixes
A deep stratum of blackish, saline, sulphureous earth
That appears to be of an aluminous or vitriolic quality.
Next are layers of pyrites, belemnites, markasites,
Sulphureous nodules shining like brass. Mica gleams
In slagpiles, layered as the pages of a book. Then              250
On the surface come the storied middens of ancient
People: conical mounts and terraces; and remains
Of fortresses in all kinds, Galphin says former
Camps of the Spanish who came here with hopes
Of finding in mounds of silver a reason to live.

"Perhaps one day, men will find where you lived
And think it as majestic and filled with stories
As this," I say, pointing to a conical mound before us.
He smiles, then laughs. "They well might, William."

He then shows me a stupendous formation called 260
Fort Moore, and I am speechless with admiration
For it all. While I wait for the ferry to take me over,
I come to the carcass of a calf, which others tell me
Fell from a precipice above while looking down
To see the rich grass in which I now stand. How sad
I think; I should memorialize his hunger and how
The depth-perception of his eyes misled him. I
Do not wonder of the same predicament in which
I now find myself with each new and passing day.
I kneel before the bones, but I do not, cannot pray. 270

    Augusta, now before me, lies in a fruitful
Temperate region. The river, which begins
As the Tugaloo and Broad, breaks over shoals
At this town; ships of twenty tons can
Navigate the river from here to Savannah.
It may one day become the capital of Georgia
From its fine setting. Most travelers go
By a different route to the Cherokee country,
Through the town of Ninety-Six on a well-worn
Road, but by traveling along the river I can see 280
And study steep banks, vast swamps, the various
Soils, and all things mineral, vegetable, animal.
Had I gone the other way I would not have seen
Fifteen miles south of this place an amazing
Sight: a great hill country of fossil oyster shells.

    The heaps of these ancient vessels lie seventy
Feet deep or more, covered with glens
Of deep-green magnolias and aromatic groves
Of fragrant callicanthus, rhododendron,
Many more. Who would have dreamed 290
To see such grandeur in this hot climate?
I have come into a different land here and now,
But am I the same man as in the deep garden
Back home in Kingsessing? I want to know where
I am bound and why, and if my life will have
Meaning for anyone else.

They looking back, all th' Eastern side beheld
Of Paradise, so late their happie seat,
Wav'd over by that flaming Brand, the Gate
With dreadful Faces throng'd and fierie Armes:                    300
Some natural tears they drop'd, but wip'd them soon;
The World was all before them, where to choose
Their place of rest, and Providence their guide:
They hand in hand with wandring steps and slow,
Through Eden took their solitarie way.

                                        Am I the vessel, am I
                              The lye, am I the pestle or mortar
                                        I
                              want to know if the rain
                                        or if the snow                    310
                              will tax disorder or like gold
                              glow in the moongilt night
                                        I want to know where I'm
                              bound, if I'll hear a
                              sound that will betray my fear
                                        or my stride, if I will
                              lose the emblem I hope,
                              I seek, I shout, I claim:


I feel the town at my back but do not turn around
to see it grow small. The flowers bloom me on.                    320

                              Nothing is written.

# CANTO TWELVE

1.

*N*ow, in the sixtieth year of my life, my own flowers
In their fading day, I, Philip Lee Williams, join the ride
With Bartram up from Augusta toward the wild valley
Of the Keowee River that I tramped when I was ten,
The village-site on one side and the long-lost fort
On the other. And that world was young and indelible,
Filled with flowers and pale sunlight, not urgent
But urgently wished for, and I daydreamed the young
Man, the Flower Seeker, into my solitary days.
How many uncountable hours I spent wandering                     10
Those hills and fragrant fields; younger brother,
Youngest son, I shaded my eyes and looked where
The village had lain two hundred years before,
Then old man Ferguson's farm. And on his porch,
Screened and waiting for a glass of iced tea,
He lined up cannon balls, huge cracked potsherds,
Transfer- and stem-ware—messages from a story
I retold myself each time we tramped the furrows.

Into that rich history I daydreamed myself, burrowed
Deep and deeper. In winter, the fields turned hoary             20
With rime, the water of the river sharp, cold, words
Coming out of our mouths in feathers. We were free
As boys could live in those days, summer scorch
Or autumn and its thousand-colored (and more)
Forests painted up the mountainsides. In my core
The quick delight of fish in current, one, another
Turning sharply in the sun. I would be lost, sauntering
Away from my father in the arch of that quiet praise,
But he would call to me, and the river's soft sung
Voice would rise, too, the flowers all convergent             30
With sky and water; beneath the shoals an incredible
Change came over me: I was home in any port
That included Nature and wild things: fish, wren,
The rich alluvial soil, the fern, the bobbing lily.

And I did not understand how time would soon collide
With my daydreamed calm, my finest hours.

My father had lived nearby, a few miles away, most
Of his life and had never driven there; when I was
Young he read about it in a book at my Aunt Laura's
House and thought: I should go see what is left there.                    40
So he took my brother Mark and me one spring day
To the valley, and O it was a place of deep delight,
A wide river-bottom for corn and history. Here—
Our father walking off presumed distance—near
Where this mulberry tree now grew—was famous
Fort Prince George. I stood in mute shock, eyes wide
With the imagination in which I would come to live.
There, back over Nimmons Bridge, was the village
Of Keowee, close enough, you see, to be shelled from
The fort, which it was during the Cherokee Wars. I        50
Thought: buckskin and tomahawks. No, he lectured,
These were British soldiers who garrisoned the walls
Of the Fort, and by then traders and others surely wore
Clothing of spun cloth. I knelt to smell the rich soil.

I felt frozen with utter joy; I would let nothing spoil
The moment. Sun, a slight wind, an armory, a store
Where soldiers drew supplies, bunks, a center well:
I could see it all. And yet it stretched for many hectares,
The fort, the village, the road, the surrounding sky,
That eminence on which our best days come from.        60
I saw how the valley had resisted white men's pillage
For two centuries, could not have known that the river
Ten years on would vanish, its blue and flowing tide
Stilled by the waters of Duke Power, the same as
Other village sites had been inundated in the years
Between 1950 and 1980. Where did the bear and deer
Go then? Where the Cherokee went, the old light
Of centuries burned out in a wink. Only a lake stayed,
Speedboats burning diesel fuel, and history's stair
Sawed off and lost. The days when a summer chorus        70
Of crickets gave me all the purpose and the cause

They needed to stay drowned at a small, pathetic cost.

But that was years away. Now, as father and brother
Talk the probable length of bastion walls, I walk
Down to the river by myself, turn and smell what
Bartram smelled: the lovely earth, the closer hint
Of water, the greenery in the wind, the old oaks
That seem to step across the land toward me.
There is more to me than history in this bright
Acrostic countryside. I come to the ford at the river's
Edge and kneel: this is where the commandant,
Lt. Coytmore, was shot to death in an ambush
In 1760, and when it came, the soldiers slaughtered
Nearly two dozen captives held in the fort, tore
Them piece by piece apart. Not long after that,
My father buys a book I'd never seen: the *Travels*
By William Bartram, and I sit on winter nights
And read the book with outrageous delight,
Camp with him at the Battle Lagoon, walk on
From one species to another, filled with joy.

I am no longer that adventuring young boy
And yet I feel as if I'm near an incandescent dawn
Some days, that all I knew of loss and cold fright
Could be winding down around me. Nature's lights
Illuminate the manuscripts of pool and river gravel,
Flit around me like the unplanned flight of a bat.
And yet the wonderment and summer love I wore
Among those days has never once failed or faltered
In my life. The Keowee River with its sweet rush
Was always a memory away. So William's want
Must have been satisfied in his last days, a giver's
Gifts immortalized in print. His dance was my delight,
His small rivers spread as wide in mind as the sea.
Like a rain that comes to stay awhile and soaks
The earth, his pleasure sinks down deep. The mint
Bushes of his time live in mine. Like a prism-shot,

Color drenches me shade to shade. Each hot stalk
That speaks of him talks to me, his distant Other.


2.
Everything coalesced in my mind: Nature, history,
Music, poetry, fiction, art, family—and I knew                    110
How to walk through my life for the first time.

I would see all things through the green lens
Of the natural world, through history and art,
Bound to the free mysteries of science—a ring

Of confluences that still brightens all my days.
Spring, summer, fall, winter, we walked along
The trails of traders and Indians, and in those

Days only a few people could be seen anywhere
Around there. We might stride out into fields,
Up the close mountainslopes to the airy tops                     120

That overlooked Keowee and that fine lovely
River and see not one moving human; dirt roads
Veined the land, and the occasional car spiraled

Loops of dust behind it and was then gone.
I walked leaning over to peer for potsherds,
Those gorgeous paddle-stamped bits of glory,

To place my bootmarks in the imaginary heels
Of soldiers and dancing Cherokees. I sat down
By the river and in solemn silence at being alive

In the filtered sunlight of boyhood while our                    130
Father lectured on history and the chemistry
And mystery of the landscape before us.

Long before we helped excavate the fort itself
We knew from his research how it looked,
The diamond-shaped bastions, the parapets,

How the well likely lay. Locals knew where
The fort was, where the village was, but no one
Had ever dug down to see what lay beneath

The surface of that farming land. Nearly half
A century has passed since then. And my eye                           140
Draws the valley as William would, filled up

With the solitary contexts of a quiet life.
Once you love a place that much all else
Breaks down, prisms of memory breaking up

The spectrum of history and nature, gleam
To spectacular gleam. Once you feel the pain
From their starvation, from their harsh disease,

From their displacement forever from that land
Of lovely sunrise and haunting moonsong,
You cannot bear more; that is the sensitive end                      150

Of the sorrow you can bear, and you suffer it
Or die. So everything coalesced in my mind
And that color, aroma, taste, sound, touch—

That sensory world braided by a stony river
Became the drumming of my history and heartbeat;
I was branded to it for the dawns of this life.


3.
I was the slow boy with a shimmer in his eyes
I was the boy who felt the Cherokee surrender
          as genuine pain that would not fade;
I was the boy who walked with the fluid motion
          of music and wind and flowing water;

I was the hushed boy who knew to stand back
    when my brother and our father fought
    congenially over fact and supposition;
I was the dreamy child who turned to see if he
    stood behind me, William Bartram,                  10
    the Flower Seeker, whose travels
    came to haunt me with their quietness;
    who thought of Mother and Laura Jane
    back home, rushed to tell them what I saw;
I was the boy who imagined the stained flanks
    of well-worked horses that snorted, sailed
    through the pastures of my imagination
    from fort to town and then back again;
I was the Flower Seeker's son, who learned to sit
    and watch for hours without moving, who        20
    could stay still in the cradling limbs of a cedar
    and see nothing go past for half a day and love
    that emptiness as if it were parading saints;
I was the dancing lad tuned to the music of drums;
I was the prince of unwasted motion, who knew
    how to be still and not want, to hear birds
    and separate them song to song, who knew
    the trickling anonymity of water as brother;
I was airfoil before the wind, seed-pod, rumor,
    Luna moth, the sound of grief when the time        30
    came to move forever away from the valley
    where the Keowee River lapped the stones;
I was the vowed enemy of power companies that
    destroy history and the gorgeousness all
    Bartrams should have still and never can
    again, not as I saw it in those spangled days;
I was the boy with a shimmer in his eyes.

FULL IN THE MIDDLE OF THIS PLEASANTNESS
THERE STOOD A MARBLE ALTAR, WITH A TRESS
OF FLOWERS BUDDED NEWLY; AND THE DEW        40
HAD TAKEN FAIRY PHANTASIES TO STREW
DAISIES UPON THE SACRED SWARD LAST EVE . . .

4.
"When Bartram came here,
Fort Prince George was
No more than trading post,"
My father says. I am twelve

Years old, 1962, and we have
Been coming here for awhile
Now, tracking down all the
Nearby Cherokee towns

That have no historical markers
Or local stories left to tell.                                    10
I nod, knowing how little
I can know beyond what I

Feel on this summer afternoon.
We find Estatoe, Sugar Town,
New Keowee, strung beads
Of towns up and down

The Keowee River. The word
*Keowee* turns into blood
That pumps up my veins;
I daydream myself village                                    20

To village, hold in my palm
The black and white trade beads
We find scattered everywhere,
The characteristic Cherokee

Potsherds with their paddle-stamped
Designs. I learn projectile points
Are from more ancient cultures,
Had laid along these acres for

Two thousand years or more
When the Cherokee came. They                                    30

Called them the Ancients, and
They were. I want to know now

Who my Penelope is, who I
Fly back toward, place or
Girl, grace, or some courage
I can never quite uncover;

No, I was born for this, quiet
Days of listening and looking,
For the poetry of things dressed
With the past, giddy with possible                                    40

Meanings; I am their translator,
Their clear companion in prophecy;
I am the one who sits alone
At the village edge, seeking visions

Of the way our world will end,
Of the evil men who will one day
Come to cut down all the trees,
To ignore the cries of this land

As they fill the valley up for their
Goddamn lake. I am the one who                                        50
Will break it down with my mind
If I could. I would. I would cause

It to crack and collapse at least
In the landscaped strictures of a poem.
I am the beadless one who is
Left alone to find a path not here

In a world raked with many paths
That go everywhere and nowhere.
I am the annointed boy who could sing
The past and future at the same time,                                 60

Who could bloom into a sign.

5.

Rain dreams down my window this November morning
Long before dawn, announcing itself by sound only.
I beg the subvention of my dead, the filled vase
Of Bartram's blooms, for the kind of rural ecstasies
I felt as a boy in that now-lost valley. The ladders
Of our double helices intertwine; base-pairs link
Name to name. I take this to mean the fictions
Of this world are the real verities, inventions closer
To what is true than our precious facts. What I say
Is what becomes True, the silt of generations rising                    10
In my unworried power. It is not arrogance or insight
That gives me such a right but the boy who walked
The hills and the valley, who sat by the river, heard
The voices William heard, who could chant himself
Into the fragrant cups of all petals. Out there in rain
The young man sits up in his lean-to, sees his fire
Has been washed out, but he is not afraid to face it.
We are illimitable, striding, face-forward, and free.

If we fear the rain, we fear the creek and then the sea.
If we understand the richness of the past, we trace it                   20
Back into dates and names but no faces, that desire
Turning into scope and passage. Somehow I have gained
An ability to raise the dead, not from their shelf
Of antiquity and breathless wonder but from a word
Into the Word, the central mythologies we talked
Around campfires for ten thousand years. I delight
In joining my journey to his, twin heart, an uprising
Of brotherhood and Linnæan pretense. It is day
And yet night; we are each statue and its old poser;
We are the fluid to flow for centuries and its friction.                 30
And yet it is all gone in the turn of a shoulder, a wink,
An emendation of sleep. And I will turn no sadder
For it all: we are the Flower Seekers and all indices
Point toward the intuition of roses, the frilled chase
For petiole and amanuensis to help stem the lonely
Days with unfolding springs and pitiless mourning.

6.
Know I hold your hand
In the fearful land's-end,
Rise up through the lake
With shaft and blade.
It is symmetry we made
These days together, sake
For sake, friend to friend,
We do not even fear the sand:

Integritas, consonantia, claritas

# CANTO THIRTEEN

1.

*T*HE land before me hums with harmony.
I ride with jolting joy among the hoofstepped
Hedges and their arching oak armory.

I feel as if I have somehow overslept
And then awakened into all enchantment
Like a dreamer whose stories have crept

On him with the stealth of an encampment
Awakened by sudden warriors at night.
I am all learning and soft contentment

These days. I find a hundred charms at night                    10
And in the shaded wakings of the dawn;
I am filled with magnificent sound and sight

And cannot bear the fact that I'll be gone
Some day from this life. The steep and rocky
Precipices abound. Like the flute and shawm,

Birds band for music. I wade, get my stockings
Damp to see a bluegill filter in the aqua tomb
Of flowing water; the water goes on rocking

As it runs south. I feel as if I have my own womb,
As if I'll give birth to a new kind of creature                    20
With so much fur to preen and to groom

That it will glisten in the changing feature
Of all light. I head to the land of magic,
Where Nature shall be my only teacher.

I set out next morning north on the tragic
Path the Cherokee abandoned, towns
Empty but for broken bits of clay bowls.

This wild country in its greening gowns
Has been depopulated; the vast wood
On chains of hills, full of gnawed bones                          30

Of ancient buffalo, fleet foxes who could
Outrun the most brazen wind. Purling rills,
Fleeing brooks, dark caverns cut deep

Into the land: every leaf I see here fills
My imagination with terrible urgency.
I ride and roam. The streamy moisture

Turns to mist that coolly falls, an emergency
Of dampness that halts my eye in wonder.
Aromatic shrub, incarnate flower, I see

Callicanthus and rhododendron. Thunder                           40
Echoes among the white and wavy mantle
Of delicate inodorous and fiery azalea.

Toward evening, the sun my only candle,
I cross the Broad River at a shallow ford
And arrive at Fort James: a four-square

Stockade with salient bastions and gourd
Dippers hung on its worn-up windlass.
Inside is an acre of ground, the good house

Of the commandant. I am not friendless
As they let me in. I see the officer quarters,                    50
Barracks for the garrison—fifty rangers,

Each with a horse, a rifle, and their shorter
Dragoon-pistol, powder-horn, shot-sliver,
And tomahawk. The fort stands on an eminence

In the forks between the Savannah River
And the Broad. Above here it grows wild
And I cannot wait to ride among its species.

2.

I begin to feel the old          need for a new disorder
    In the country of my      riding bones, a breath
        Gone out into a      world beyond eye
           And hand, the monuments
             Of the ancient ones
              A glory to me.

With the surgeon of the        garrison, I ride five
    Miles above the        fort to see great
        Conical mounds     of earth, four huge
          Terraces, too, and around            10
            The mound a spiral
             Path to the top.

Four niches in the side        of the mounds point
    The cardinal direction      of Aeolus's winds,
        And were meant     perhaps to look out
          Over the land around
           The river bottom.
             The fields

Surrounding are now          planted with Indian corn,
    And even the mound      is fertile enough to            20
        Grow huge loads     of ears each year.
          Thousands of workers must
           Have worked to
            Build it up.

My wings spread here;        my pleasure is vast as
    Great mounds them-     selves, and I pick up
        A huge pottery     slab with swirling
          Decorations like wings
           Or the many stars
            Of clear night.                 30

3.

*Old men, do not hide your monuments.*
*Do not disappear without telling us stories*
*We can take with us along the far path*
*Of our lives. Old men, you want silence*
*Now when we need the shape of dreams*
*To light our lives in the camping nights*
*That await us. I am your elderly confrere,*
*Your whitening companion on the route;*
*Listen to my chants and recipes so you*
*Can take the fire to one more new town*                          10
*Along the path. Tell it for your coming*
*Philip or Mark, who re-remember your*
*Riding days with giddy and inappropriate*
*But joyful surrender. Do not be afraid*
*To be timid or unsure, even tender when*
*You set out on a journey; tell us what*
*You fear and why, and we will love you*
*For it. Tell us of your sunny sloping days*
*When every path lay downhill and bright*
*Before you. Old men, do not take away*                          20
*Pity for the monuments you see ahead.*

YET I LOVE GLORY; -- GLORY'S A GREAT THING: --
THINK WHAT IT IS TO BE IN YOUR OLD AGE
MAINTAIN'D AT THE EXPENSE OF YOUR GOOD KING:
A MODERATE PENSION SHAKES FULL MANY A SAGE,
AND HEROES ARE BUT MADE FOR BARDS TO SING,
WHICH IS STILL BETTER; THUS IN VERSE TO WAGE
YOUR WARS ETERNALLY, BESIDES ENJOYING
HALF-PAY FOR LIFE, MAKE MANKIND WORTH DESTROYING.

4.

My saddlebags bulge with new collections; my horse
        is anxious for the trail. We stamp out the older dance
the Indians must have once stepped along the high mounds.

Mid-May has come with its delicious fecundity. I set off
     for Keowee now, toward that fabled valley where Cherokee
lately lived and fought with their British neighbors in snow

and bitter cold. The world springs fully into fragrant green
     before me. I recross the river back into Carolina, feel my
pulse brighten with a prospector's often-disappointed glee.

For I cannot not find what I seek: the highland river that flows       10
     with bubbling music over stones, the farm fields, flintlock
mutinies among animal and plant. I head for the drama of all

Nature; she cannot fail me. Up the road not five miles, a great
     drum of thunder plays from vale to door, and I seek a house
to keep from being lightning-struck, find an isolated farmer

and his goodwife who let me in. We stable up my grateful horse,
     give him a bagful of sweetgrass. "Come in fast now," he says,
and I follow the farmer on to the porch of his trembling house.

His churchmouse wife, almost pretty but very much afraid now,
     takes my wet sleeve and almost pulls me inside, shuts the door     20
behind us, sits trembling by the unlit fire in a crude rocking chair.

"We shall die, Eli," she says raspily to her husband. I look around
     for children, see or hear none. (Is she barren, have they died as
so many children do in the back-country? I cannot say, won't ask.)

"We will fare well of it," I say, smiling to her. "Tell me what you
     know of Keowee and Fort Prince George, the destination of my
travels in this country. I am a naturalist come to catch plants and

and animals, to draw what's hereabouts for my patron in London."
     She looks as if she's seen a madman. "Grace, he is a good man,"
her husband says. "Don't be afraid none." He holds her. Lightning hits     30

nearby, and the crack and rumble of thunder make the house shake.
     She cries aloud. I see how modest their belongings are: crude
chairs, a badly nailed table, and in one corner a cradle turned upside down.

5.

I tell them of my Florida days.
They tell me of their farm.
"We have dug three graves
Now," says Eli. "No charm

Of any kind could save
Our babies' sweet lives.
We have tried to be brave.
We keep a few sweet hives

For honey, grow our corn.
For the rest of it we hide                                    10
From the storms. We are born
For suffering, go on and ride

Out our pain with no stop
To hear a summer child
Pull a string on his red top
To spin, to drive us wild."


6.

Having finished my collections and observations
And my conversation with the poor farmer and
His quiet, frightened wife, I ride on into the rain,
And though the thunder's stopped, the showers
Pour down the creeks and dry geological folds.
My horse Tom plods on, his head hanging down,
Clop to clop, and I do not rush him. All waters
Rise as the rain runs ceaselessly downslope:
Branch, creek, rivulet, and river; fordings bloat
Like blisters on the water. The country is uneven,          10
Its surface undulated by ridges or chains of hills
Sometimes rough with rocks or stones, yet still
Green with deep and heavy forests: fine hickory,
Chinquapin, magnolia, viburnum, and azalea

Intertwined. Finally, thirty-five miles of riding
Have passed, it is almost dark, and I see before
Me the commissary for Indian affairs and its
Commander, Mr. Cameron, sitting and smoking

On the dripping front porch. He sits there stroking
A huge, green-eyed black and purring cat that fits                    20
His lap as lips fit a mouth. He stands, the door
Behind him opens, the cat jumps down; striding
Out comes a rough-faced, bearded trader trailing
A huge and bearish dog that wags me up. My trickery
To get the animal to shake my hand fails; its will
Is stronger than mine. Its owner's laughter fills
The rainlight with gruff glee. I feel almost feverish.
"Tell 'im he's got the world's finest goddamn coat,
And he'll shake," the trader says. "He needs hope
You'll at least give 'im a compliment." It bothers                    30
Me, but I do it, though leave out the curse, frown
To show I will not use such language. The cur unfolds
A grin and lifts his paw. "I'll be damned," I glower,
Stunned at my own profanity. They laugh. Strain
Fades between us, the dog shakes and rolls, hand
Striking out to touch mine, his gentle ministrations

Fulfilled as I sit and tell Commissioner Cameron
Who I am, take out my letters of introduction
From John Stewart, the area superintendent who
Lives in Charleston, announcing my business                          40
In the upcountry. Cameron reads it as the rough
Trader and his dog trickle off. Rain comes harder.
"You've come to collect flowers and roots, plants,
Stems, small animal pelts, and to render them on
Paper, is that right?" Cameron asks doubtfully. Put
This way it feels foolish, but I assent. He sends his
Boy for a mug of toasted rum, and I think to defer
Because I am a Friend, but then I take it, and warmth
Spills through me like escape from my final fears.
"That's right," I say. "My employer, Mr. Fothergill                  50
Of London has hired me to seek out new worlds

Among the plants and animals and by doing so tell
The world their shape and form." Unexpectedly,
Cameron claps his hands, says, "By God! Wonders

Of the world so described and writ!" The thunder
Claps and dooms the darkening day. So affected is he
That he claps again. "An idea after my heart, and well-
Said, Bartram. I have often named plants and hurled
On them my own cognomen: Brighton's Purple Pill,
Achilles' Shield, Angelwort, the Soldiers' Tears!                60
I cannot wait for the changes in the sun, in the month
So I can see the shift in flora. The Cherokee concur
There are creatures unseen by white men; 'tis
The Uktena I remember best, scales, claws to cut
Up the unwary man to ribbons just before dawn
In a waterflow. And huge aggressive ants
That saw leaves to take into their mounds and larders.
Can you draw me sitting here, boot eye to cuff,
Bartram?" He's been drinking. His dizziness
Is mild and makes him more agreeable, a true                    70
Good man, so I take out a pencil. My production
Pleases him. Like a flashing, slammed hammer one

Bangs upon a stone, he claps his hands. A gunshot
Goes off in the woods at the same time, and I jump.
Cameron laughs. "You'll learn not to flinch when
You hear gunfire in these parts, Bartram." I laugh
At myself. A stable-boy comes for my horse, takes
Him off to feed out of the storm. "You'll stay here
Until the rain calms down." I tell him I am bound
For Fort Prince George and Keowee. He lights up           80
His long pipe and nods gravely. "I hear its glory
Days are long gone, the fort I mean." He concurs,
Tells me: "The parapets inside have largely fallen
Off now; the swivel guns taken to the Overhills
Towns, Keowee abandoned. And yet there's mystery
There, an intangible sense of profound unknowing.
I've seen walls glowing with foxfire lichens to light

A man's nighttime ride. Amazing things. Be prepared
To feel what you have never felt before as you ride
Through that country." I *feel* an unasked-for shiver.　　　　90

Is this the place toward which I have been driven
In my life so far? The word *Cherokee* thrills, collides
In a fruitful way with all I've ever dreamed or cared
For. It is different from *Seminole* or *Creek*, a height
From which I feel I can look down, know I'm going
The right direction in my life. I am bound to learn history
As well as botany, the old fights, the sorrows, the thrills
Of unexpected peace. I can hear the flora calling
To me, deer tramping out my name. Do I deserve
This bounty, this perpetual rain? Will William's story　　　100
Be worth telling a hundred years from now? I sup
With Cameron, and we do not talk about it. Crowned
In my private chambers, though, regent, no mere
Artist or descriptor, I know what lies ahead. Lakes
Of dreamwater pour over me in the night. The chaff
Of my past pilfers all my false fears. My own kin
Live in this fastidious wilderness—stump to stump
My kind abuts the greenery, this my silvery lot.

Three days pass and the water stays too high
For me to travel, but I ride around the post　　　　　　110
And collect ginseng, malva, delphinium
Whose flowers are a fine deep blue color
Much like the common larkspur of gardens
In my North. I sit to drip and draw. On the third
Day, the sun comes out and Cameron says,
"William, remember what I told you of what
You will feel in that transcendent valley, how
The mystery will fill you as a well fills after rain."
We shake hands. I remember Eli and his Grace,
Solemn souls with a yardful of babies' graves,　　　　　120
And I wonder if I ride toward my own death
And if so how soon it might be. And yet I head
Up country with a kind of unknowing ecstasy,

A sense that I could suffer, starve, be broken
In my body's bones and still feel more delight
Than most men feel in a hundred imagined lives.


7.
"This is John, a slave, and he will
Direct you to Seneca to keep
You on the trail, for it is ill-kept
In the rain," says Cameron, and I
thank him but feel a chill creep.
He's just a boy, black as obsidian,
My angel, my true Gideon.
We head north. My heart fills.
The trail grows muddy, steep
In places. I could happily die                    10
Here: This is the world toward
Which I have dreamed myself
All my life. It is a place almost
Too delightful for common thoughts
To supplement. I kick my horse
And ride into these golden hills.

# CANTO FOURTEEN

## 1.

*How can I delay the approaching subtle raptures of my story, friend,*
*How can I make clear the way Nature wrapped me*
*In such sought-for madness*
*That each breath propelled*
*Me birdward into blue*
*So that I charmed even*
*The impartial mudslick*
*Trail with my singing*
*That birds gave way*
*Knowing they could*           10
*Not penetrate the film*
*Of epic pleasure, how*
*Can I say that each*
*Hoof- and footstep*
*Left me higher off*
*The ground than*
*Anything a man*
*Had ever yet*
*Conceived—I*
*Do believe it*           20
*Would be possible*
*For all love,*
*Fire, happy*
*Thoughts on*
*Earth became*
*Mine for days*
*All mine for all days and*
*I would years later here inside in the midday heat feel*
*The impenetrable flowering of memorial breathless*
*Galloping, my horse unable to slow down*           30
*From the sheer scent of the tramp*
*In our muscular young years—God,*
*What we have and do not know*
*That we possess until we are old*
*As I am now, dreaming of going back*
*Out in the later day of this July.*
*For I no longer see an old man*

*When I lean to look down into our*
*Pond, hair frost and snowstorm, but I see*
*The magnificence of my young, well*
*Days—the glow and gleam of hope—*
*Let me feel that wonder once more,*
*Old, old, and older William Bartram.*

40

2.

And can I, Philip Lee Williams, clock out of this life
and ride alongside the other William as he leaves
Cameron's post and heads north toward the valley
       of which he's dreamed

all his life, all my life? I say, "William, I am the
Flower Seeker's son come to help you collect
and recollect this world of our young manhood
       so how can we derive

the alpine rupture of our plainer days to rise up
and filter out what is not Nature and history or
art or music or literature from all other things
       that bind us?"

10

3.

It is mid-May as I set out from Lough-abber,
The home of Mr. Cameron, ride north with the slave
Boy, cross on our first day several rivers and brooks.
This is now called the Keowee River, and we trace
It, beds to beds of pebbles, and its holy water flows
Over painted-still bream with their rainbow sides,
And they glide or hide in their travels, each sliver
Of their flighty shapes seen to us miraculous, glazed
With shafts of sunpaint, carved without dross,
The river-spray dampening our stamping fetlock days.

10

We are looking for Seneca, the first Cherokee town,
And though I know from the Seminoles what such
Towns resemble, there is a dense uneasiness now
With this colony's temerity toward independence
Brightening it stream to stream, fold to rocky fold.
I stop to draw a vast clustering of *Vitis vinifera*,
Grape vines that ramble and spread themselves
In low trees. The air is all wine, the brooks seams
Or stitchery in the land, and no frightening shout
Seals our turnaround dreams. We gallop delight.          20

Now we see Seneca, a very respectable settlement
On the east bank of the Keowee River; our flight
Is a swirling flume, fine fettle, brown riverbottom
Soil unwashed away by storms and silver squalls.
The chief's house and those of the nearby traders
Sit atop a mound not far from the freshet stream;
Since the late Cherokee wars, Seneca is rebuilt
Body and soul-less, though Indians still lounge
Around, children swinging corn-shuck dolls in circles
Of newly planted squash and corn. The Fire-Giver          30

Brightens lodges against the coming night; mouse
And mockingbird mull the angled axe and musket.
The Lower and Middle towns were broken in war
By Middleton, and now but a few Cherokees dance
Out their lives here. There are not more than a hundred
Warriors in all these former thriving towns; safety
Creeps among the whites like an unseen disease.
Bodies were mangled, copses rent. The old gods
Did not send salvation to them. Is there a worse day
When God or the many gods fail a whole people?          40

It is afternoon when I ride out of Seneca through
This flower-dripping valley, scented with ripeness
And the filtering lights of sunshowers in the treetops.
Bushes, bent like mops in the recent rains, stand up
In their shimmering Indian beads of water, drench
My eyes with what cannot frighten me. A boy prances

His horse not far away—I cannot tell if he is Cherokee
Or white or if it matters in the end. I see Montgomery
In my mind marching up this river shoulder, headed
For the blooded grief of war. An unflickering star                    50

Holds fast in the waning sky. It should be, it should be,
It should be not far now . . . the crumbing parapets,
Spavined barracks, the wide-diamond bastions, and,
Across the river, the town of Keowee, which they say
Is now a village filled with ghosts alone. It should be,
It should be . . . how far have I gone now, fifteen miles,
Sixteen miles? I ride to the river and see that gorgeous
Flow, bright with sunlit stones and the unwrinkling sound
Of water flowing south. Suddenly, there it is before me:
The walls themselves, my goal, old Fort Prince George.             60


                    4.


(Mark and I find paddle-stamped potsherds almost
At the same time, and we take them to our Father,
And he beams them equally with his proud smile.
I want to walk every inch of this valley's miles,
To rout out every point and cannonball, to tame
All the hidden stories of how it looked, its boast
Of pomp and power when William Bartram came.)


                    5.


They now call the villages before me
Fort Prince George Keowee, as if the white men
Thought to take an *equal* portion of the flowers
And their roots and stems. They came to take
It *all* as they always do and have here, too.
Cherokees still wander round the trading post,
And the whites dress as I have never seen before,
Rough to the point of utter rustication. And yet
I wander back to the river, cross its ford, find

Fruitful strawberry banks, aromatic Calycanthean                10
Groves, the moor fowl thundering in the distant
Echoing hills and the nearby ascents from which
A military surprise seems impossible. The shrill
Perpetual voice of the whippoorwill rings me
With its three notes repeated in endless need.
What is *my* endless need here a thousand miles
From all I have ever really known in the world?
In places the river flows gently, but its shoals

Of whitewater make most of its course. Foals
Fan out near the old fort, kick their now unfurled            20
And faintless cry. No prison could hold my smile
As I watch their emptying pleasure. A new seed
Has been planted to empty this land of Cherokee,
And the few around the trading post do not fulfill
What I had expected of a mighty people. The ditch
That once encircled the fort has filled in; the misty
Mountains beyond are blue, and their gray anthems
Blend with the coming darkness. Tales now unwind
From the whites of how Virginians have come, set
Indian against Indian, white to white. A hawk soars          30
Around the main gate whose hinges do not boast
A swing for mousetrap's close. A man named Drew
Says, "The Cherokee do not like whites who make
Pilgrimages into their mountains. If it's flowers
You seek as they say, be wary and plan to send
For help as a sailor cries when sinking on the sea."

6.

Inside the fort, the stench arouses my sorrow.
Outside, in the late day I build a fine campfire,
And to feed it I go camp to camp and borrow
Old plants and deadfall. Instead of the higher

Pleasure that such a lovely place could afford,
It is, in all, a sadly worn-out vale, the shoulder

Of the land unplanted and burned. The cord
Is cut from mother to man. It is much colder

To the eye than I would have ever dreamed.
From Sugar Town to the north, a small village,
Then far south, the land is drained and seamed                    10
With multiple regrets of a people's pillage

And the Cherokee moving farther north
In the night. The remains of their houses are
Visible but not a woman or a child, source
Or destination, remains. They have gone far,

Over the hills and far away. Night comes
And I do not hear the sound of voices,
Do not hear the raged insistence of drums;
I have few desires and even fewer choices.


                    7.


And yet not long after dark, when the stars bathe in the blue-dark sky,
                    and cricket anthems rum the air
                with their snickering roundelay,
            two Indian men come before me,
        stand in the hem of my firelight, say
    without words that I must come with
them, and I nod and do not say: yes, yes,
        take me with you, and I will not ask a
            question of what you wish of me, I will
                do whatever you ask. We walk in the dark,            10
                    and I turn once to see the crumbling fort, head
                        off with them in a place I cannot see or know.
                    I hear the torn wool of a cat's maddened growl,
                I feel the sound of it in my throat and my arms;
            the two men walk on either side close enough
        for me to feel the swish of their flesh. I can smell
their smoky flesh, the oil of some creature on hair
        and in their skin. We walk north, and they start

to sing in the Cherokee tongue, but I cannot know
  what tales they make. How do they know who I am,   20
    and why have they come to my campside in the night?
     We reach a hidden place by the Keowee River
    where a small lodge has been built and inside I see
   a white-haired old woman dancing on her rump, a hum
  coming from deep inside her wrinkling body, and I turn
 to my captors and raise one eyebrow, and they nod to let
me know I shall not be harmed. An equally old man drips a
palmful of gunpowder in the fire, grain by grain, and the flash
 fills the lodge, which has an open roof, with the daydreamed smell
  of battle. They hold hanks of grass tied up with thongs of  30
   of ripped-up blue silk, and it burns on the ends, and they
    inhale it, wave it into their open, chanting mouths.

    I smell
    the smoke from
   the grass, inhale it, too,
   and then they give me another
  handful of dark vegetable matter and show
  me that I should chew it up and swallow it, and without
 thinking, I do it, and for a moment nothing happens at all except
 I feel dizzy but then O haven, heaven, sparks go off inside  40
  my mind, and they prop me up and give me a black
  and bitter drink, and I quaff it off, and I vomit
   it up, but the lodge begins to fill with
    images of monsters and girls
     of beads dancing
     by themselves
     around this
     tomb.

WHAT DWELLING SHALL RECEIVE ME? IN WHAT VALE
SHALL BE MY HARBOUR? UNDERNEATH WHAT GROVE  50
SHALL I TAKE UP MY HOME? AND WHAT CLEAR STREAM
SHALL WITH ITS MURMUR LULL ME INTO REST?
THE EARTH IS ALL BEFORE ME. WITH A HEART
JOYOUS, NOR SCARED AT ITS OWN LIBERTY,
I LOOK ABOUT; AND SHOULD THE CHOSEN GUIDE

Bᴇ ɴᴏᴛʜɪɴɢ ʙᴇᴛᴛᴇʀ ᴛʜᴀɴ ᴀ ᴡᴀɴᴅᴇʀɪɴɢ ᴄʟᴏᴜᴅ,
I ᴄᴀɴɴᴏᴛ ᴍɪss ᴍʏ ᴡᴀʏ. I ʙʀᴇᴀᴛʜᴇ ᴀɢᴀɪɴ!

I fight for order bu          t          I feel mys          elf
    losing          con          tact          w          ith
        it          an          d          yet                                        60
      sw          ans          glid          e
        befo          re          m          e
          and na          ked gi
              rl
              s
      swi  ng          their there they're dance
        danc          ing!

𝔴𝔥𝔞𝔱 (δο) 𝔶𝔬𝔲
see one says
in Eng                              lash                                        70
    𝔴𝔥𝔞𝔱 δℯ𝔴 𝔶𝔞𝔴 𝔰ℯ𝔞
      in Engl
        itch
           and I sea wave          s
        ris  ing          and          fall-
        ing
And sudden, sudden, suddenly, a bright *ecstasy!* explodes over me
And all makes sense and comes into a mosaic pattern, and
A drowsy numbness dilates my bones, a trembling hickory smell
    *burns!* in me and I grow taller than all moons                    80

And far beyond all stars and I want to live forever in this place
I want to come down from the Mountain to in in instruct each
Lost soul who can no longer *find!* Nature and tell Her how sweet
    her fortunes glow without consuming a bloom or a *bone!*

But the          n I sea it is it is it is
    a fal  se  ord          er
      se  ord          er
that a man alone          ne+++++++eds
    no or=der to sir vive and now the stars ex

                                        plain                        90
                                        plode
and I see dan
     ci
     ng
                    before me, her body pain
          ted                    (no pain for me)   *a naked girl!*


                         and my
                         and my desire
                         arrives quite hot &
                         b(right) with need, she                    100
                         is painted wildcat black
                         I sea      now    nd I am
                         writhing writ(h)ing  the
                         steed of      wild water
                         she  falls to a skin  mat
                         my head explodes)!! in
                         crockery shards bobs to
                         her rhyt(hymn) the men
                         help me down to her  O
                         what am I (G     odd) is                    110
                         this a maze a joke amaze
                         me with the sea    villainy
               can't stop                myst. wild
               brain filled                with a wake
               of white flew              ed she pulls me
               into her b(odd)dy          who have become
               I am the fl(whore)          seeper I am going
               to I am going to            I am goin    g to
          can't help   then can't             the others drum
               and Im moanoooon              ing for herd         120
               and they stand            me upupupup
                    and strip off          my skin
                         no and it      hot in
                         hear (hell     and
                              fare    wail)


and I swim in the interior sea of her

body oh God, and now I rush outward again
beyond a billion trillion willing moons
through the rings of Heaven, and constellations
reach out to touch me as I                                    130
pass

and O myth I swim in the interior ocean
of her, and she dances on me
and sings, and the others dance round
us sing and and and sink rich (uals)
and I see all things are

= = = = = = = = = = = = = =

and the girl and I *explo!*(ding from the fort in war)
to
gather roots and bobbing flow-her heads              140
and all things are = = = = = = = = = = = = = =


all things are un= = = =


gasping now, death of Venus
but the release last on and on
for both of us until I can't
bear bare it & run *scream!* (ing)
from the lode thrash through tearing
under
bru(a)sh
fall heart-first                                            150
into the laughing
river



8.


*I sit at my sunny desk now smiling*
*At the suffering I gave myself that*
*Night. I awoke on the shore in the river,*
*An equally tattered and skinny brindle cat*

*Staring at me. I pushed up. I was naked*

*Completely, groaning. What felt like fleas*
*Sought a trail home through my hair.*
*I was all injury then and all disease.*

*I sat up in the edge of the current,*
*And the cat fled. I could not believe*          10
*What I had done; to be this weak*
*Is not what I had planned. We deceive*

*Ourselves if we think we are strong*
*Enough to turn dishuman, to stride*
*Above what species, genus turn us*
*To become. If you must turn, deride*

*Me for that weakness, I understand,*
*But each of us becomes one night*
*What it is we most fear; so I bathed*
*In the river and had shame, fright,*          20

*And yet felt more alive than I knew*
*Ever before in my life. I can say,*
*Too, that I understood quite well*
*That I would be alone the days*

*Of my life after that, and I have.*
*For I knew too much of beasts*
*And their desires to do anything else;*
*I had taken famines and feasts*

*And understood I needed nothing*
*More than a glimpse of what mars*          30
*Character to avoid it; I knew my*
*Eyes were angled more for stars.*

9.

I come naked up the riverbank and creep among
The strong shady cuff of trees along the flow
Until I see a plowing farmer and hail him, tell
Him my story. He laughs so hard I fear he will
Be sick then goes back to his house and retrieves
Me trousers and a shirt, rough-spun stockings,
And a pair of serviceable boots. "They take your
Money, if you have any," he says, "a kind of
Initiation they put unwary travelers through.
You're supposed to have seen visions—that's                    10
What the others say, anyway." I tell him I had
Little in the way of money, and my other things
Are in the saddlebags on my horse at the fort.
"*Fort?* You mean the trading post?" he coughs,
Laughing. We reach his house, and his good wife
Comes out, eyes grinning but with manners too
Refined to mock me. "Hasn't been a fort for years
Now. It was once a fine, grand place. But the world
Changes around us, does it not?" I tell him I did not
Have a vision exactly, but that the universe seemed          20
To explode and whirl in my mind and that I may have
Laid with an Indian girl. "Many a man's refreshed
Himself after a long ride thus," he says, clapping me
On the back. His wife, nettled, says, "Gideon, stop
With your stupidity and go plow. I'll make him food."

He slaps me on the back, and I fall down to one knee,
Still wobbly from the night. He goes off whistling.
I come inside to their rough table, and she gives
Me dried beef and cold cornbread, well-water
Clear and fresh as a March sky. I cannot look            30
Her in the eyes, and she knows it. "There's no
Shame in acting as we must time to time," she
Says. I am in such shock I do not know what
To say. In Philadelphia, among the Friends, no one
Forgives any sin; indeed I'm told that is for God
Alone and only if He pleases. "Now remove your

Shirt and let me balm your cuts, for I see the blood
Leaking through the old shirt I sent out for you."
At first I say to myself that I will refuse, but then
I realize it is a different world I have come into
And that I do not know what is right or wrong.        40
She treats me as I eat, daubing on caustic sodas,
And at least two small plasters. "There. Dress
Again. That should heal properly. By the way,
I'm Emma." I turn to her and say, "And my name
Is William Bartram, and I am a traveling fool
Who would be grateful if you did not tell anyone
Else what has befallen me." Two children, boy
And girl, tumble in, roughly dressed and grinning
At their mother, but she shoos them back outside.     50

"Do not worry, William. Get strong again and
Healthy, find a guide to go with you. Though you
Do not see Indian dwellings in plain sight here,
The Cherokees abound in the protection of night
And deep places. Mr. Homes at the trading post
Can tell you of one who might guide you into
The higher mountains where the tribe has gone
After all the wars and coming white people."

I tell her I will, and after finishing my food
I rise in my ill-fitting clothes and walk to the ford     60
Nearby on the river and cross to where the village
Of Keowee was. The site is abandoned now, high-
Spots for council house and celebrations covered
With burned remnants of their now-passed glory.
Broken bits of pottery lie everywhere, bones,
And opportune plants growing in the places where
Dances once enlivened their lives.

## 10.

I wait three days around the fort to find
A guide who's said to be returning soon.
To my mischief, everyone seems blind,

And I walk on hills beneath the moon
That bathes the river silvery and gold.
What will be too late or then too soon?

I cannot know. I talk to one who's old,
A trader white as ripped and grizzled rime.
He tells me how the Cherokee were bold

In their best days, how they watched for signs          10
From the weather and the flesh of light.
I say God is patient with designs,

And he smiles and says, "*God*, the bright
Boy who lets his children starve to death
With pox when winter's deep upon the night?

Mountains are paths to fainter breath,
And God will watch you plunge a waterfall
And die without a cross or funeral wreath."

And yet I love the silence when it calls
Without a sound, and so I'm lured upslope          20
Into the forest with its fragrant halls.

So I wait alone from hope to hope,
I scan horizons like a boy at sea.
And for meaning in this life I grope.

11.

Finally I can wait for this guide no more
And so I set out alone, determined to run
The risks for myself. I cross the sunned river,
The Keowee, at the ford below the fort
And ride through the rushing whitewater
That's only fetlock deep. The day is sunny,
And the spring air rings with delightful
Strawberry plains and gently swelling green
Hills that begin to ascend the steep and more
Rocky ridges. I ride to the top of the hills                    10
And can see below me the former site
Of the Keowee village and the serpentine
River speeding through the lucid plains:
They seem right beneath my stirruped feet.
I turn away from what I have come to love
With such conflicted passion and head up
The trade trail alone, wondering if danger
Awaits me, though this one from mankind.

A rider here could be lost and completely blind
And still love the land as a familiar ranger                    20
Would. For four miles I cross rivulets and brooks,
Come to the edge of rocky precipices. A dove
Coos her welcome and her warning. If I meet
Another rider what will I say? None remain
About, though. I come into a charming scene,
A meadow embellished with a river of all delight
Glittering in the sun. Grass rides these rills
And will be cropped for hay. I see the lost store
Of antiquities, towns of the Ancients between
The river and the slope. Once the frightful                     30
Sound of blood-revenge, the aroma of honey
To warriors bent on war, rose. The daughters
Of chiefs would have cried aloud to support
Their warring ways. And the village vision-giver
Would glower in the tumuli from moon to sun
Into knowledge's secret and hidden core.

Every flower seems to be in bloom. Each village
I pass has been burned or lost to crumbling time.
Now at once the mount divides, and I can see
The ample Oconee glen, encircled by a wreath                    40
Of uniform hills. I begin to ascend the mountain
Of that same name, and at its base is old Oconee
Town or the ruins of it—char smears of roofs
And council houses, scattered broken pots,
And occasional cracked-up axe heads carved
From smoothed and shapely stone. I take out
My notebook and write down a dozens species
Of plants before me, *Fraxinus excelsior, Annona
Glabra, Aesculus sylvatica*, and even a new kind
Of *Robinia* fine to me, though perhaps it is the one               50
Described by Catesby in his book. I ride on to
The top of the Oconee Mountain, and from there
The view is inexpressibly marvelous, the finest
Magnificence I recall. I linger awhile to dream

Of what this place must have been when a beam
Of prosperity shaped the Cherokee to their highest
Level of strength and influence. Each village bears
The marks of death and dissolution, of Time who
Gave them over to rot. Here is the same warm sun
That stilled their summer days, the same designs                   60
Of water and wind. And like the Bible's Jonah
They were swallowed by the dark. And no Jesus
Came to save them. I am sickened by the thought.
Yet they lived and they loved, and daily they farmed
These rich bottomlands. And then white men blot
Out that life in a blink. There's not a single truth
In how we tell the story, I know. Each Indian pony
Was stolen or shot. There are no crystal fountains
Here as in Florida to keep the rivers for belief
Instead of blood. I hear the unworried hum of bees                 70
Around me. I hope to find some kind of new sign
For this New World, but all I see is rot and pillage.

12.

My good mind and finer pen:
*Vitis vinifera, Olea Europea, Amygdalus communis,*
*Ficus carica, Punica granatum, Amygdalus Persica,*
*Prunus, Pyrus, Pinus strobus, Pinus sylvestris,*
*Pinus abies, Acer saccharinum, Acer striatum,*
*Populus trimula, Betula nigra, yellow Jessamine,*
*Halesia diptera, mountain Stewartia, Styrax,*
*Ptelea,* and *Aesculus pavia.* Now I enter
A charming scene whose happy banks tumble
With shrub and vine, mountain brooks                          10
Of inestimable charm.
And:
An ample high meadow on the left
Embroidered by the shade of a high circular
Amphitheater of the hills, the circular ridges
Rising magnificently one over the other;
On the green turfy bases of these ascents
Appear the ruins of a town of the Ancients,
And the upper end of this spacious plain
Is divided by a spur of the ridges before me;              20
And:
My road leads me up into an opening
Of the ascents through which the glittering brook
That waters the meadows runs down dashing
And roaring over high rocky steps;
And:
I gain the top of an elevated ridge
And there appears before me an opening
Between other more lofty ascents,
Through which continuing as the rocky road              30
Led me, close by the winding banks
Of a large, rapid brook, I ride with mad joy,
And the brook at length turns to its left,
Pouring down rocky precipices, gliding off
Through dark groves and high forests,
Conveying streams of fertility and pleasure
To the fields below;

And:
I cannot bear to be in such beauty
Or to leave it for I know that no finer days                    40
Can await me, no more lustrous adventure,
No richer diversity of species and footpaths.
How can a man arrange to leave his Earthly
Life at such a moment of supreme delight
Without causing it himself and thereby
Sinning against such beauty all around?
If the great Cherokee warriors could not
Do it, why a modest Flower Seeker
Who has lived so deeply yet erred so much
On his journeys across this great land's              50
Tropic South?
And:
I cannot stay if I hope to gain genus
And species, and so I strike onward,
And the surface of the land for miles
Is level yet uneven, occasioned by natural
Rocky knobs but covered with good earth
Which affords forests of timber trees that sway
In the small pleasure of a northwest wind.
And:                                                  60
I descend from the highest trail and travel
Slowly for miles, clop on enviable clop,
Through grand forests, dark detached groves,
And meadows with exuberant pasturage
For cattle, and on the bases of the surrounding hills
Flowering plants, fruitful strawberry beds,
And as always the abandoned habitations
Of the Ancients.
And:
Now I cross the delightful Tugaloo River              70
And once again I begin my ascent, first over
Rills and stately forests and then to the top
Of Mount Magnolia, the highest point here,
Separating the waters of the Savannah River
From those of the Tennessee. (Do not look
For Mount Magnolia on a map for I have just

This moment named it, as is the right of each
Discoverer!) I call it so from a new species
I have found of that celebrated family
Of flowering trees. I realize as I stand                    80
Here how hot and thirsty I have become;
My good mind, my finer pen,
My lulling fields of strawberry petals
And their pendulant berries.

# CANTO FIFTEEN

*4th October, 1756*

*Sir, There was three Chickesaws came in Keowee four Nights agone with a Message and Talk to these People and went immediately away over the Hills for Chottee about Midnight. They staid no longer than to deliver their Message, the Truth I have not heard as yet, as there was no White Person there to hear what it concerned, only a flying Report from the Indians, that the Creeks had been foul of the White People.*

*The Creeks, it seems, fired on the White People first and wounded three of them, and the Whites fired on them and killed three Indians. But you may be assured, and I am certain, that it is not all they are come after. I advise you to have a good Look Out to know the Truth, for it is about no Good they are come, for these Indians keeps it all hid from me, and will not tell me all.*

*I am Sir with due Respects,*

*Your very humble Servant,*                                    *JAMES BEAMER*


*P.S. Please, sir to give my Compliments to all the Gentleman in Company with you. As soon as their Things comes up and my Horses comes down, I shall send them of directly over the Hills again, and I believe I shall come with them myself.*

*Yours &c.*

And:
Me pulling Bartram back toward Keowee
When I was fifteen, trying to halt him
And ask him to stay, to see if, twenty years
After Beamer's letter, he could put an ear
To this sacred ground and hear what runes
He could make undessicate and reflower
For our own family explorations. For I wanted
To be the one to find one important artifact
That Bartram might have seen on his visit
To what was left of Fort Prince George

And so in some small way become the victor
Of our own explorations.

There was not a time I did not know
Of Howard Carter's double exclamation
On opening the dusty doors a few weeks
After our father's birth in 1922, and so
How could I, too, find wonderful things?

A.

*Old age does not bathe each day in its wretchedness,*
*My visiting Friend; I sense a coming kinship with a boy*
*Who might trace my tramping days, who might care*
*To blossom from inquiry as I did into consequential joy*
*From what I learned of petal and fragrant, fleshy leaf.*

*There is in every land an unsettling and immemorial reef*
*Of that which cannot be explained. I do not see the reason*
*For this old age, for the daily awakening into new sun*
*And silky rainfall. I do not see why the changing season*
*Should find me still alive, but it does, and I am one*    10

*Who can bear it until my final sleep. I am not done*
*With the tale this summer day. But my fainter breath*
*Informs me well enough that my time has come apart*
*And unknits in this warm house. My old friend Death*
*Warms me, too, eye to eye, and hand to my heart.*

B.

We would cross a stream bridge into the valley,
Mark and I wearing jeans, our father in broadcloth
Khaki trousers, all booted. Mark and our father
Spoke of science alone, the tangible proofs of history,
But I let my boy's life wander, sensations of sun
And council-house shouts filling the multi-voiced

Inner ear I carried with me always, even in those days.
They spoke of angles of fire from FPG into Keowee,
And I watched the slow creep of sun in winter seed
When the fields lay fallow in the coldest part of winter.          10
I saw how yellow mocks lemon, how cloud shadows
Marbled every foot of the village site with its hillock
In the middle, site of power, no doubt. Even then
I was The Listener, the one who held an outside
Place among a crowd, The Watcher, a thousand
Ideas and sensations firing at once until I knew how
To separate them from incipient madness. I could
Feel history peel back in a bright stratigraphy,

Understand that even in the damaged mind geography
Operates with its own logic. Mark and Daddy would          20
Talk of subsoil glories and they might even allow
Imagined features to enter possibility. I saw cows and
Their stippled shadows on the Kodacolor hillsides,
The impossibility of some terrible and enduring sin
In a world of such forgiving grandeur. Air was silk
As we walked in Ferguson's fields and meadows,
If there was a door to any past, we could enter.
Already in the winter soil we felt the hum of seeds
In their botanical memory, and on my young knees
I put my ear to the Earth and heard them praise          30
Bartram, for they had been passing down by choice
The story of his travels for centuries. I might run
A hundred yards because I could. The brief mystery
Of it might make our Father glance up, not bother
To wave or ask what made me race. I stood, soft
In understanding, sweet slave in a sunny galley.


C.


My spirits flag as I tire from walking
          north from old Fort Prince George,
and my thirst grows geometrically. Now past
          midday I seek a cool, shaded retreat

where there is water for refreshment, grazing
        for my horse and time to rest
for my faithful companion, a black slave
        who has caught up with me on horseback,
        sent to show me the way just ahead, speechless.
            We now enter into a dark forest            10
            and its charming solitude. Shades
            are animated by sun, cloud, wind.
            Greek columns of huge trees
        rise before us. And rushing from rocky ridges
under the shade of the pensile hills is the unparalleled
cascade of
            Falling
            Creek.


Rolling and leaping off the rocks, the water
        glows like brands from a campfire in deep      20
night. It lands below in a huge sheeted pool,
        spreading a broad, glittering pane of crystal
waters over a vast convex elevation of plain,
        smooth rocks. The basin that catches it all
trembles in the center through hurry and agitation
        then gently subsides, encircling the painted,
            still verge, and out of it glides a small
            but delightful river. I sit here upon
            the moss-clad rocks, under the shade
            of spreading trees and floriferous fragrant    30
        shrubs in full view of the cascades.
I feel lost to time and direction and am in no hurry
            to go
            anywhere.

D.

*Magnolia auriculata*
*Rhododendron ferruginium*
*Kalmia latifolia*
*Robinia montana*
*Azalea flammula*
*Rosa paniculata*
*Calycanthus Floridus*
*Philadelphus inodorus*
*Anemone hepatica*
*Trillium sessile*                                                      10
*Trillium cesnum*
*Viola*
*Mitchella repens*
*Stewartia*
*Halesia*
*Styrax*
*Lonicera*
*&c.*


E.

These beauties stroll over the mossy, shelving, humid rocks
And from far away the wavy boughs of trees bend down
Over the floods and salute their shades, play on the surface,
And some plunge their heads and bathe their flexible limbs
In the stream while others are tossed about by breezes,
Their tufts spangled with pearly and crystalline dewdrops
Collected from the mists that glisten in a rainbow archway.

F.     THE SWALLOW WARRIOR TO CAPTAIN RAYMOND DEMERÉ

*September 5th, 1756*

*This Day James Beamer Trader of the Town of Eastitoa waited on Captain Demeré in Fort Prince George. He brought with him the Head Warrior of that Town by Name the Swallow Warrior, who informed Captain Demeré of the following Particulars in the Presence of Capt. John Stuart, Capt. John Postell, John Chevillette, Esq., and Lieut. Robert Wall.*

*James Beamer and John Hatton, Linguisters.*

*He says that a Fellow called the Thigh who was formerly a Prisoner of the Savannahs and lived sometime among them and speaks the Savannah Language very well has lately brought in News to the Cherokees to join the Savannahs. He says that the Thigh has brought with him from the Nuntueyaws a Belt of Wampum which was given them from Chota a long Time ago and that it is now sent to the Headmen of Chotee from the Nuntueyaws to signify their Willingness to make a Peace and that they expect on the Sight thereof the Cherockees will immediately join them.*

*He says that the French Indians met in a very numerous Council at the Savannahs Town consisting of all the Headmen and Warriours of the following towns (viz.)*

*The Squaghkeaws, Nuntueyaws, Twichtweyaws, Yankesheyaws, Savannahs, Tau'wees, Yawhtenous, Cowghkeyaws who all agreed and consented to send the Belt of Wampum aforesaid.*

*He says that Old Hop has sent for the People in the Middle Settlements to go to War but that they did not go to Hop. He says that there is a Party of the Cherockees shortly designed for Charles Town and another Party is going to Virginia. He says that Old Hop has sent ten Men to the Nations above mentioned to confirm a Peace with them, and that there is a Party from Great Tellico going to the French to perform a Peace with them. He says that all the Headmen of the Cherokees have been informed of this and have desired that the same may be kept secret from all the White People.*

G.

I was a slow boy in those days,
and my quiet fluttering filled
the valley with the sound of wings
while my father and brother
shouted out streams of science;
Bartram's crystalline dewdrops
climbed along my outstretched arms
like rewards for my silence
while they joyfully argued facts.
My own Valley of the Kings                                    10
with its saffron-scented breeze,
the ford that Bartram crossed
that I sat alongside so many times
and listened; the bee-trees,
the absolute inability of songbirds
to understand cruelty or impose it.
Whose shadows had passed there
before me, and was I worthy
to shift in that always falling shade?
I wandered away from them                                    20
and thought: O God, let me live
forever in this place, where
I feel like a floating thing, wings
spread, and catching lift on the barest
wind, rising in my dreams across
the Keowee River to the Fort
settling in a field of wild strawberries
with William Bartram and saying:
Tell me, tell me, sing my summer,
pipe my dawn, walk with me                                   30
if only a little while by the river
and then beyond it; always spring,
forever summer, the flowers
always opening into full bloom,
*Stewartia*
*Halesia*
*Styrax*
*Lonicera*

## H.

Having collected some valuable specimens
    I continue my lonely pilgrimage,
My road for some time winding and turning
    About the steep and rocky hills.
The descent of many is troublesome, rough
    As a plunging corkscrew. The rocks
Beneath my feet are friable fragments,
    Slippery clay and talc. Yet soon I see
Beneath my steps another level surface
    And before my eyes a pretty, grassy way    10
Close by the banks of a most delightful creek
    That falls over steps of rock and glides
Gently with serpentine meanders through meadows.

Snow-white cascades glitter on the sides
    Of distant hills. Feathered singers
Pave the way ply on ply with their melodies.
    Then, without my noticing it, a deep shade creeps
Over all the land, and thunder begins to drum vast
    Warnings before me and behind. I see
An Indian standing by the stream alone, a Cherokee,    20
    And he's holding up his peaceful palm,
And I come forward. In clipped and accented English
    He says, "Great storm. Please come." He takes
My hand and I follow him up the streambed,
    And by now the explosions wrack the trees
Around us. Rain pelts our skin like hot shot.

I THINK HEROIC DEEDS WERE ALL CONCEIV'D IN THE OPEN AIR, AND ALL GREAT POEMS
    ALSO;
I THINK I COULD STOP HERE MYSELF, AND DO MIRACLES;
(MY JUDGMENTS, THOUGHTS, I HENCEFORTH TRY BY THE OPEN AIR, THE ROAD;)
I THINK WHATEVER I SHALL MEET ON THE ROAD I SHALL LIKE, AND WHOEVER BEHOLDS
    ME SHALL LIKE ME;
I THINK WHOEVER I SEE MUST BE HAPPY.

Suddenly, all goes silent.
The birds are afraid. We
Await the coming violent
Rage; the purpling sea

Of storm clouds begins
To pour rain just as my
Companion leads me in,
Out of the storm's eye                                    40

Into a deep, mossy cave
Where he squats next
To an old fire, the nave
Of a holy place, a text

Of stone and distant fire.
"You lost?" he asks, turns
To me, puzzled. "Up higher
The sky's firewood burns

Even more brightly." What
Can he mean? I sit with him                               50
To ride out the storm, not
Knowing how this hymn

Of Cherokee inquiry may
End for me. "I have ever
Been lost," I stop to say
Softly. "I am here to sever

Any connection with that
World beyond." He draws
In the dirt. A small bat
Flits out. Thunder saws                                   60

On its fearful storm.
Rainwater cascades over
The cave's mouth, warm
With spring, dripping clover.

He goes outside as the rain slightly abates, and when,
    After a few moments he does not return, I walk out
To find he has vanished, and the shore of sand and stormcloud
    Form a sharp line of demarcation in the sky
Over the dripping trail. I walk back to where I had
    Tied my horse to a clump of shrubbery, and he      70
Is eating placidly, dripping, wetly indifferent to the blaze
    Lately heaved upon the dark sea of the spring sky.
To my astonishment I see upslope a now-abandoned
    Indian hunting cabin, and I ride up there and clop
Slowly around it and see the slave, who is here already,
    So I take possession and turn my trustworthy horse
Out into the sweetgrass of the adjoining meadow to graze.

I.     LACHLAN MACINTOSH TO GOVERNOR LYTTLETON

---

*Fort Prince George, 16th Jan., 1758*

*MAY IT PLEASE YOUR EXCELLENCY, The within Copies came to my Hands a Fortnight ago with the Officer and the Party from Fort Dobbs and the Indians mentioned therein. They belong to Keowee though they are directed to the Upper Nation. They have been here at the Fort every other Day since they came. They talk of returning so soon as the Head Men come from Hunting.*

*I had the Honour to write your Excellency ten Days ago with Brown, a Soldier of this Command, as I could not get another foot Person to send with the Express as Capt. Demeré gave me strict Orders to send one off directly.*

*There are a few of the Indians coming in and I'm very ill off here for Want of an Interpreter, for Mr. Hatton, the Person Lieut. Shaw recommended, has been never one Day sober since Lieut. Shaw left this, and I cannot depend one Moment upon him. He made a Promise before Lieut. Shaw came here not to drink and behaved very well. But at the time Lieut. Shaw left this, he broke out his Promise and never has been sober Day nor Night since, and the Indian Traders passing leave him always Rum. There is Nothing else material every Thing is peaceable and quiet here, and I have the Honour to be with the most profound Respect, may it please your Excellency,*

*Your Excellency's most obedient and obliged Servant,*

*LACH MACKINTOSH*

## J.

I lay a fine fire in the loose-limbed fireplace
Inside the abandoned Indian cabin. My face

Grows warm from the flames. I find pleasure
In my biscuit and dried beef, a fine treasure,

But then I dig deep in my leather rucksack
And find a small piece of cheese, sides black

With mold that I scrape away. I brought it
All the way from Charleston. I sought it

Out at a quiet mercantile to have when time
Wears heavily. Now I eat it. Small mice mime          10

Genuflections in the corner. I toss to them
The last tiny rind. Over it, they kneel and hymn.

The slave stays outside, will not come to cross
The threshold; his companionship is my loss.

The night is clear, calm, and cool, and I head
Outside into the meadow where every dead

Spirit rises like stars before me. My horse
Kicks with unreasoning rapture, no course

Left but natural delight. The Cherokee gods
Throw a meteoric spear three hundred rods,          20

And its fiery streak of fine etching lingers
For three seconds. I catch it with my fingers.

This is my song now, my antiphon, healing,
And every pact I make with Nature is a sealing

Of promises past and to come. One dark day
Down the years I will turn in bed and softly say

I had one great day and one greater night;
I stood in every country. I glowed with every light.


K.

I awaken to the *keer* of the social nighthawk
            and merry mockingbird.
            The sun gilds the tops
of towering hills, and the hills ring with shouts

from the cheerful tenants of this rising landscape.
            And O the vast pinnatifid
            leaves and expansive umbels
of snow-white flowers, and on the swelling bases

of the surrounding hills the fragrant red strawberry
            in painted beds on many                                    10
            acres of rolling surface.
I mount my horse and ride the high country.

Before I can reach the dead town of Stecoe,
            three drunken men in
            rough frontier clothing
come riding from the dark forest, halt me.

I pull my horse to a sudden stop, and he
            senses with a flare
            the peril ignited here
before us, tries to run away, but I hold on                         20

to the reins. The roaring drunks ride up
            laughing and circling,
            and one waves a long-
barreled pistol beneath my chin. I say

quietly to my mount, "Hold," and he does.
      "Ain't she pretty?"
      The dirtiest one
asks, and suddenly there's a sharp report

from the handgun, and one of the men
      falls off his horse,
      writhes and moans
in the dust, bucking with bright red pain.                    30

The others dismount, and I kick my horse
      and ride as fast as
      I can, and one mounts
and comes after me but rides straight into

a low limb and knocks himself off, hard.
      The gutshot man cries
      in hideous pain behind
us. I pass on until their sounds fade, disappear.            40

My heart clatters with the pointlessness of it
      all. I thought I was
      alone. I thought I had
nothing in this inclining world to make me fear.


L.

Word: Duke Power Company will biblically flood
      The whole valley, cut down hundreds of acres
Of trees, maul the river, rip it all into wretchedness.

The water will rise over it all, dozens of village sites,
      A world of artifacts from thousands of years past,
Bartram's trees and hills, the abandoned Indian cabin

Where he spent his life-everloving night as his horse
      Pranced with plummy ecstasies of muscled youth.
Our father paces in a cold rage, incites his sons' riots

With multiple damnations of any men who could destroy                                     10
          With such ease the history that belongs to us all.
The next time we return, I stroll away from them to the river

Alone, and walk from the ford back to Nimmons Bridge
          And summon ghosts. Do I believe in the persistence
Of spirit? Is that against science? I understand I am not cut

From the same pattern as those who simply reassemble facts,
          Necessary as that is. I feel ten thousand ideas, sensations,
Facts fill me at every second, and some days the bright

Mystery of it all is hardly bearable for the sun it gives me,
          And others I am so sensitive to light, sound, memory,                           20
Image, that I find simply being alive almost excruciating.

Word: How can they get away with doing this?
          Power? Of course we must have it, but to destroy
This paradise with diesel-spewing cats, with saws

Whining day and night as they cut down forests that
          Have been on this stream for millennia? I call upon
The Cherokee to curse them. I call upon the spirits

Of my own dead to rise and crack the mirrors of all
          Who destroy the Keowee River valley. And yet
I cannot. I am the quiet boy who feels a thousand things                                  30

Simultaneously, and I will not add hate. I will turn it into
          Sorrow and agony. I will suffer and take on more suffering
For what we lose. And I will turn that agony into art.

Word: They will pay to excavate Fort Prince George
          And our father wonders: How can we get in on that
And help them with what they find? The Great Adventure

Begins that way.

M.

Fear has not shriven me
        I feel the world rise in me
                I feel a perpetual knowledge
                        And an eternal sense of loss
                                I ride along the crystal valley
                                        And see the ruins of Stecoe
                                                A vast Indian mount
                                        Or tumulus, a great terrace
                                On which stood a council
                        House, with banks encompassing                    10
                Their circus, old peach and plum
        Orchards, some of the trees still
Thriving and fruitful now.
        I kick my horse, ride onward
                Higher, westward out of
                        The valley, into the Cowee,
                                A land of meadows, brooks,
                                        Sheerest delights, sunny
                                                Dappled shadows, eyes
                                        Of shy animals upon me,                    20
                                Streams foaming over their
                        Rocky beds and lashing the crags
                With the speech of speechless things.
        I continue my serpentine path,
Over the meadows and fields
        Crossing the riverbed twice,
                Three times or more now,
                        The fields divided into green
                                And turfy beds, forming
                                        Into vistas and parterres,                    30
                                Verdant swelling knolls,
                        With so many strawberries
                Their rich juice dyes my
        Horse's feet and ankles.
The mountains seem to be
        Continually in motion as I
                Watch them from my horse

And the Tennessee River
Gets larger each step
From the conflux                                    40
Of rivulets and brooks,
Forming a spacious river
Of wild passions and flow.
Now I begin to pass over
The mountains, and the vale
Expands my winding way.
A waterfall beyond belief
Appears as a vast edifice
With sharp crystal font
Or a field of ice lying                              50
On the shoulder of the hill.


N.          MEMORANDUM OF JAMES BEAMER, TRADER

*April 20th, 1758*

*A Memorandum ... that I, James Beamer, was a going to Jore with Colonel Byrd and Colonel Howarth, we mett an Indian Fellow at the Clay Pitts nigh Stecowee Old Town. Colonel Howarth and I stopt. Colonel Howarth desired me to ask the Indian if those in the Middle Settlements were ready to go according to their promise (to him) to Virginia with Colonel Byrd. He said he could not tell, they were almost all out a Hunting and that the White Man of Cowee (James May) told them not to mind the Talk of the Warriours that came from Virginia and Carolina, but to remember how many of your People has dyed going to Carolina and to the Assistance of the White People at different Times, and that there Bones lay white upon the Road, and if you go with these Warriours to Virginia, it's so far that you will dye or be killed for not a Man of you will ever return.*

*(Signed)*
*JAMES BEAMER*

O.

In the beginning there was no fire,
And the world was cold until the Thunders
Who lived up in Galunlati sent their
Lightning and put fire into the bottom
Of a hollow sycamore tree which
Grew on an island. The animals knew
It was there because they could see
The smoke coming out of the top,
But they could not get to it because
Of the water, so they held a council                                    10
To decide what to do. This was
A long time ago.

Every animal that could fly was
So anxious to go after the fire.
The Raven volunteered, and because
He was so large and strong they thought
He could surely do the work so he was
Sent first. He flew high and far across
The water and lighted on the sycamore tree,
But while he was wondering what to do                                    20
Next, the heat scorched all his feathers
Black, and he was frightened and came back
Without the fire.

P.

I am never homesick when I am in the Keowee Valley.
I am never alone when I walk in the Keowee Valley.
Let me stand in the high places and watch the water flow out
Forever so that the river returns and the shrubs return
And the trees come back with their dappling shade
And the crow returns with fire in his beak, with direction
To the stories that will save the valley from this if fools
Ever again plan such destruction in the name of power.

## Q.

We come to a river. My servant wants to flow back
To the Fort, and I let him go, ask if he knows the way,
And he says: "I have been this way many times, and
I would not stay in the wilderness to starve, sir. I hope
You will fare well." I say, "And I hope you will find
Freedom, my friend, and agree I have not used you
Ill for the state of your slavery." He looks at me as if
I have gone mad then kicks his horse around and is gone.
Will he return to the trading post and fort? I cannot
Know. I ease my horse into the ford to cross the river,                    10
And I can see from the debris along its lace-edge
That it has fallen several feet from its floodtide stage,
And that glittering pebbles bed the floor, so I walk
My horse out into it, and toward the middle I must
Swim him, and we are both soaked before his feet hit
Bottom again. He never once asks to turn back or doubts
Me. There is a fine meadow just across, and I strip
My clothes and lay them in the grass to dry with my books,
And my specimens. I walk naked as Adam into the fields
Of strawberries and eat those plump fruits while watching          20
Wild turkey and capricious deer roam freely without fear
Of me. They seems to ask that I join them in a meal,
In these happy fields as a fellow creature of slow pleasures
And no obvious rage.

## R.

Dried out, refreshed with fine fruit
I gather my grazing horse and ride
On through the meadow and decide
This way is as fine as any route.

I come to a stunning sight along
The road: huge mounds on either
Side of the trail. Birds' low song
Speeds me. I am bound by neither

Loyalty nor fear to this strange sight
But I know they are Indian graves                                    10
That are mounded in the lean light
Of late afternoon. Dead, no more slaves

To human necessities, I almost envy
Them. I pass on by, move slowly past
The serpentine Tennessee, can last
A long time in the quiet keening

Of hawk and the perpetual moaning
Of mourning doves. We are homing,

All of us, heading back wombward
In the day, heading on, tombward.                                    20


S.


The excavations begin: we have a year or less
To survey the valley. Already the diesel growl
Of chainsaws begins with its feral amplitude
From skyline to eyeline. Shovel-testing begins
Where Fort Prince George should be, and we come
Down on the northwest bastion. My father's high
Delight knows no boundaries. We watch as outlines
Bare themselves, each diamond bastion, post-
Molds of the soldiers' bunkhouse, other structures
And even the rock-filled cellar of a stone house.                   10
And the one day we are emptying it, taking by
Wheelbarrows all the rock walls pushed into the filled
Basement out, and when I dump my load near the road
I see in the sharp sunlight that has just broken through
Fog clear numbers: 1761. I carry it back to the others,
And the jubilation is beyond shouting. Our voices
Carry down the now-treeless valley. This cornerstone
No doubt stood when Bartram came through; his eyes
May have roamed it. I am eighteen summers. They
Look at me, the boy who walked in silence alone                     20

Who has found the most important artifact yet,
And I swell for a moment and then take a walk, grow
Quiet, kneel in the rich soil that will soon drown
In the valley. I would be the stone's linguister,
Its sole translator to the living world. I would tell
Stories of the New World, of the oldest known paths
To human destruction or resurrection; I would
Raise my staff and break up what breaks down
The Garden—my boyhood, the solitary fruit of days,
And the Flower Seeker with his backpacked roots                    30
And blooms, his journal, his pure ignorance with
Its eternal addiction and stories of our ancient fire.


T.

I ride for fifteen miles and see coming
Across the river toward me a white man
In a swift canoe. "Where are you bound?"

He asks, and I say Cowee. He hits land
With a smile and says he lives nearby
And that I should come across the sand

And dine with his family. I see his wife
Is a Cherokee, pretty and slim, and they
Have cattle and fine farm, a good life

In all. Toward sunset Indian girls sashay                          10
Into sight as if dancing, bringing baskets
Of strawberries as a gift. They do not stay

Long. Next morning we have good biscuits,
Coffee, venison, corncakes, butter, cheese,
And I eat my fill. I set out again, will risk it

Even though the weather has clouded, leaves
Rattle warnings, and one of the Cherokee girls
Appears alone and watches me. Hived bees

Hum on, hum on, hum on.
And I kick my horse and am gone.                                        20


U.                              ADVERTISEMENT

> *Notice is hereby given that the Directors for carrying on Trade with the Cherokee Indians, on Account of the Publick of this Province according to Law will, on Wednesday, the 23d of this Instant February between the Hours of eleven and twelve in the Forenoon, at or near the usual Place on the Bay at Charles Town, expose for Sale for ready Money to the highest Bidders, a Parcel of merchantable Indian drest Deer Skins and a few Bever, in Lots which may be viewed at the Day Place of Sale, by any Person or Persons minded to do so.*
>
> 
>
> *Charles Town*
> *February 10, 1763*
>
> *Thomas Lamboll*
> *Thomas Shubrick*
> *Thomas Smith*
> *John Savage*
> DIRECTORS
>
> 


V.


*What is left when a man reaches my age?*
*Is awakening once more from a nap*
*The same blossoming as a long horseback*
*Journey when a young man, a time when all*
*Was possible, even probable if strength*
*Held and the road north were navigable?*

*My friend Mervonne has left now,*
*Driven off in his carriage, slumping down*
*As he stood straight just long enough*
*To be the man he once was. His stars*                                 10

*Are in eclipse; neither of us will meet*
*Again in this life, our snow years*

*Full upon us and time slipping past*
*With its gliding sleigh toward history.*
*Who will see the Keowee Valley*
*Two hundred years from now, a boy*
*And his father trying to imagine how*
*Fort Prince George slowly fell apart*

*When the Cherokees in Keowee moved*
*North forever? Some day soon they will*                    20
*Be forced West to some desolate dusty*
*Nowhere, without mountains or flowers,*
*Where stories of fire and water lose*
*The surface shimmer of their loveliness.*

*Father, son, remember me. Father, son,*
*Kneel by the ford I crossed and hear*
*The hoofbeats of my splashing horse*
*As I crossed the river heading north.*
*Come with me to Florida and hear*
*The clear gush of the Crystal Basin.*                       30

*And my own father, John Bartram?*
*I pray you love me into the New World*
*Where our shades will float in blooms*
*Too fragrant for the living to bear.*
*I pray you love the life I tried to live,*
*In full witness and fuller purpose*

*Than imagination could once have taught*
*Me. I bring you roots and leaves.*
*I bring you genus and species, fur*
*And feather, tendril and rough bark.*                       40
*I bring you the false simplicity of love.*

W.

*Durate et vosmet rebus servate secundis*
(I say as I ride toward the town of Echoe)

*Ipsa scientia potestas est*
(I say as I ride through fields and plantations)

*Dum spiro, spero*
(I say as I pass through Echoe, Nucasse, Whatoga)

*Perfer et obdura; dolor hic tibi proderit olim*
(I say as I reach the council house in new words)


X.

Not knowing where to turn, I see a young man
Who motions me forward with a fine smile
Across a small meadow and stream to the council house
Where the chief welcomes me, giving the care
Of my horse to his handsome sons. These happy people
Treat me with respect and perfect welcome. My host
Leads me into an airy and cool apartment. Women
Bring me a meal of sodden venison, hot corncakes,
And a pleasant cooling liquor made of boiled hominy
Mixed afterward with milk. The men come in,                    10
Bringing tobacco pipes, especially one whose stem
Must be four feet in length and sheathed
With the skin of a speckled snake and adorned
With feathers and strings of beads, and one lights
And puffs first toward the sun then to the four
Cardinal points, and finally over my chest, hands
It to me to partake as well. And:

Do you come from Charleston?
Do you personally know John Stuart?
How has it been since you left Charleston?                     20
*Are you lost?*

I tell him I have lost the road to Cowee,
And I need help to find it. He says
He himself will lead me on the way,
And then he orders grain fed to my horse,
A great honor to a traveler I understand.
I lead my mount by its bridle, and we walk
Together nearly two miles to the right path,
And we shake hands.

Are you happy as a man?                                                    30
Do you believe you will find what you seek?
Can you understand the birds' songs?
Will you hunt flowers all your life?

He must be sixty years of age and so
Can recall when few white men
Came in these parts and is yet so pacific
And equable that I envy the peace
That emanates from inside.
*Am I happy as a man?*
Will I hunt flowers all my life?                                           40
I know where to turn: he has
Shown me how not to be lost.
When you have reached Eden
You do not need directions
Anywhere.


Y.


Floodtide: spring of 1968
                    Duke closes their god-
dam, and slowly the water
                    begins to fill the valley
like a bathtub, bubbling up
                    over the banks of the river
and the shorn hills, all trees cut,
                    earth bulldozed, houses torn

down, and the fort we excavated
                    gliding beneath the sheet                              10
of glassy water, time capsule our
                    father buried in a bastion
in sheets of soldered lead there for
                    all time marking the site of
Fort Prince George and the trading post
                    it had become when Bartram
came through in 1775, when signs of the village
                    across the river remained.
And Woody, our father, standing on a high place
                    above the flooding valley and giving           20
his best military salute as the fort flows below
                    what will become Lake Keowee,
in the valley of damned things,
                    this valley of destroyed history
this valley of no more flowers,
                    ever, where the only thing left
to collect is blue water, and so
                    I curse the company that ruined
the valley; I dance around fire
                    and ring wretchedness down on            30
their corporate heads for this;
                    when will the last witness
of the valley die so that in
                    pictures alone will
the Keowee River exist?
                    Except our father took
his tape recorder to the ford
                    where Bartram crossed
And rolled it for half an hour,
                    and now I still listen                             40
And try to quell the pale rage
                    and bring back the bright-
ness of all flowers, all journeys.

## Z.

I leave my thoughtful friend and arrive finally at Cowee
About noon, a lovely town situated at the base of hills
On both sides of the river. This is the end of the great
Cowee Valley, crowds of greenery, silt worth silver,
And sharp slits in the cloudline; the feet of mountains
Bathe in the golden flow of the Tennessee. Far ahead,
A blue ridge unravels beneath the spring sky, chanting
Geology and geography with runic impatience. The chief
Trader is Callahan, gray and respected for his age and equity,
And he welcomes me; I can see the Cherokees revere him          10
For his humanity toward them. Most white traders, I know
Too well, are trash and scoundrels, a disgrace to human-
Kind, but Callahan walks as if ground forgives his steps
Upon it with gentle understanding and future forbearance.
I blush for my countrymen, know that the Indians have
Cause to hate us. I hate what we sometimes are and can
Become, the corporate nation of united hatreds, suited
Up to destroy or run off those unlike them. Callahan is
Unlike the others who have ruined the Indians' lives,
Seized their property, killed them, or driven them out          20
Of the peaceful lands they have owned for centuries.


It is now the ever-night,
Stunned with stars,
Constellations flowing
And turning as pastured
Colts kick and prance.
I walk into the meadow
Behind Cowee and inhale
The jeweled magnificence
Of my explorations. How                                          30
I wish I could move more,
Unceasing, rowing land
All my life into old age
If I am granted such.
Here in the ever-night
With flowers unfolding

Scents and colors to me,
With pearled waterfalls
Skipping in the starlight,
I say: let me live forever,
You with the power to
Let men miss an early date
With death. Let me rise
With the moon and dance.
Let me lean back beneath
The bright beads of stars
With the moon and dance.

40

It is the next day now, and having crossed the river
In a canoe, I join another trader for a tour of the land
I see in                    disbelief, new corn
Eighteen                    inches above the ground,
New beans                   sprouting in the mounds
Around corn                 and we turn to mountains
And ride through         a delightful mead among
Pyramidal hills, brisk    flowing creeks, blooming
Cluster roses, blushing rhododendron, and fair lily.

50

We rise and ride, higher and higher upslope until we
Reach the top of the world here, and I can see below
River and                   fertile valley, lawns,
Crops, green                crowns of tree species,
And beyond the             misted mountains, high
As a dream, cloud           banked, built for breath
And hung, purpled, lie    great clouds of grapes for
The quick picking, for a   day in which all things are
Possible for man and creature and all of Creation.

60

We descend now from this genial height, ride back
And forth on switchbacks to a fine pasture far below
Where we                   park our horses and
The trader has             in his hands salt, and
Dozens of head             of horses suddenly appear
From nowhere and           laugh up to take a mineral
From the trader's hand    as if it were dessert on

70

The richest table in all      the world. I have never seen
More beautiful horses in any green place as these are.

We return toward town and see
Cherokee girls gathering strawberries,
Some of their baskets already filled
To overflowing, and strolling about
Them flocks of turkeys and herds of deer
So that the scene is one of the greatest                                    80
Peacefulness and beauty. Some girls
Lie back beneath the shade trees
And rest, tease each other to laughter.
Some bathe their arms and legs
In the cool, fleeting stream-water.
Others chase attendant boys,
And many have red lips, stained
From eating strawberries beneath
The day's perfect arch of sunlight
And wind and a slight and lovely                                           90
Breeze. Is this primitive innocence?
I want to believe it. When else in
Life could we believe in half so much
As in our own youth when we think
Life goes on almost to the edge
Of forever? I want to play with them,
To feel their arms intertwine mine,
And I find myself walking toward them
And might have come into their meadow
Except for the sudden arrival                                             100
Of scowling older women who chase
Me away with a sodden glance.
And yet they now see me come
Toward them, and with permission
Of their guardian aunts, they step
Forward and present me with a basket
Of fine, plump strawberries. My friend
And I accept the basket, sit down on
A carpet of green and eat our fill.

Now, our thanks having been given
Properly in view of the guardians
And the laughing girls, my young
Trader friend and I mount our horses
And ride up the mountains, passing
Acres of flowers in their bright cloaks,
Arriving back in town in the cool
Clarity of the evening, into salvation.

110

# CANTO SIXTEEN

# I.

*M*IDDAY *has passed, and I awaken from a nap.*
*Alive? I am still in this world, and its fruit*
*Hangs in the garden, by which I mean leaf*
*And vinous growth, root, stem, petiole, air*
*Rich with the aroma of reason and passion*
*Which together make of this ancient world*
*A purposeful journey. I have been dreaming*
*Of Keowee and how trickery made me think*
*I was welcomed when I visited the inner*
*Workings of madness and found myself*                               10
*Naked in the river's wake the next morning.*
*And I saw Patrick in my dream, too, bright*
*As new day, undead, and the girl who came*
*To me in Florida that night, and McIntosh*
*And the traders on the road to Cowee, all*
*Formed and reformed into different persons*
*As if I were casting spells to make my life*
*Make the sense it often has not when I am wary.*

*I am in my chair where I dozed away. Sara,*
*The girl-servant I employ, asks if I would like*      20
*A glass of water: no. The pains that curse one*
*My age are blissfully absent now; a lifted pall*
*Makes the early afternoon shine. The squash,*
*Other cucurbits ripen in my garden; the rain*
*Will come back in a day or two. And in night*
*Moon and stars will mix their discerning*
*Measures of fine grace for all things. Shelves*
*Will sag with fruit in fall, even if by winter*
*I am no longer here to enjoy them. "A drink*
*Of wine might be nice," I say to Sara, scheming*      30
*To see her pretty face again. Now I unfurl*
*Myself from the chair and stretch. A ration*
*For such things as wine is not necessary where*
*Age owns one so deeply. I get the current sheaf*
*Of my writing and look through it. Can roots*
*Still give a man happiness? Clouds come, lap*

*The shingles and the sills. Sara brings to me*
*A crystal glass of Madeira and it fills to light*
*My dark fears. In dreams, one can be young*
*Again, strong, bone-hungry, muscles lithe*                    40
*Enough to pull one up a mountain. So it was in*
*Those days at Cowee when I saw all the girls*
*Picking strawberries and dancing for the sheer*
*Pleasure of their bodies. I saw how they knew*
*Without knowing, really, the Ancients' mounds,*
*The flower carpets, the blush of sunrise, wind*
*Tickling the treetops. I saw the flumes of mica*
*In the creekbeds, pebbles and possibilities,*
*The coming rapture of rain, how all empties*
*Out and is filled again in time. But how can*      50
*An old man be filled again? Is there a dream*
*I have overlooked in this life that I might*
*Walk into this afternoon? I cannot know, so*
*I simply stand before the window and dream.*

*The glassy feeling comes in my chest, a gleam*
*Of transition and lasting sleep, and I will go*
*There without fear. I have long forgiven fright*
*For the spurs it dug in me. The sun's beams*
*Break stories through window glass; a man*
*Must translate them as he will, his old eddies*          60
*Still slightly moving, if at all. All my frailties*
*Together cannot make me weep, move one pica*
*Toward shame or despair. I will use my mind*
*Until sleep stills me. I will walk these grounds*
*Of my past and present beneath the high blue*
*Of summer's last sky. Look hard: no fear*
*Comes off me. For I have walked in worlds*
*Of sublime blossoming, seen lark and wren,*
*Fierce nights, balsam days. My final tithe*
*Is given. My last song is so nearly sung*          70
*To the garden and the stream. It is delight*
*That I still own, deep as, deeper than the sea.*

I wait for two days at Cowee for a promised guide
That never comes and so set out as I have before:
Alone on the trail to the Overhill Cherokee towns
Where the Indians are said to be angry if not at war
With whites. At the last moment my old friend
Callahan joins me and rides fifteen miles onward,
And we pass through the village of Jore, where I
Observe a little grove of *Casine yapon*, the only          80
Place I have seen it grow in the Cherokee country.
The Indians call it *Beloved Tree*, and I understand
Why. They keep it cultivated and pruned, drink
A strong tea from the leaves, buds, and branches.
We begin to ascend the mountains again, a stream
Accompanying us by roaring over rocky precipices.
We now reach the traders' path to the Overhills
And Callahan says: "William, there's the way you
Must travel, and I must head back now to Cowee.
I hope you fare well and are not killed by sunset."          90

And I am left alone as I have been, like one met
By himself alone or death in the dark. The oo-whee
Of a hawk harries me. Not pathless entirely, but few
Well-tramped tracks precede me. I grow blue gills
To breathe the watered air, or should; my guesses
As to avenues for study elude me, and I just dream
My way ahead. For the first time, the broken patches
Of humanity behind me seem desirable. I sink
With deep and sudden fear of loneliness, right hand
Holding my left to still its shakes. All and sundry          100
Terrors rise. Like Nebuchadnezzar sent lonely
From other men to roam in the wilderness, sigh
To sigh, night to night, feast to beast: one word
From humankind in any tongue would now send
Me into raptures. I walk faster, I run then I soar
As if winged down the path. Sharp sunlight crowns
The tops of trees; let me step through a new door
For safety's sake; I do not want to run or to hide.

Sheer terror quells itself. I come down the path
To a beautiful stream, the only ford crowded up                    110
With shelving rocks full of holes and deep cliffs.
I walk onward, glade to glade, brook to brook,
And after hours stop and turn my horse at meadow
Out to graze. I loll in the greenage, greet doves,
Pillage the song of windy clover. I take out now
A meal of biscuit, cheese, and ox tongue. I doze
Nearly to sleep when I realize an Indian stands
Not far away with a rifle and two dogs. I brace
For the shout or shot, but none comes. He smiles,
Holds up a friendly hand and comes over to me.                     120
We heartily shake hands, but soon I realize that
He speaks only Cherokee, as he must realize I
Have only English. We both shrug, and I give him
Choice tobacco and try to ask if I am going the right
Way to the Overhill towns. He does not understand
Me, though. We shake and his dogs romp ahead

As he sings his way on, Ꮡꭉ-ꭎꮂ, ꭽꭉ-ꭎꮂ, sped
On his way by the bounding of his hounds. A man
Could live in a worse way. I take with all delight
The dozens of species around me, write the hymn                    130
Of their singing in my book. Filled with food, eye
On the higher reaches, I ride onward now, hat
Cocked rakishly, sun buttering my face, trees
Huge with ancient girth. I reach the crest miles
From Jore now and am astonished that I face
An unexpected vista of magnificence, lands
Few white men have spied. An unfolding rose,
Its fragrance bathes me; the air cools. My vow
Of fear fades. What does not bloom in coves
Hereabouts already blooms south. A shadow                          140
Passes before the sun. I shudder. Can a book
Reproduce such diurnal ecstasies? Shade sifts
Light from light. With my hands I make a cup
And drink from the cold stream flowing past.

How can
I plan to recall
Such grandeur in years
To come? How can my ride
Now down the western side of the
Mountains be brought back whole, the air,                                    150
The needled paths, the quick glimpse of antlers
And scuttling bear fur? My descent is gradual, through
Grassy, open forests, but then I come to a difficult place, a
Steep, rocky hill over which I must ride for nearly a mile downslope,
These shattered mountains now presenting tremendous obstacles to my horse
And myself. And there are oozy springs along the way, stagnant rills sinking
In micaceous earth; some steps along the path seem to crumble away
Hoof to hoof so that my mount steps too warily to move fast on
Our way. In these moldering cliffs I discover veins or strata
Of *Mica nitida* with its faint bluish and pearl gleam like                  160
Little cliffs or the wavy crests of new-fallen snow-
Drifts. Also I see strata of lead, black and heavy
As the night of a loved one's death. I camp
Finally beside a stream and think: O
God, I am so alone here, outside
The sound of a man's voice
And I imagine she is here,
The Indian girl who
Comes to me in
Darkness.                                                                    170


O
Look at
Me in this filled
Land, William Bartram whose
Heart is amass with moonlit lanes
And golden coins of stars on the water;
Remember me, I tell no one, take me to love,
To home, to heart. Bring me into your keeping, hear
These old stories, translate me into black bear or pale dove
And let me tear flesh, fly, cut sharp circles in the cold current            180
That flows below my campsite in the night. Remember my words
That I speak to her alone, with only my heedless horse to hear. Take me

As one who heard the antiphons of wild streams and sang back
With a wilder human song. Tall hemlocks with their tiny
Cones ring the place where I had laid down my blanket
And these spruce specimens whisper with cool wind
And speak my name: *Willll-iam, Whillll-iammmm.*
I think I hear the sound of men moving in dark
Shadows, but perhaps it is a deer or squirrel,
A hare come to see the miracle of fire                           190
From my camplight. I rise and walk
Around the edges of my world.
Who have I become here in
This vast fullness of time?
I want to stay here, now
Forever, to lie under
Bedspread stars,
Far from
Time.

*Am I awake here*                   200
*And now by the window*
*Looking into my garden which*
*I must reach before the darkness comes?*
*Or have I gone bodily back into that night when*
*I was alone on the Tennessee beneath a familiar face,*
*Meaning all stars in their ancient constellations, brightwork*
*Brilliance blended with the sparking fire upon the curving water?*
*Old man, old men, winter gone, winter that will never come again:*
*Bend down, I say, for your benedictions. Kneel to whisper*
*Everything that cannot be a soft distraction in the world*        210
*Left to you. Believe the unbelievable transit back*
*To youth when no height was too steep for*
*Quick ascent. Be awake here and sing,*
*Hear the wood-birds, the wrinkling*
*Of water and wind; smell hemlock*
*And fir and pine and old rose*
*From other memories. Rise*
*Ritually, wring clouds*
*For their pale blue*
*Water, go back,*                   220

*Go back,*
*And back.*

II.

I come to a ford on the Tennessee River: giggling
Water, little gods of spoken sunlight whose sheen
Sweetens all the cedared air. A company of Indians
Rides toward me in the water, led by a fine man
I recognize at once as the Little Carpenter, strong,
Unadorned, and clearly in lead of these strong troops.
He smiles and raises a hand, comes to an elegant halt
Near me: "I am Attakullakulla," he says, speaking
His name in Cherokee, "and you are welcome alone
In this land." I bow my head in the simple formula            10
Of humility, say: "The Great Spirit has spoken to me,
And tells me you are the high chief of the People,
And so I honor you. I am your friend, will always
Be friend to the Cherokee." He smiles, rides around
Me on his prancing horse, which is draped with ribbons
And strips of painted leather thongs. I expect his
Formulas, his formal greetings, and to my surprise
He says: "Is John Stuart, my superintendent friend,

Well?" He notices my amusement, comes to lend
My horse a steadying hand. "We share no lies,"              20
I say, "and he is well, for I know him, aimless
As I seem riding here." "We love Stuart; he enlivens
Discourse, does not dishonor us in our own round
Council House; what is it that you in your days
Have come for in the Overhills?" Hemlocks steeple
Over us; mild wind dreams. "You must now see
That I am a Flower Seeker, that I stand in your umbra
With humility to find blooms in their color and tone
And name them again." He narrows his eyes, making
Sense of me, then I see his pleasure. He finds no fault       30
In me. "We are going to Charleston now." He stoops
After dismounting and hands me a blossom, its long
Petiole bobbing in the wind. I take it, and he gains

His mount once more, and I know he is sending
Me onward, and I ride. Like a sunny sudden dream
I go through woods and streams, fish wriggling

In the silvered flow. After riding most of the day
I dismount and build a fine campfire, feel cool
Air sifting down. I see suddenly before me a white girl
In Cherokee dress, gleaming in the brands of my fire,     40
And I sit up sharply, beg her not to run away now.
"Who *are* you?" I ask softly. She speaks in Cherokee

But I cannot understand her. She steps to the lea
Side of the fire, and I can see that no matter how
I show her I am harmless, she fears me. Her eyes
Harden with alarm. She sobs once; pain uncurls
From her strong glance. "Wait, I am not a fool
Who will harm you." Then she is gone, gone away.

I am afraid. Say it: *I am afraid*. What have I done
To come here in the night? I seek another sun.     50


### III.

Heavy rains (dreams of fire, actual fire
          silvery spilling of dousing fire and deep dreams
             a n d   a   b e a r  scrambling up a tree)
      Streams or dreams? Are they? Will they?
O                 And:
  let me know the right way to turn
                              f
      & the rapidity of frothing w a t e r
                            l
                            l                              10
                          s
             cruciform fixtures the uncustomary
    i l
  r l s
          the flowing days and riverfalls,

       rifleshots, smooth pebbles
    in the screams that flow=along down
the needleside mountainrange=

O let me know the right way to dream
            the                         10

         shape           of the circle
      in the center        of the Earth
      where it lies    and grows
      graphic sphere     such sense
      makes of light      makes of
             the light

to wake briefly, see the fire out
    then back=dreams & to find myself floating
        footless on the streets
           of Charles TO              10
              WN

Paddle the river
  paddle the river
    paddle the river
      paddle the river
           Oh God, William WH
               AT
                have you gotten yourself into
           this ≈≈≈≈≈≈≈≈≈≈≈≈ wave
        of one water one life one death=      10

O let me know the right way to dream

Heavy rains, awakening and resleeping
back in Florida and awakening to the roar
    of toxic jaws

O let me not to thy love admit impediments
     *wake up wake up wake up*
  Dark         still         rain gone
    fire          out

**O let me know the right way to dream**

IV.

Tell me why I was chosen to be the witness
of these native glories, and I will believe you.

Tell me why I was chosen to rank the flora and its
lovely Latin nomenclature, fauna leaping lightly
through the Cherokee glens, and I will believe you.
Through the abundant secrecy of all watercourses,
through the clarity of crystal basins and bead-blue

skies, I am the surveyor of iris and am the clarity
given back to dreams. If you could hold my tread
timeless in your slanting paths I would take your hand
and peel back the coldest years of your young life.

Tell me why I was chosen to ride south through
this roseate glow of bursting buds, acidic howling
of swamps with their million-voiced unsuffering
insect choruses—and I will believe you. It is now

just-morning, the dream shakes itself as my horse
shakes the dew from his mane, and I sit up and ask
you who may or may not imprecisely wander
these hills with me why I was chosen to be one
who sees the last days of the Cherokee nation,
the one who haunts the hart-paths, the scumble-tread
of turtles and otters in their daily dash from harm.

Tell me what is the name of the eldest Flower
and what is the tint of the rose, where the current rolls
the rich debris and the roe in rictus downward
toward the sea and Frederica. Let me tract all
who roam the ridges with no gun or condemnation
of kind or kin; let me be the prey and predator,

the Seeker and the huntress, tame as wilderness,
shouting out youth with all my days.

10

20

30

## V.

Finally awake, I sit up in this mountain glen
And find myself more alone than anyone
Has been in any desert life. I know I must

Turn back. Death and frost rime the crust
Of my world now. Fog fills me, no sun
To crack or kindle darkness into friend.

Madness came for me last night. Go back,
Return, my conscience tells me now,
Crow-omen, grave-maw, seeking-arrow.

Messages from the moss and the sparrow                          10
Are the same: you have found the prow
Of the ship ahead, sailed out into black

Stars and not been maimed. I gather my book
And bag, cue my grazing horse to prepare
For departure. Another season, I must argue

To myself, is a better time to come bargain
With these mountains for facts. A rare
Truth might expose itself then, new look

At the world and how it works. I hear that
An expedition sets out soon for the west,                       20
And that is the heat I seek, not this curdled

Madness. So with fear I'm gutted, girdled,
And admit it. Now I climb in the fog, chest
Shuddering with suppositions. Like a bat,

I slip into the gloom of deepest nightly day
And point my horse south, am Cowee-bound
Once again. I cannot do this anymore.

And, out of nothing, a breathing,
     hot breath on my ankles,
Beasts like shadows in glass,                  30
     a furred tail upon nothingness.

# CANTO SEVENTEEN

1.

*I* MUST control both fear and rapture if I
Am to see this world plain. I must forget
The soft curves of women, the bondsmen
Friends: to go alone is to be free to learn
Even though I must also with it bear pain.
I feel shame to have turned back to Cowee
And yet I am alive for another day, and sun
Burns off the gloom of fog and my suspicion
That death awaited me in the deep Overhills.

My friend Callahan meets me at the edge                    10
Of town: "William, I'm surprised you're
Back so soon. Trouble?" I start to say yes,
There were attacks, omens, cascades, injury,
But instead I hear my voice speak: "I was
Afraid." The truth of it stuns me. He claps
Me on the back. "It takes more courage
To turn back for that than a hundred wolves
Gnawing up toward your fearful heartbeat,"

He says. "Do not be troubled by the truth
Of this. A man who does not listen to his own         20
Fear is a fool for it. Would you like to meet
The Chief of Cowee, who since you left us,
Has returned from the hunt?" I feel the fear
Break in me like sun through a wild storm.
"Yes, my friend, and tell me what I may learn
Here before I leave." He tells me to come, and a
Lovely Cherokee girl comes with us, sweet-

Eyed, tenderly untouched, I believe, smile lit
From within by interest in me. The town, I see
Now, has about one hundred houses up              30
Nearly to the edge of the Tennessee River.
Each dwelling is built longly of logs in three
Apartments, with inner doors to communicate,

And nearby a conical earthen Winter House
For sweats and the revelation of strong visions.
The Council House is in a large rotunda, can

Hold several hundred people, stands on top
Of an ancient mound heaped up by ancestors
To the Cherokee, so at the top the whole edifice
Is sixty feet above the common ground. I pass                    40
The day looking through this and other places
In Cowee, and the pretty girl is never too far
Away from me. I do not come closer to her,
Though, for fear of crossing some social border
That may exist between us. But her eyes shine.

Night comes, and I find a grand festival of dancing
And music has been planned for us—Callahan,
The other white traders, and most especially for me.
He has told them I am an honored guest, a man
Who herds flowers and leaves and speaks to them,            50
And I find the Cherokee understand instantly why
A man would do such a thing. I tell one my name
From the Seminoles, and by nightfall all of them
Are calling me "Flower Seeker" in English. One

Could never tell from their delight there has been
Trouble between our people. And here I can forget
That my own people are nearing troubles with
Britain and facing possible war. As men live, they
Also fight, a thing the Cherokee will understand,
From ancient enmities or familial fists. I find              60
That the next day a great Ball Game is due against
Another town, and they now stamp out the dance
They make to spur victory. The people assemble.

They sit in what appears to be a predetermined
Order, and the musicians, having taken their
Station, the play opens first with a long oration
From a white-haired chief, who speaks to them
Of many brilliant victories their ball team has

Won in years past over other towns. "I myself
Was among the strongest who scored our win
Before the cries of all The People," he says,
Arms out to his side. "And other gray-haired           70

Men before you were heroes of our town, too,
Strong, young, and able before Time spilled
His years among their bones. What does it
Mean to win one such small victory? Now,
When we feel the way The People have lived
For all memorial time in danger, the smallest
Victories may be the ones we will tell around
Our fires a hundred years on when all of us          80
Here, even the smallest child, are nothing more

Than mossy bones. You young men must bear
Us on your shoulders, too. We await your fine
Victory in the morning. We ask the Great Spirit
For the swiftness of your legs, the strength of your
Arms, the fitness of your breath, and the keen
Sharpness of your eyes. Great Spirit, come down."
With this he sits, and I can tell the others are
Greatly moved, and the young men flex their
Muscles and clench strong fists, ready to field          90

Their team to play. His speech finished, music
Begins, vocal and instrumental, and a company
Of girls in clean white robes, hand in hand and
Led by the girl who watched me all this day,
Comes before us dancing. They wear many beads
And bracelets, a profusion of gay ribbons, and
As they enter the Council House door they sing
In a low, sweet voice and form themselves in a
Semicircular file in two ranks back to back,

Facing the spectators and the musicians. They          100
Move slowly round and round, singing softly,
Until we are stunned by the sudden scream
Of a company of boys who run in, one after

The other with their racquets in hand. They,
Too, are dressed in finery: silver bracelets,
Gorgets and wampum, neatly cut moccasins,
And high, waving plumes in their diadems.
They form a rank in front of the girls and dance.

Before them in the same way
One end of                        the line rises            110
Toe to heel                       toe to heel
And it flows                      down the line
Of boys and                       girls until they
Finish and                        it goes back
The other                         way. This
Is the ball                       game dance,
The chant for                     victory and I
Am stilled,                       stunned, filled
With a joy                        I cannot tell.
I feel my                         own body ask           120
Me to rise                        and almost do
But catch myself at the last.

They now begin other dances, and the men caper
    In odd and even ridiculous ways that all enjoy
        And that have meaning I cannot deeply know.
            Some are martial, others appear to be tragic,
                And I look to Callahan, and if he understands
                    The meaning, his eyes do not share it to me.
                Now the boys act out a sexual farce, and I am
            Unsure how to react, but the men howl in happiness        130
        And women, though blushing, find it none too offensive
    And so I learn again how their world is different from mine.
I turn to Callahan and shout how much I enjoy the dance
    And the festival, but he cannot hear me and so I know that
        This night is one I must remember for myself alone, that
            I will never again in this life see such a thing, a dance
                Of pure delight for a thing so inconsequential or
                    Important as a neighborly game of ball between
                Cherokee towns. They finally filter off to bed
            After midnight and I walk along the river and hear         140

Bright sounds that might be the whispering of gods.

    These things
astonish me beyond words.

Early the next morning I set off on the road,
And in two safe days arrive back near Keowee
At the base of the rocky hills. And ascending
From the riverbanks, I take note of a great
Number of singular antiquities, the work
Of the Ancients, constructed perhaps for
Sacrifices or sepulchers: four flat stones,                  150
Two set on edge for the sides, a large
Stone for the top, one end closed and
One left open. The trader says they might
Have been the Ovens of the Ancients, and
No one knows otherwise. I make a note
Of this in my sheaf of papers, decide to stay
Two more days around Fort Prince George
And what is left of the village of Keowee.


2.


I go there in dreams: we all do; floating
without narrative down the river, over shoals
and cultivated fields, sitting with old man Ferguson
on the screened porch with its ranks of artifacts
plowed up from the village site for many years.
We are young again as Bartram must have felt
On the last day of his life when he came inside
from the heat to work on a monograph, think
back to that night in Cowee when the Ball Dance
took place to spur the town to victory. Now,              10
two centuries past, all evidence of those towns
has vanished. Keowee and Fort Prince George
lie beneath a hundred feet of blue water, and
I resurrect them in my dreams and see them
rising from the watery plains, speaking to me.

At what point is one life separate
From all others? I walk my path
From the village site to the ford
Filled with unexpected light,
Stones in my hands rubbed round                              20
By a thousand current years.

I try to stretch my stride past
William's to be one who does not
Lie and listen to the speaking water
And spoken rocks, but I take in
My hand a palmful of flowers, bring
Them up to graze on high fragrance.

I go mad in a moonbeam. I lean
Into the culled and gathered hay
Before it's shocked and bundled                              30
Against the wind. Mostly I hum
Myself dreaming into sneakers,
Into the slow dance of retrieval

And return. I drain all the waters
Of the world and the trees grow back
Along the old watercourse-night.
I bear penitence for those who killed
The Cherokees' footprints, who tore
William's way from our scrapbooks.

I walk along the river in mottled day                        40
And sing the source of unsavage
Histories back to their plaintive birth.
Bear me once again. Bear me new
Into the risen hills. Lay me now upon
Their mammary heights, not alone

Not alone even as we lie to sleep.
Not even as the rain comes back
To weep and run the ruts, turn riot
With silvery dances, spun-silk days.

3.

So Francis Harper by the twilit stove,
By the coffeed January day to gain precision
Over William's carelessness in the *Travels*:

  xv. follows = follow (families)
xvii. [Palms and Magnolia] strikes = strike
xvii. Comma inserted after Linum
 xxii. (larva and plant) rises = rise, increases = increase, arrives = arrive
 xxii. (difference) are = is
 xxv. (fruit) are = is
xxix. spider, on a leaf-spider on a leaf                                    10
 xxi-xxii. (harmony) animate = animate
et seq. as to misplaced, superfluous, or omitted words

And so earlier, as to "merely archaic, obsolete, dialectal, or rare variants" minus
corrections:

*ancle*
*antient*
*bason*
*cabbin*
*centinels*
*chearful*                                                                 20
*Eastermost*
*frolick*
*gulph*
*inchanting*
*inthral*
*poney*
*shew*
*spirted*
*steril*
*tinct*                                                                    30

Ample evidence of Bartram's
deficiencies and inconsistencies
in orthography

*authorgraphy*
aim is to take
a minimum of liberties
in virtually every case to ascertain
the form or the original
Publickation

4.

And will I return to order now, to journey
South back toward Charleston and then to
Georgia? My sore ankle is healing as I bid
My goodbyes to the Keowee Valley and
Its ancient mounds and village sites. I ford
The shimmering basin of the river one last
Time where shoals frolic over smooth stones.
I feel a cheerful fullness as I ride on, gulf
Between my present and past losing its pain.
By the easternmost side of the river I head                    10
On, turning back once to see the valley and
Its enchanting slopes, my stout pony standing
In patience to await me. Show me Thy ways,
O Lord, show me, teach me Thy paths, and
I will follow the ways of Your world forever.
The world does not weary of me. It flowers
Beneath my steps. Yea, though I walk through
The valley of all beauty, I flower until the end.

5.

Tired. Ride on with the traders
all the way to the Seneca village
where we find the commissary
and the Indian chiefs in counsel.
Remain there some time, weary
of riding, sleep too much, go
out into the fields and woods

to collect materials for Fothergill,
Indians unsettled in their determination
to keep their land and not in a good                          10
humor. Must head south, perhaps
then west? I do not have enough
to go home yet. I have failed again
and know it. I tell myself it was
too dangerous to have gone farther
in the Overhills, and perhaps it was,
but I let fear overcome me again.
Tired. Exhausted, in fact. Which
means push on, push onward
through it or I will forever regret                           20
my cowardice. I will regret it.


6.

*Echoe, Nucasse, Whatoga, Cowee,*
*Ticoloosa, Jore, Conisca, Nowe,*
*Tomothle, Noewe, Tellico, Clennuse,*
*Ocunnolufte, Chewe, Quanuse, Tellowe,*
*Tellico (second), Chatuga, Hiwassee,*
*Chewase, Nuanha, Tallase, Chelowe,*
*Sette, Chose great, Joco, Tahassee,*
*Tamahle, Tuskete, Big Island, Nilaque,*
*Niowe, Seneca, Keowee, Kulsage,*
*Tugaloo, Estotowe, Qualatche, Chote,*                       10
*Great Estatowe, Alagae, Jore (second),*
*Nae oche.*

My list as I sit here beneath
A tree on my last day in the Cherokee
Country. I stoke myself for adventures,
Wonder what swings west, if I shall
See the Great Waters in more than
These dreams.

# Canto Eighteen

$\mathcal{B}$ECAUSE I am well-rested and ready to stride westward
Because it is nearly summer and the heat rubs me lovely
Because the botanical excursion I make near Fort Charlotte
        Is of small value only and cannot slow me greatly
Because my horse is stamply ready to wander onward west:

We set out *en caravan*, Mr. Whitfield in the lead, and travel
        Twenty miles to the home of M. St. Pierre, Français,
We set out for his mansion on a hill near the Savannah River
        That overlooks his plantation
We set out to see his Indian corn, rice, wheat, oats, indigo, potatoes          10
We set out to sip the sights of his thriving vineyard:

And we head into the green world after breakfast
And we head ten miles farther down the river and stop
        At another plantation and are joined by others
And we head, after eating, another six miles then cross
        Over into Georgia and the great Trading Path
And we head down it toward the Creek Nation, and:

For several days the products of all Nature are the same
For several days the soil and rocks and roots and minerals
        Are all the same                                              20
For several days I write nothing down for nothing is new
        In my sight that I have not studied or collected before:

Early this evening we arrive at the Flat Rock where we lodge
Early this evening we study this horizontal formation near
        The delightful rivulet of excellent water which is one
        Of the head branches of the Great Ogeechee River
Early this evening I study the curious herbaceous plants
        Around the Flat Rock, and one I love, a species
        Of *Ipomea* three feet high with strong stem,
        Decorated in plumed leaves resembling delphinium          30
Early this evening I kneel to ask God to refill me with curiosity
        And I tremble with the knowledge of new knowledge!
Early this evening I candle myself into a nearby canebreak
Early this evening I love the growing strength of my hands:

We are joined by two companies of traders in firelight
        Headed for the Creek Nation as we are
We are joined and decide we might travel together
        On the great path that runs across Georgia
We are joined for they have many horses to spare
        And others only lightly loaded                                    40
We are joined for several of our horses are now jaded
        From travel and unable to haul more for days
We are joined for we have no more days to wait:

Because my new packhorse will not stand still for it
Because he throws off my notebook and collections
        I do as old packers say and catch his ear smartly
        Between my teeth and hold on, and he grows still
        Until he's completely loaded for my travels.

We are twenty men and sixty horses
We are strong enough to repel outlaws or Indian bands
We are setting out on high gravelly ridges, and I note          50
        With brazen joyfulness a new catalog of species:

And I am the Flower Seeker, happy as the woodlands
And I am the man who collects by eye *Quercus rubra*
And I am the instrument on which the wind plays

On July 1 we camp on the bank of the Oconee River
On July 1 we laze in a grove of oak, ash, mulberry, hickory
        Black walnut, elm, sassafras, and *Gleditsia*
On July 1 I walk through a nearby patch of high forest
On July 1 I attend Indian fields and plantations                60

We camp on the site of old Oconee Town, which was
        Abandoned by the Indians at least sixty years past
We camp where they lived before moving north to another
        Town site which they also then abandoned and
        Turned southeast toward the seacoast along
        The extensive plains of the Alachua and named
        Their new town Cuscowilla
We camp where they lived before fleeing to the new land

Claimed by the Tomocos, Utinas, Calloosas, Yamasees
And other remnant tribes of ancient Floridians                                70
And northern refugees driven away by Carolinians
And Spanish and other tribes, press to pressure
We camp in the cool shade where no tribe now lives
We camp where sorrow, silky as sunrise, whispers my name

Georgia: Creek-lapped loam and the lilt of folded breezes
Georgia: by ford across the Oconee River two hundred and fifty
    Yards and clopping onward team to team, horses
    Bright with froth and sweet-smelling sweat-flanks
Georgia: heat of summer baking our slick skins, man-smells,
    The yeeeen of mosquitoes that we swat in our saddles          80
Georgia light and drumming sun, fetlock creeks and unnamed
    River courses, branches to the Oconee River
Georgia: expansive illumined green fields, native meadow,
    Canebreak, vegetables, trees, shrubs and plants
    The same as we have seen so far in this land
    Without new stories or material variations
Georgia: on and onward, rough jokes from the teamsters
Georgia: waves of heat on the road, brown water,
    Green water, low floating lake-rivers
Georgia: finally to the Ocmulgee River, map-work                               90
    And geography catching up with my eyes

We reach stately mounds and lower ones studded
    With bones of deer and turkey and their men
    Cracked pots, gilded gorgets, oaks like clubs
    Warning us to keep away, which we always do
We reach the edge of the Ocmulgee and seek a ford
We reach a ford in the river quite soon and step off
We reach our line of horses and men into the cooling water
We reach mid-ford and reckon the whole transit some
    Three or four hundred yards across, no holes                       100

We see before us conspicuous remains of the ancients
We see the ruins of a capital town and settlement
We see vast artificial hills and terraces now forty miles
    From the Oconee River, also like the Ocmulgee

An arm of the great and descending Altamaha
We see in the evening our campsite near the banks
      Of Stony Creek, a large and rapid water six miles
      Beyond the river.

I ask my friend Andrews to walk with me in the evening
      In the hot and clouding evening with rain nearing      110
I ask my friend Andrews if he is ever afraid so far from home
      And he says, "Home? Home is the earth beneath
      My bedroll, William," and I nod, know it is so
      For me and not so, either. He is a kind boy, not yet
      Twenty, teamstering west, hoping to see, as he
      Says, "Things a white man has not seen before."
I ask my friend Andrews if he has ever had a girl, and he
      Stares quietly and says, "A wife in Charleston
      Two years past, sweet-eyed and kindly, dead
      This twelvemonth of infection in the lungs."      120
I ask my friend Andrews if he misses her, and his eyes
      Fill with spilling rivulets, and he can only sigh
      And stand to throw stones in Stony Creek

Onward and onward we ride, next day reaching
      The Great and Little Toboschte Creeks
Onward and outward we get to a large brook called
      Sweet Water, its glittering wavy flood passing
      Over a bed of pebbles and gravel, so beautiful
      So beautiful here and now, and I ask of Andrews
Onward and goneward, a man named Isaac tells me,      130
      He turned around in the early day and headed
      By himself back the way we came, and I know he
      Was thinking of his lost wife and cannot journey
      Farther from her in this world or any other

I observe species to calm my need to brood, kneel down
      And see a singular and beautiful shrub, I suppose
      A species of hydrangea that grows in coppices
      Or clumps on the banks of rivers and creeks
      (O what have I done, God grant me distraction
      From the undistractable parts of my many lives)      140

I observe many stems arise from one root of this plant
I observe how it spreads itself with suckers and offsets
I observe how these tendrils decline or diverge from each other
I observe how they are covered with several barks or rinds
      The last of which being a cinereous dirt color
      And they crack and peel off each year like papyrus
I observe how the stems divide regularly and oppositely
I observe how they are supported by slender petioles
      And are of a fine, full green color in sharp sun
I observe how I observe myself observing, the pretense      150
      Of science when I am but a catalog-man here
I observe our campfires lit like fireflies umbra to umbra
I observe how Nature pushes sorrow away even now
      Where I am lost and solitary even with other men


In the summer of my days I cross the Flint River next day
In the summer of my days I feel the oven heat cramp my arms
In the summer of my days I wade through cane forests
      *Arundo gigantea* and a species of *Hypericum*
      Of extraordinary show and beauty, but the heat!
In the summer of my days I drip with perspiration and wonder      160
      How men will farm this fertile land in such steam
      And blistering blanching; our man Smith falls from
      His saddle, overcome with it, and we find a tepid
      Slow-moving creek in which to submerge his body
      And he trembles as if freezing or frozen until he
      Slowly comes to his senses, and bugs sip blood
      From us all, from Smith who cannot even slap
      Back at them, his weakness is so vast and deep


WHEN BELLS CAME LIKE BOATS
OVER THE OIL-SLICKS, MILKWEED      170
HULLS


Why did I not stay in the cool and shaded land of the Cherokees
Why did I not stay in Charleston with rooms and inns for food
Why did I not stay in Cowee where the Ball Dance enchanted me
      And that one girl watched me with clear pleasure all that
      Afternoon and into the night, who saw me as she danced

Why did I come to this itching land with its million biting insects
Why did I ride where the heat and burning flies torment our horses
      To such a degree as to excite compassion even in the hardest-
      Hearted of our pack-horsemen                         180
Why did I come here where several species of flying, biting creatures
      Torment us all, a vast cloud of them from first light to last
      So thick that they obscure every distant object, and horses
      In the van bearing brunt of the conflict, head, neck,
      Shoulders of the lead horses continually in a gore of blood
      Some of these flies large as bumblebees, armed with lances
      With which they instantly pierce the veins of creatures
      From whence the blood springs in large drops, rolling down
      Like tears from daggered flesh; and there is a fierce aching
      For a long time after the wound is taken; their sting is like    190
      The stab of a red-hot needle or a glowing fire on the skin
      These are called Burning Flies and tear our arms apart
Why did I come here where we cannot find a place to escape
Why did I come here where even in the shade of a stream
      Millions spin out to scratch us bleeding and bloody
      Like Evil Spirits that continually follow us over hot
      Desert ridges and plains, even the mouth-filling gnats
      That do not sting but harry man and animal to screaming

O God it is beyond bearing, the dreadful constant hum of it
O God our flesh is torn and we blossom flowers of blood         200
O God we camp and build huge fires and hope to drive away
      These monstrous foes but we cannot and even beneath
      A blanket, soaked with sweat, they find our sweet flesh
      And a man named Duncan leaps up screaming, runs
      Tearing his flesh into the dark and with a sickening thunk
      Runs into a sentinel pine and knocks himself cold
O God next morning we rise to find it unbelievably worse and
      We mount and ride miserably onward, and I ask Death

We think we can bear it but I do not believe I can bear it the world is blood and the blood is a sharp thorn of nature that is made to torture us and what I ask is this land will ever be the same for our going through it and if this is its vengeance, to tear flesh off our bones, to rip us into bloody hanks in swarms of insects that have been sent to keep us from knowing the secrets of each hillock and valley, each stream and river, each secret tongue spoken by those who once lived here and have been chased away forever, what is then the price of our trespass, my good friend? We dive in the water and come up in the water of insect clouds; we lie beneath where we cannot breathe and then surface to find we breathe wings and carapaces and a thousand stinging creatures in their trespassed rage. Would the Cherokee do the same if they could, cut us into hanks with spears and hatchets for what

We think we can bear it, the foam
  of fear, the tearing light,
madness that rips us
                    we think we can
run for the higher ground beneath the
lower water
            but we can't I am going
mad now with need to rip up the
animals      that      rip      me

O God we climb into the pellucid
brooks before us
    But when we rise from
beneath
the glimmering flow
    The tearing insects await us
again, and men groan
    And cry aloud to thee, and we
fall into a mortal torpor

The men groan and now the earth
trembles          under the peals of
incessant distant thunder
                    the storm
comes roaring into our presence
and I am shocked again to life

  I raise my head and rub open my
eyes,  p a i n e d  with gleams
    and flashes of lightning; floods
break over us  vast  rivers of ethereal
fire! And instantly I am struck!
          dumb
inactive and benumbed & death seems
a welcome friend
                    the wild insect-
swarm seems to abate slightly
    when the clouds crack open
        and flood us with rain,

We think we can bear it but **I** do not **believe** I can bear it **the world** is blood and the blood **is** a sharp thorn of nature that is **made** to torture us and what I ask is this land will ever be the same for our going through it and if this is its vengeance, to tear flesh off our bones, to rip us into bloody hanks in swarms of insects that have been sent to **keep us** from **knowing the secrets of each hillock and valley,** each stream and river, each secret tongue spoken by those who once lived here and have been chased away forever, **what is then the price** of our trespass, my good friend? We dive in the water and come up **in the water** of insect clouds; **we** lie beneath where we cannot breathe and then surface to find **we breathe wings** and carapaces and a thousand stinging creatures in their trespassed rage. Would the Cherokee do the same if **we** could, cut us into hanks with spears

we do and have done
to their land? Would
Nature tear us apart
for what we have
done to her land here
near the Flint River
in Georgia? O God,
forgive us our tres-
passes as we

sweetened rain, and slowly we rise
man to man and     feel (is it true?)
        the insects begin to let us go
to stop chewing our bones, sweet rain
        sweet silver floods mixing with our
blood as the afternoon moans
        on      as the afternoon moans on
and on with such sweet sorrow

and hatchets for what
we **know** and have
done to their land?
Would Nature tear
us apart for what we
have done to her land
here near the Flint
River in Georgia? O
**Love**, forgive us our

If he has come for me, if now is the time for me to fade
        Into dusky oblivion because I cannot stand it, I cannot
O God we halt at noon unable to bear it any longer, the moans
        And cries coming unto thee, and we are as high on a ridge
        As we can get and still they come in clouds with blood arrows
The pulse of life begins to vibrate again
The pulse of animal spirits begins to exert its powers
The pulse of my unstung places begins to revive me slowly
The pulse of the storm begins to pass and the world drips                    260
        And drains from limb to our limbs, and we gather
        A great quantity of wood to make a huge fire
The pulse of the flames at sunset cuts a clear circle
        Around us where insects do not go, and we raise
        The pyre higher and higher, and the heat is terrible
        But so far less worse than the whining hum of bugs
        That we raise it broad and high enough for Ulysses
        To see on his return voyage to his Penelope

We collect pine knots with their strong sap to keep
        The fire dripping and sizzling with strong flames                     270
We collect clearings in which to dry our clothes as we
        Dance half naked like savages before fire
We collect our trade merchandise and dry it out, too
We collect our wits and try to laugh off the mountain-range
        Welts that line our arms and backs and legs
        From the stings of insects insane for the taste of blood

We awaken into a cool morning with nearly all insects gone
We awaken into a cheerful freedom from suffering and fear

We awaken into air with elasticity and vivific spirits
We awaken to see that the natural world seems to smile                    280
We awaken to see sparking crystal dew on the sipping plants

Birds sing merrily in the groves
Deer whistle as they bound over meads and green turfy hills
Cane meadows roll down long swimming rows of mounds
A branch of the Chattahoochee River finds us near sundown

Next day we find on hard stones the pictures of ancients
Next day we see the dawn and the dusk, stars, constellations
Next day we clear away the buds of rocks, the shine of rock faces
Next day we shout to sweep away the dropped needles
Next day we have come into the New World                    290
Next day we walk to wonder who could have carved this farm of animals
        And signs before us into the parchment of stone
Next day we shout that here is another to translate
Next day we argue over what we see before us
        In the slant-sun decryption, we damp it down
        With water to make it stand out better to read
Next day we cannot read what we can surely see
Next day we stand before the scroll in true wonder:

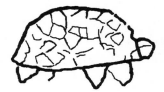

Our pack train moves onward past the stones
Our pack train jingles merrily as it moves without stinging                          300
       Insects now as we near the great Chattahoochee River
       And sense the wealth and breadth of huge water
       That separates one land from another land
Our pack train passes the summits of rough ridges with
       Ferruginous rocks in high cliffs and fragments
Our pack train passes high cliffs of stiff, reddish brown clay
       With strata of stones and veins of purest ochre

And now, another day passed, we ride on through
       A delightful territory, primitive and greenly descending
       Toward the river through easy declivities                          310
       And magnificent terraces with forests, fields, and groves
And now we arrive at the banks of the Chattahoochee, magnificent
       And broad as Heaven and there beyond it and across, just
       As we had navigated the Indian town of Uche, and we sit
       For a time to measure the depth of our undulating wonder.

In my eighty-fifth year, in this final glassy summer
I have found in memory my true pack-train back
To the ecstasies of those days. Faces come to me
In their dozens, faces and the signatures of letters
Arriving always at Kingsessing after my Travels                    320
Came out. I chant the names like Linnæn species:
Jefferson, Franklin, Lyell, Baldwin, Marshall,
Rush, Say, Nuttall, Madison, Michaux; I recall
The day that Audubon & Mason came to my garden.
Darlington visited recently to see after my health,
And we joyfully went through my copies of maps
Of the South and spoke of how in those days as
A colony all things were different, and I say now
I fear for the Cherokee and their dwindling land
After our late war and that they will be forced                    330
To move as all red men have been swept west
Since we first set foot on this wondering land
Those hundred years in the siftings of the past.

Nothing red in this mapless world can last.
Names mean nothing in the end, only the hand
That led one out of darkness to our final rest.
If the species that I found were not sourced
Properly, so be it. I do not need glory, that sand
Which slips so quickly in its cracking sun-vow
Dial. If I do not know the weak old man's face                     340
In his shaving mirror, I had my miles and traps,
My younger days. And all the country's wealth
Cannot keep me breathing: that is now certain.
But I remember salvation from insects, a squall
That blew out the power of their cloud, how partial
We became to scorched skin in the bright and deepest

We unload our horses
and Indians come over
the river for us in large
canoes, bright bowed
wood with upturned
prows

We unload our horses
and take the packs off to
shift into the bottoms of
the huge canoes, and the
Indians are friendly to us
as they know we have
brought trade goods in
abundance for them

We unload the worries
we have borne for days,
the insect bites, the sides
of our faces reddened by
the great flames of the
fire we built

I turn and see behind us
that the Indians have
driven the horses into the
river to swim, and now
here they come, mythic
sea creatures striking the
foamy water with hoofs
iron-hard

I turn back and see the
banks before me of this
New World, and I am
stronger than I have ever
been in this life before

*The heat on my house is
lovely; I can feel it
through the walls and in
the windows. It strokes
its way across the plank
floor my father had laid
so long past.*

*The heat is fine on
ancient bones, on petals
and branches, on limbs
that arch to shade the
living and the living.*

*I begin to separate
myself from all that I
saw as a man, for I will
become incorporeal soon
and be laid breathless
beneath the sod of this
garden*

*I will be part of what
grows and no one will
know which flower is
William and which is
John, and I will bloom in
the spring and be
harvested by winter's
white hand*

*Birds are mad for
singing, the melodic
context of all that I have
been in this life; birds
are mad for bringing me
their untranslated myths
and tales as the
Cherokee did and O that*

To be Philip sitting here
at the end of December,
half lost with Bartram
old and Bartram new is
a grace I could not
guess.

He has crossed my state
some miles to the south,
flesh torn by insects,
eyes glazed with hordes
of hellish gnats, and yet
he rides on, onward, to
the edge of the
Chattahoochee and
across it

I unload the packhorse
worries of my days and
prepare to cross with
him to one life or
another, from one river
bank to another or from
light to light beneath the
light of summer soil

I begin to separate
myself from all that I
saw as a man, for I will
be driven into the river
to swim or drown like a
mythic sea creature
striking the foamy water
with my hoofs.

The canoe in which I
ride now is large and
filled with sun's rays,
and I feel them dance

And the horses gain on          *girl whose eyes watched me*          my bones, bring me the
us from fear or necessity        *in Cowee, and her hands as*          supposition of eternal
And the whole scene is           *she did not come to me in the*       life.
of such magnificence I           *night to hold me*
cannot believe it

*Melodies of fire. I do not mind the names unravel*
*As I say them. Though weak I shake my fetters*
*Into jingling links. I will soon be surely free*
*From pain and flowers. I have already packed*                         400
*A mockingbird to take with me, and a hummer.*

The river here is three or four hundred yards across
The river is filled with stroking canoes and swimming horses
     That with strong thrusts push the water back behind them
The river is strong and splashes its cool water on our arms
     And it is deep and splashing with fish, and I feel as if
     I could myself dance across it as the horses now do

And as he rides, the canoe fills with all pasts and futures:

The ant's a centaur in his dragon world.
Pull down thy vanity, it is not man                                    410
Made, or made order, or made grace
E quindi uscimmo a riveder la stele
But nathelees, whil I have tyme and space,
Er that I ferther in this tale pace,
Me thynketh it acordaunt to resoun
To telle yow al the condicioun
Of ech of hem, so as it semed me,
And whiche they weren, and of what degree,
And eek in what array that they were inne;
And at a knyght than wol I first bigynne.                              420
From the hag and hungry goblin
That into rags would rend ye,
     All the spirits that stand
     By the naked man
In the book of moon, defend ye

Tell me, O Muse, of the man of many devices,
Who wandered full many ways after he had sacked
The sacred citadel of Troy. There were many men
Whose cities he saw and whose mind he learned
Indeed, and many the woes he suffered in his heart                    430
Upon the sea, seeking to win his own life
And the return of his shipmates. Yet even so
He did not save his friends, though he wanted
To badly, for through their own blind folly
They died—fools who ate the Oxen of the Sun
But he took from them the day of their returning.
I didn't think I'd shake the pumpkin, not here and now
In the Old Days the terrapin had a fine whistle
But the partridge had none
Say it! No ideas but in things                                       440
Migrations that must needs void memory,
Inventions that cobblestone the heart:
A little onward lend thy guiding hand
To these dark steps, a little further on;
For yonder banks hath choice of sun or shade;
There I am wont to sit
Nel mezzo del cammini di nostra vita
Mi ritrovai per una selva oscura,
Che la diritta via era smaritta.


I cross the current of the river to Uche                             450
I cross the vast plain on which the town is finely located
I cross the gradual ascent into the largest, most compact
        And best situated Indian town I have ever seen
I cross to the houses built of wooden frames and then
        Lathed and plastered inside and out with a
        Reddish, well-tempered music of clay mortar
I cross to the structures roofed with cypress bark
I cross into the teeming streets of women and children
        And men, perhaps more than a thousand of them
I cross to a headman and ask the number of warriors               460
        And he says perhaps five hundred—formidable
        Force against any foe, *en masse* or *en defilade*
I cross to listen as they converse and it is a radically different

Tongue from any I have heard, not Creek or Muscogulge
But Savannah or Savanuca, and traders tell me it is
The same dialect as the Shawnees, and they are in
Confederacy with the Creeks but do not mix with them

We share the trade goods we have bought
We share the story of the dark nightmare of stinging insects
      And how they drove us nearly mad, and they nod        470
      And say they, too, have such suffering on hot days
      And well-grease themselves to dissuade the mosquitoes
      And gnats from driving them into communal madness
We share food with them, and they bring us meat and drink
We share the knowledge that we must move on

And they accept our swift departure with elegant grace
And they briefly dance for us and in their art swim air
      With as much forethought as they decorate their pottery
      With the flowing movements of water and ships
      With the swiftness of unchased deer running for delight      480

*Where was it we went then?*
We head from Uche for Apalachucla through beautiful plains
*What did we see on our way?*
We see ancient Indian plantations, groves, and lawns
And I have crossed the river near there yet do not know it
We rode onward into the western light
(Into the light of all the western stars)
*What kind of town did it turn out to be?*
It is the capital of the Creek Confederacy
Where no captives are put to death or human blood spilled      490
*Can you recall the colors there?*
I know that part of the state in summer.
*But there was another town . . .*
The great Coweta town twelve miles up the river
Is called the Bloody Town where Micos chiefs
And warriors assemble when a general war is proposed
And here captives and criminals are put to death
*Oh yes, I recall it now in my sunny study:*
*The color of blood in their trilling language.*

We stay here near this town for a week                                      500
We stay so I can walk with the chief trader of Apalachucla
        To walk a mile and a half down the river to view the ruins
        Of that magnificent city built on a peninsula by a doubling
        Of the river; huge artificial mounds and terraces lie every
        Direction. While built by the Ancients it was used until
        Twenty years past and then evacuated by common consent
We stay to hear that it had grown an unhealthy place to live
We stay to learn the people had grown timorous and dejected
        And, they thought, haunted and possessed by vengeful spirits
        By reason of human blood spilled without reason here          510
        And the people had been warned by apparitions
        And in dreams to leave the town

And when the day came for them to leave their home
And when the time came for them to disperse
        They separated from each other forming several bands
        Each under the leadership of a chief of family or tribe
And the greatest number chose to build the New Apalachucla
        Upon a high bank in the river above the floods
        And beyond the mounds of their unhealthy Babel
And the other bands went their own ways down the river          510
        Toward the seacoast to the Lower Creeks in East Florida
And I ask my friend what he knows of them and he says:

"They needed new land for plantations and to evade evil spirits
They needed extensive ranges to hunt where game was abundant
They needed land that did not touch the ancestral haunts of enemies."

I think now that the reasons our red brothers
        Fought and moved is no different from the Greeks and Romans
I think we are more alike to them than we wish to say
I think what some white men call madness and cruelty
        Is no different from our own motivation and that the gifts          530
        We condescendingly give to them, a duffield blanket,
        A polished rifle gun, or embroidered mantle, are no more
        Than they are to us—not magic, not thunder, not evidence
        Of our white superiority; all who think so are fooled and foolish

O the great plant production of this fertile land
      Amazes me with its fecundity and magnificence:
      *Populus heterophylla, Laurus sassafras, Liriodendron tulipifera*
      *Salax fluvialis, Ulmus campestris, Æsculus pavia*
      *Hopea tinctoria, Fagus sylvatica, the forest trees*
      *Halesia, Ptelea, Circis, Cornus Florida, Amorpha*        540

O I am the eyes to see, the hand to write of the high ridges
      That divide the waters of the great rivers from each other
      And from which arise numerous branches that pour forth
      From the vast humid forests and shaded prolific hills
      And lastly flow with an easy, meandering, steady course
      Into the river to which they pay tribute

Our horses, fed well and refreshed, and we filled
With history and Nature: we leave our hosts and head
Onward southeast toward Mobile with fresh provisions
The number in our train is pared down as we lose several      550
Who head into the other towns of this nation

And I see one final shrub that I do not know
And I so badly want to name it; it grows five or six feet
      With many stems ascending and a smooth whitish bark
      (What is it) The branches wreathe and twist about
      With five lanceolate serrated leaves (What is it)
And I see it has one general long slender petiole
And it terminates in a panicle of white flowers with an agreeable scent
And from the character of it, I think it may be a species
      Of *Æsculus* or *Pavia*, but as I see few of the flowers      560
      (They are out of season and imperfect) (What is it)
      I do not know I do not know, I am not certain
And in the shade of my motion I simply *simply* do not know
      I am the eyes to see, the hand to write

# CANTO NINETEEN

*T*HE steam of July lets us slip southward here,
And I begin to feel my age and the miles that
Weigh upon my arms and legs. And yet so
Young a man is torn by such incessant travel,
By the raving of insect clouds, by alligators
Roaring and splashing in the thunder-dark;
He is gifted with the clear waters of the Cherokee
And the bustling streets of Charleston, seabirds
Billowing lane to lane. I dream of going home.

Yet there's more that I have come to see,                                    10
      A dazzling species, flowers' sin-white crowns;
Has a young man ever been more free
      Than I to move in countryside or towns?

I do not feel one with my own time or day.
The Age of Science lures but cannot quite enthrall me.
On, I ride on with my trading friends this July 13,
And we clop and sway onward three days
Before we reach Talasse, a town on the Tallapoosa River.
This is a wet and soaking land, rivulets, streams,
Small rivers, great ones, and we must change course,                          20
And we take the left hand, continually in sight
Of Indian towns and mounds of the perpetual Ancients.

Town to town and present time to past
      We ride; I walk among the milkweed range
And brush the tops of flowers that can't last.
      Every day's unstable and will change.

In an agreeable Indian town we refit and freshen
Ourselves and our horses, lean to taste the Tallapoosa River
And find it clear, agreeable to the tongue, salubrious.
We hire a new guide to set us on the great Trading Path                       30
For West Florida and early in the morning we set out
Toward Mobile and ride all the oven day in as much shade
As we can find, though often we must cross rich savannah

And grass-green plains. Toward dusk we find a place to camp
In oaks whose limbs are loaded with waving Spanish moss.

Who am I and what will I do now?
        Storm-clouds gather, lightning cracks the sky.
Should I make or take another vow?
        And when will be the day that I shall die?

The storm warns us. Yet we learn nothing.                           40
Next morning at the edge of a great plain
Our men rouse a sleeping litter of puppy-wolves
And chase them, catch one by the hind leg
And beat its brains out with the butt of a rifle.
I turn away, sick to my soul at white men,
At the unquestioned savagery of our own race
In such a murder as an Indian would never partake.
Barbarous sport: I am sick against a pine tree.

*I dream the wolf-cub back into his life.*
        *He hunts the man who tore his leg apart.*                   50
*I cannot shed the anger or the grief,*
        *And aim disgust, an arrow, at his heart.*

Ride, we ride across the course of serpentine creeks,
That are directed across the plain with gentle knolls.
Vegetation changes with our latitude, and I see
Wild Crab, Wild Plum, vast acreages of strawberries
That turn our horses' ankles jam-red as we ride through
Just as the berries did at Keowee—that seems so long
Past now. The most beautiful we agree is a tall species
Of *Silphium*: the radical leaves are large, long               60
And lightly sinuated, but those on the limb less so.

What do I accomplish in my riding
        Days? I want to find God in a stream-
Bed where He bathes His face, and gliding
        Past is all Heaven a man could ever dream.

Now we come into a remarkable grove of dogwood trees
That continues for nine or ten miles unchanged
Except for here and there a towering magnolia.
The land of this flowering haven is completely level,
The surface a shallow, loose black mould. So dense                    70
And humid is this place, so concealed in shadows
That neither sunbeams or any other kind of plant
Grows along the rich earth. And so the Indians call
It the Dog Woods formally to honor its delights.

Madison's dogwood blossoms turn the streets
          White and pink in the spring; I recall
Driving out of town in summer's heat,
          Heading up to Keowee, enthralled.

We ride through natural gardens no man could make
In his brightest dream. We come to camp on                            80
The banks of a glittering rivulet amid a spicy grove
Of the aptly named *Illisium Floridanum*. A new friend,
David Cahill, whom the others call Pericles for his
Strength and naturally handsome face, sits with me
In the edge of a starry field on this unusually clear night.
I tell him *Pericles* means *surrounded by glory*, but instead
He is only surrounded by us. He laughs and says,
"William, this here's the glory of things, these woods,
Their boughs of wildflowers, the wonder of house-thick
Trunks and water flowing like liquid jewels—what more               90

Glory could a man be wanting?" Then he turns
          Contemplative, says the ones who killed
The wolf pup should be left among the ferns
          To rot or be consumed at wild dogs' will.

"Let us watch the stars instead and know that they
Will have justice some day for that barbarous act,
David," I soothe, patting him on the shoulder. He
Looks up strongly in the light reflected from the water
And there is Periclean strength about him that I had not
Seen before. "For all its beauty, this is a savage place,"             100

He says. "And for that I am ashamed to say I will miss it
When our journey is done. I cannot bear the civility
Of cities, William; that is my chief curse, that I can only
Flower in the wild." I say, "If that is a curse, then I
Have it as well, for I would not set foot in a city
Unless made to by necessity or the funeral of a friend."

We throw stones like boys into the stream;
          We skip flint upon the flaking flow.
Starfields cross the sky from beam to beam.
          And we know what we can never know.                              110

Another day, gathering our horses, another
Day sore in the saddle through miles of land
Few in our party know well enough even to get
Lost. Cane meadows, swelling ridges, and at evening
We ford the Schambe River, a shallow stream
That flows outward into Pensacola Bay. We camp,
But before the fire has burned down, I know I am
Ill, and that a fever has seized me madly and that I burn
From the inside out. David sits up with me, dabbing
My brow with river water sopped up in a heavy rag.                         120
Lightning wracks the sky. Thick clouds wash up
On our shore like omens of worse yet to come.

I begin to tremble as if cold
          Has swept upon us with an icy hand.
I feel brittle and so very old,
          Rain begins to pelt the fireside sand.

AS ON THE VERY WALL FLAME RIPPLED UP
HYPNOTIC WAVE ON WAVE, A LULLABY

*Oh God*, I cry, and now they bring me back inside
A tent where the chill begins to break my bones                           130
With a shuddering ache. I try to sleep, but I am awake
Through the night. David gives me a sip of rum,
And it helps somewhat to spark my sense, but once
Its beneficial sting has gone, I feel worse than before.

The storm blows down all the trees, all the undergrowth,
And destroys all the living world, amen. David shakes
Me, trying to restore my sense, but by now the fever
Turns me         into       a   m
                                 a
                                 d                                       140
                    Man who cannot count or dream peace
           Who loses the order he begs the world to supply.


Poor William has a William has a has a
        Fever, cannot, fever, cannot rise.
Poor William has a William has a has a
        Fever, cannot—deceiver and his lies!


I rave and my friends support me, check for pox,
I sing: Over the hills and far away, run without
        Moving
Run through imaginary            clo                    150
                      ver

**O**-ver the hills and fade a        way out
Of this? Oh God O God O God O God Hmm hmmm
hmmm hmmm and hmmm hmmm hmmm
More! Rum! Me! A! Quaker!
hmmm hmmm and hmmm hmmm hmmm


# OOoo


Come into my tent URSA MAJOR


ɦe! ɦaγuγa'ɦani wą'
ɦe! ɦaγuγa'ɦani wą'
ɦe! ɦaγuγa'ɦani wą'                                    160
ɦe! ɦaγuγa'ɦani wą'
In Tsístu'γi you were conceiveð—γoɦo!
In Tsístu'γi you were conceiveð—γoɦo!

Ħe! Ħayuya'ħani wą'
Ħe! Ħayuya'ħani wą'
Ħe! Ħayuya'ħani wą'
Ħe! Ħayuya'ħani wą'
In Tsistu'yi you were conceived—Yoħo!
In Tsistu'yi you were conceived—Yoħo!                                    170

Then the drumming coming
Ora sen va per un secreto calle,
tra 'l muro dela terra e lie martiri,
lo mio maestro
Then the drumming coming
David! OOOOOOOOO God!
oh God of my fathers

                                   *


Awaken to a limitless breeze, weaker than a child:
Take me outside, David, into the world that still lives.
Beneath my arms they lift me outward to the fire                          180
Where hot tea brews, and the languorous lilt of wind
Billows my sopped hair and clothes. I cannot stand.
They prop me beneath a scratchy-barked pine tree,
And I take a deep breath and realize the fever has
Abandoned me for older grounds, old men, those
It can take with more ease. David feeds me soup
And tea and says, "William, we thought we'd lost
You in your ravings in the night." I ask all to forgive
Me for anything I might have said against them, and

Each says that I was mannerly, if mad                                     190
        But I can see within their morning eyes
How close I came to being naught but sad
        Memories. How blue now are the skies!

Later in the morning Pericles takes me to walk,
Supporting my weak legs with his strong arms,
And we stride by the stream, rest on flat rocks,
Speak of family and daydreamed futures. I ask

If I was really quite so close to death as he said,
And he replies: "We despaired of you. Two men
Wept and cried aloud to God to spare you, and          200
I did as well." I say, "But I am of almost no value
To this as a trading expedition, David. Why do
They care for me this much?" He strokes the still
Water with his hand and makes it wave stories
To us: "Because you are what most of us will never
Be: a gentle man in love with beauty and knowledge
And without a need to gain money or gain an edge
With white man or red. That is your difference, Billy."

*You called me by my childhood name, dear friend,*
    *Spoke to me as if my mother called.*          210
*You made me know how different in the end*
    *I am from others, how my heart's unwalled.*

"I am quiet, that I've always known, a boy
And then a man given to his solitudes, to silken days
And the complicated magnificence of spider webs;
A new leaf is greater to me than a new man.
I know my raptures are undignified, that when I praise
Water and wind and the Cherokees and Seminoles
I will lose all measure and exult with excitations
More apt for a bucking colt or an untutored boy;          220
I know my exhilarated shouts shatter all decorum;
And yet I feel as if I am open every moment at all
The senses like a blossom in high spring. I spill out
Like a cataract, flow over memorial boulders to fall
A hundred feet in the white swan of water's-wings.
I know few men can understand the sensitivity
That owns me pore to pore, that haunts each step.

I cannot hope to know such days again.
    I cannot rise to wing among the clouds.
I cannot touch azalea, pine, and waving fin          230
    Or find my greening way among the crowds.

    *

Later in the day, I'm well enough to mount
My horse: we head out south to find Mobile.
Gently ascending a hilly district we reach
A high bluff on the eastern channel of the Mobile River
About thirty miles above Fort Conde and the city
Of Mobile itself at the head of the bay. Next day
I get in a boat with others and glide along the banks
Of the islands for twenty vast miles, seeing there
The rich and fecund plantations of French gentlemen.                240
The city of Mobile through which I stroll is now chiefly
In ruins, many houses vacant and moldering
To earth. But a few good buildings remain,
Inhabited by French, English, Scotch, and Irish,
Immigrants from the northern British colonies.
Fort Conde is made of brick and sturdy and seems
To be copied from the villages of the Creeks;
And none there seem to find any irony.
It's 87 degrees: thunder, showers, morning, night.

Several days will pass before I'll find                              250
        Transport to the British town of Manchac.
So I pass the time canoeing, blind
        To paths that might allow me to turn back.

O my soul I'm missing that home in the North,
Family, the sound of their words and their names,
The enclosed environs of Father's garden, the scree
Of carriage wheels on the road before our house.
Before despair grows in me, my transport comes,
And on August 5 within dense humidity and heat
I ride the trading boat to Taensa Bluff, the seat               260
Of Major Farmer who has invited me to spend a few
Days with his family. I say goodbye to David who
Is going other ways, and we clap arms, and I thank
Him for saving me from mad illness in the night.
"Remember me as a brother," he says. Taensa
Is on the site of an ancient Indian settlement
And covered with mounds and battlements
And the French families that are the Major's chief

Tenants. Days pass. I paddle myself up the great
Tombigbee River: lagoons, plants, the vast geology                    270
Of rivers and the men who tickle their broad backs.

I feel a scratch that troubles throat and eyes.
      A fever grows upon me like a sheet.
I wonder if the man who curls and dies
      Hears Death whispering so sweet, so sweet.

        *

Once again I am sick
to dying; want to feel
one day of good health
and promise to recall
how it feels the rest of                                              280
my life. The Major's
lady gives me a dose
of purgative, and it helps
me finally, though for
a few days I toddle
around his plantation
like a child. And yet
I feel alone, so alone!
O God do not let me
live and die alone:                                                  290
give me a girl to
hold my hand when
I am afraid, to stroke
my hand when I am
afraid. I will give her
an eye to love Nature
in her finest dress; will
you come to me in mist?
Will you give me this?

Slowly my strength returns, and I feel                               300
Like taking a short trip, and one man
Says I could find the plant that saved

My life upstream a ways, and I think
That may be a worthy trek, and I set off
One morning with a black man to take
Care and pilot me to this place. His name
Is Jesse, and I ask if he is free or slave:
"Slave, sir, but there is a kind of freedom
In learning what others do not know, so."

He is powerful, admirable in every way.                                    310
We ride side by side. "This is a hard land
To live on," he admits. "Wet, hot, filled
With insects and wild beasts to tear up
Your flesh into eating strips of blood
And bone. It takes a hard man to live here
And flourish." I am quite impressed with Jesse
And his word *flourish* and wonder what
Children may grow from Jesse's stem but
Do not ask. We ride for miles without speaking

Then come to a clearing where he dismounts                                 320
And kneels before what I believe is a species
Of *Collinsonia*. He says: "It is a carminative
And esteemed febrifuge." I look at him in wonder
And his eyes smile at my surprise. No wonder
Slavery is madness when a man so intelligent
Can be owned by another. Yet he is allowed
To travel free, and so there is a measure of kindness
Here that I do not yet understand. I gather a large
Number of specimens for my pack, and he says:

"There's a place I know not far away where we                              330
Can stay for the night." We ride in the gloaming,
And I am happier for his companionship than
I can say. It chases all fear from me. For the first
Time in a week I feel strong and well. A young
Man comes riding out from a plantation near
The river to greet us, shouting, "Welcome and
Be glad you weren't just shot! Jesse! It's good

To see you once again!" The man smiles, is strong
And wildly built, gun up, howling with strength.

We ride in for dinner just as darkness gathers,                                340
And I realize that I am not well, that the illness
That I had considered gone has returned to haunt me
With weakness and a dizzy feeling in the head.
Am I to be an invalid for the remainder of my days?
At the plantation is a bear-strong grizzled man
And his three sons, all famous hunters, and skins
Decorate every bare space in his rough house,
And I find myself dozing, and his good wife
Nurses me with drugs of her own making, rubs

My feet while her men sit and smoke, laughing                                  350
At the day's adventures. Next day Jesse and I
Ride back, and I mark tall blue sage growing
And feel delight despite the illness that continues
To plague me. We return to Manchac, and I find
My sickness endures and my spirits lag; a sick
Man is no companion, and I thank Jesse and
Say I hope he fares well, and he bids me the same.
I am sick for days and despite the help of doctors
And medicines, I feel as if permanently weakened.

Yet I take time to travel by boat to Pensacola,                                360
But I am too weak to stay and head under sail
Back to Mobile.

The steam of August lets us slip westward here,
And more and more I feel my age and the miles that
Weigh upon my arms and legs. And yet so
Young a man is torn by such incessant travel,
By the raving of insect clouds, by alligators
Roaring and splashing in the thunder-dark;
He is gifted with the clear waters of the Cherokee
And the bustling streets of Charleston, seabirds                               370
Billowing lane to lane. I dream of going home.

The same words torment me in the night:
*I dream of going home.*

# CANTO TWENTY

THE *heat of the day makes wreckage of fear*
*In my study now. I thought I was ill then*
*In my journey west, but I could not know*
*The pain and sorrow that was to come*
*And that Man can live through so much more.*
*Even now, eighty-four years old, I suffer*
*From the illness I bore on my trip west across*
*The South—the unhealthy air, the vast swamp*
*Of gorgeous and humanly miserable land.*
*And yet I somehow in memory adore it, too,*            10
*The dripping richness, the utter lack of order*
*That young men find so entrancing—I recall*
*How it felt to be sick and free at the same time*
*And there was a wildness to it beyond eye,*
*A shadow of the solitary's thrill with journey*
*And lethal adventure. My waxy limbs rejoin*
*Memory here in the summer heat; my chest*
*Swells with impermeable treasures into light.*

*I am broken and yet endure. My eye's the blight*
*From my trailing days then; all the rest*            20
*Is pleasurable, but the pain dances like a coin*
*On the river before me. Sharp light, the burning*
*That bears me away, pains me like a stabbed sigh*
*Since my sickness in Mobile. I sense the sublime*
*In every petiole and bloom, yet since my fall*
*While pruning up a tree, my bones speak disorder*
*To each other and grief. What was I meant to do*
*With one blind eye and broken bones? My hand*
*Was alive to write: to tell my story, to stomp*
*The long trails once again, but the utter loss*            30
*Of my soul in that book of travels was a buffer*
*From the disapproval I feared for the deep core*
*Of what really happened. Now, like a Cowee drum*
*I bring it back in full for you, my friend, the blow*
*And the blessing, the sanctities and the sweeter sins*
*Of youth: better than purity, forgiveness so dear.*

## 1.

Next day on my return to Mobile, the pain
In my head is so severe, my fever so high,
That soon the disorder settles in my poor eyes.

I lie in bed through the summer heat and rain,                          10
Blind from the clear-bled diffusions from stab
To stab, all color drained from me, the low drab

From the rich blue or green. And yet I believe
That to lie abed is to court death, and so I soon
Sail (fool!) on a large trading boat. A low loon

Like an omen hovers over the water. I am deceived
For a day with better health, but soon I begin to writhe
In my bedclothes aboard. There is no ample tithe

To buy health, no medicine to shear my sorrow.
The owner is a Frenchman returning to plantation                       20
From below; I hold the rail and pray salvation

From today, beg I'll have one light of tomorrow
To judge or be judged by. Three large black men
Aboard navigate and sail. I, slack with sin

Or the physical equivalent of it, lie and watch
The green land pass us, eyes blurred, the word
Of my companions by splashing waves deterred.

When we finally touch that sinking silent cache,
Our Captain says, "William, come for a walk;
Surely it will make you feel better, a gentle talk                     30

To me of what it is you hunt or are hunted by."
I laugh: he sees my situation clear enough
So I sit, then stand and walk from smooth to rough

And get my land legs beneath me for a hike.
We see an ancient fortress, iron cannon, kettles
Filled to the brim with a sticky liquid, mettle

Well met to sit without harm here, a witch's
Brew in a fairy tale. "They're set out to boil tar
To pitch," my friend says. We now cross the bar

Of sand and re-board the boat, the sail twitches,                    40
We head upstream. I lie, weak and uncomplaining,
And one black man dabs my brow, explaining

Where we're bound. We dock again and I struggle
Off the barque and hold my new friend Jupiter's arm
To move. Kind man, gentle man. Can further harm

Find me here? I want to say to them: smuggle
Me anywhere for I am too weak to wander.
We eat a meal with a French farmer. I wonder

How I can go on living with this deep disease.
We sail back down the flow, but I am too ill                         50
To make observations. My right eye now spills

The sharp light up in terrible pain. Brine seas
Flow out. Blind blackness blunts vision from
That side. When we land, they see that some

Medical arts are due or I will surely die.
They bundle up, take me on to another isle,
To Mr. Rumsey's home. A woman here boils

My clothes, bathes my trembling limbs.
"O God!" I moan aloud. Let me fold and pass,
Let me be observed at the animals' Mass                              60

As sacrament and sacrifice. All light dims
Around me. Is this for killing the helpless wolf
Cub? I see beneath me a wide and depthless gulf.

2.

~~if the unto thee mine eyes my soul hath long dwelt~~
~~let my cry come unto thee my lips shall utter praise~~
~~happy is the man that hath his quiver full of them~~
~~art thou the King of the Jews slate-colored rice-bird~~
~~Prunus padus Magnolia grandiflora Lorimer &~~
~~Fothergill~~

is is is there grace sufficient sufficient
For me O chestnut why have
            I        come        to        this
place-name origins                                                    10

*Air reir 's mar tha e sgriobhte san fhaidh Isaias: seall, cuiridh mi m' aingeal roimh do*
*ghnuis, a reiticheas do shlighe romhad.*

*Guth neach ag eigheach san fhasach: Reitichibh slighe an Tighearna, agus dianaibh a*
*rathadain direach.*

            this is DEATH
                 is it
                 not
            impre*SS*ed

        green/brown flow
            of the river
                green/blue flow
                    of the Air                                           20
do you do you do you
know what suffering is is is
clean me

            Wil              Wil
            *William* was my name
ɧeɤˌɑ, ɧeɤˌɑ, ɧeɤˌɑ,
ball dance in the            council

                    h                                    30
              house
                    r      eyes as she watched
me!
gather strength Linnaeus name to the name
Father I have f f f failed you bring me
come bring me back to brotherly love
            sic transit Gloria mundane


O god let me
die
my eyes                                                  40
let me
# DIE

              or let my cry
              come unto
              *three*



              3.


Mr. Rumsey, do you have can you prepare
A blister plaster for me my soul is on fire



              4.


Is this the Great Thing thing great death
        let my order ord3er come (un
              two three)



              5.
Here here here here here
        am I the the legal rep representative
              of of of of of:

By his Excellency Peter Chester Esquire Captain
General and Governor in Chief in and over the Providence
of West Florida and the Territories depending
thereon in America. Chancellor and Vice Admiral
of the same &ca. &ca.

To all whom these presents shall come or may in any wise concern:

Greeting,

   Know ye that William Bartram Botanist having requested my Leave and Licence to Travel through the different part of this Province under my Government, in order to make Botanical and other Observations I do hereby permit him to Travel in and over the said Province for the purpose of Collecting Rare and useful productions on Botany and Natural History. And I do here Command all His Majesty's Servants and Subjects within this Province that they do not interrupt him in his lawful proceedings, but that they be abiding and assisting to him as becometh all encouragers of useful Discoveries

   Given under my hand and Seal at Arms at Pensacola the Fifth day of September in the Year of our Lord one thousand seven Hundred and Seventy Five and in the Fifteenth Year of his Majestys Reign

                                        PTR C CHESTER


By His Excellency's Command.
     Alexr, Macullagh./. D. Sec.y.

6.

There, there, there between my shoulders
put the plaster between my
there

I awaken and my suffering has abated
though I am a blind mind now
shall I be a blind man tapping with my cane
down the lanes of Kingsessing all my days
or will I have days left—are these the last
of my days and how does a man know
when the last of his days have come to him?                                    10

What have I said in my illness and was I mad?
I have not yet seen the great Mississippi River that was
my goal here, to push myself relentlessly until
          that wide body of streaming water that divides
               America come into my eyes but if I am
                         a blind man what can I know? Its aroma,
the sound of it sweeping south in grandeur, a description
by comrades? I know that I must bear my suffering like
                         a man
but O light, all light blinds and torments me                                    20
          and so I must lie in utter darkness, eyes compress'd,
                    curtains drawn to shade my sickroom
                         from the white-hot knives of light

MANY A TIME HAVE THEY AFFLICTED ME
FROM MY YOUTH: YET THEY HAVE NOT
PREVAILED AGAINST ME. THE PLOWERS PLOWED
UPON MY BACK: THEY MADE THEIR LONG FURROWS.

### 7.

All is peace and tranquility and yet my eyesight
Has vanished from my Body. When I consider
How my light is spent . . . *was* spent? The idea
Of it torments me, for how can I know productions
Of Nature without my Sight? For Touch can deceive
And Scent is ignoble in discriminating one blossom
From another. I take a staff and go outside, push
Myself, ask my friend to stay away and let me fall
If needs be so that I can gain my legs again. Blind,
However, I crash into tree trunks, step into holes,                    10
Land with a disastrous collapse on my elbows
In a rocky hole. I do not confess to it, say that my
Wounds are nobly gained; he laughs at my knight's
Vanity and lets me be. Slowly, slow as a season,
The hard summer light does not cause me unbearable
Pain as it did for weeks and vision returns to one eye
In a defective but useful way. What can I know and
How will I know it day by day on this island?

### 8.

Salt marshes and plains, six miles long, four miles wide:
Shelly heights with a rich admixture of shrubs:
*Rhamnus frangula, Sideroxilon, Myrica, Lysium salsum,*
*Zanthoxilon clava Herculis,* and particularly a new species
Of mimosa with huge long leaves that cannot be exceeded
By others in its family. High lands on the interior of the island,
Soil that looks like a heap of sea and sand, mixed with shells,
And nothing, it appears, but desert sand, and yet it produces
All vegetables of Nature and man, and especially do fruit
Trees flourish here: peach, pear, fig, plums, grape vines.              10
Praise be: I can at least now pretend to be well though
My body is still broken by its lingering illness. Praise be.

### 9.

Spread the sails: span the air, scoop the wind
From the sea-span and let me glide onward
Toward the Mississippi, to see its silver slash
Across America. Sea-wrack crackles on the shore,
Hands of my black mates man the sails and oars,
Shout sea-spun commands, sing the rich bass

Chanteys of free men. The salt scrubs my face
As the wind cheers us; seagulls bank and soar
Above us in *keering* joy. I have closed the door
To death for now, though still half blind, rash      10
To be heading out before completely secured
From illness. I know I will or will not mend.

Can the river rival the magnificence of my bright
Imagination? Not the sea at all, they say, but
Lake Ponchartrain on which we glassily glide.
And across its north shore for twenty miles we
Let the wind take us past caves of air, sirens,
Terrible deaths from creatures with blood-claws.

We settle on the shore to camp. All the flaws
Of nature cannot touch the beauties. The fire is      20
High in our camp; the black men cook. I see
With difficulty but they are my eyes, decide
When danger nears. The roar of crocodiles cuts
Across the bay. We do not even think of flight.

### 10.

All of us must die of one thing or another,
        I tell them. In Florida I saw one night
        Ten thousand alligators by camplight
And felt they knew me as a scaly brother.

The men hum melodies of Africa, and the tune
      Turns me to stories: Then they had
      To come to take me down, sweet lad
With strong meat and muscle. The old moon

Hunts us as I speak on. They hum and listen.
      And I tell them I am a flower hunter,             10
      That I mean none harm. So, asunder
They went and left me to watch the moon glisten

On the waters of Florida. And all the evening
      They roared my name in finest praise
      And promised to protect my days
Among them. There will be no deep grieving

For your death, not yet, they roared to snakes
      And poison spiders in their sticky webs.
      And all Nature moved back, the crabs
Scuttled off, wolves nodded in the canebrakes,          20

And I was Lord of the roaring darkness, sure
      To live on my journey in the sinecure
      Of alligators who knew I could endure
The deepest fear and suffering, sharp and pure.

The black men love my tale,
clap me on the back, bed down,
none of them fearful anyway,
and I know I told it more to chase
my own fears away than theirs.

I do not tell them that I am still in terrible pain.          30
I do not say that the Mississippi is what I must gain.


11.


Westward past cypress swamps and rivers
That run into the grand lake: All the way we see

New settlements, plantations, houses of men who
Cut paths or wounds—I cannot tell which yet—in
This hot land. We sail up the Taensapaoa River,
And I lose track of time, as my eyes ache in terrible
Throbbing succession. *Do not turn me blind now.*

I sleep, awaken, see farms and cultivated prows
Of cornfields above the river, the land, the thurible
Of rich and sweet aromas, the back of the Giver,                10
By which I mean this majestic land, and high fins
Cutting through the water, and the sky so blue:
I ask my black companions if we will soon be
In sight of the Mississippi. Illness back, I shiver

And they sail us into shore. I apologize for my
Sickness, but they comfort me, build a fine fire,
And try to prop me up, but soon whining armies
Of mosquitoes attack us, billions all told, and we
Cannot fight them away. "At least them gators
Will not catch us napping," one called Sam cries.              20
I swat and laugh and curl up, sick and so weary.

Next day we're off again, and I feel myself leery
Of their directions and wonder if we will all die
Here in this monstrous wilderness. Are we fated
To be lost in our final days? Is there worse? I see
Somewhat better today, though, and a charming
Clearing of entanglements ensues, and from dire
Worry I soon see a vast plantation. Sigh to sigh!

The fine Scotsman who owns the farm receives
Me with civility and invites me to stay with him               30
For a few days, but I am mildly feverish and must
See the Great River soon—I feel its wild torque
In my bones and try to tell him how I feel. He
Understands before the words are out: "Ah, all
Majestic words in the world canna' quite tell
The feelin' ye hae when first you spy the flow,"
He says, smoking his clay pipe. "Go ye, boy,

And let your eyes take their fill of the river."
We do wait until morning and set sail toward
It, and my pulse pounds like celebratory drums.                    40

The black men paddle and pump; the ship comes
Round in the river, and my eyes are now a sword
Of anticipation that would cut through, the giver
Of ecstasy to me. Now the water's swift voyage
Ends, and we must walk nine miles, legs rowing
The stream of a road, and I am weak yet can smell
The silt and soaring Father of Waters; birds call
To say we near. My heart races ahead. So free:
Can I ever have such freedom again? A hawk
Rides the wind with lordly arrogance. The rust          50
I've grown from illness flakes away. A hymn
Rises on the road. I hear past all the world's disease.

Evening nears: "Mr. Bartram, *there*," one of my
Companions says quietly, and I follow his out-
Stretched hand and see before me like molten iron
The staggering sheet of the Mississippi: I gasp, lean
Against a pine tree, feel shot with the pleasuring
That is only momentary in the flesh and the blood.
"Beyond *belief*," I pray in a hoarse whisper, and I
Rejoice my health has held me to this place. How          60
Much land this stunning flow must drain I cannot
Guess. I kneel at the riverside and all but genuflect:
I have seen it with my own eyes, and in dreams I
Will carry it onward no matter how brief or long I live.


                    12.


I cannot hope to know such days again.
          I cannot rise to wing among the clouds.
I cannot touch azalea, pine, and waving fin
          Or find my greening way among the crowds.

# CANTO TWENTY-ONE

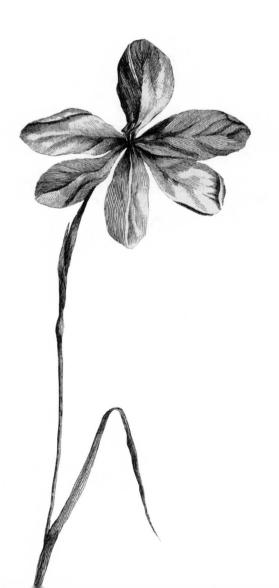

*T*HE grace of that moment, the broad sea of the rivercourse,
The deep intent of my eyes
      Still painful and sickened as my body was
The dream of a City of God, shimmering in the summer sun,
      Suddenly become less dream and something in which
      I could dip my dripping hands and cup to sip up
The dream since leaving the Cherokee Nation, to see the sway
      And roaring cataract that is so wide it seems motionless
The motion real though, magnified into a hundred rivers
      And floating full trees down the slow-winding course      10
The severe sheet of light-fire on my eyes from the slanting sun
The heart of America, for I know there are lands beyond this
      A white man has barely seen or ridden his horse upon
The slow breathing of my horse which has borne me over
      Several thousand miles uncomplaining, friend, sweating
      Companion, staring with me at the unswimmable flood:

Savannah, Keowee, Flint, Alabama, name by name by name
The rivers race in their spring-fed or summer-rained courses

I sit beside the river of rivers and ask my eyes for science
I sit in the wonder and splendid moment of the vastest torrent      20
      And ask for facts and dimensions, measurable things
I sit drenched in my constant cry for discipline, try to gauge
      Distances and depths

But O               I see in the corner of my eye
What                must be a vision if not a mystery
The        **G**      supple air, the limb-bent wind,
Treaties              with the fear inside me
So that I see          gold-silver light and know
It bears truths        I do not, cannot understand

O what            deities of soil and flower      30
What                grave suspicions that I
Bear        **O**      messages from the grave
Or back             toward life from it
Limb-bent          body, myself the
Message, not the     bearer of it from mystery

The                                          Great Waters must mean
Some                                         wonderful thing, more than
Water                    **D**               beyond all rivers and courses
A blossom                                    unfolding petal by petal
A source of                                  great mysteries to unfold          40
Name by name                                 by Latinate Linnæn name

Amite River, the Iberville, having come here to Manchac
On my faithful horse now in late October 1775, trees
Slightly, slightly shading toward an autumn glow and me

Kneeling in stained-glass praise before the Mississippi
Sentences forming and unforming like subtle currents,
And the gentleman I meet here now a fine Scotsman

William Dunbar, educated well in astronomy and mathematics
A naturalist as I am, given to dashing from one stem to the next,
And we are friends immediately, as I was with poor Patrick        50

In Florida, on his Land Grant where he is a well-known
Trader but wishes to talk scholarship and blessed blossoms
Everyone else calls him Mr. Dunbar but he delights to ask

That I call him Billy, his boyhood name, and we speak
Of his scientific observations with alacrity and joy
And I say to him: "My boyhood name was also Billy,

So we can be twin Billies and friends if that pleases you":
"It pleases me greatly," he laughs; "tomorrow in my boat
We shall sail north a ways if your health will bear it,

For I have heard that you have been ill for so very long,            60
And I know how that wears down the strongest man
And you are thin and bear watching, I am inclined to say."

He means it lightly and I take it so; soon it is the morrow
And we are in the Great River and no greater day comes
Back in my memory, and I do not speak of the mystery

That has lately glowed in my mind but remain on what
I see and sense and can write down, and we speak of that
And it is far glory enough—to have seen this river flow.

We stop at Alabama Town
On our way to Baton Rouge                                                    70
Then travel out, for he wants
Me to see the White Plains
And they are magnificent,
But my eyes and body tire
And he can see it and we rush
Onward up the river toward
His own home where we can
Rest. The three black men
Who row our boat are strong
And I wonder what tribe                                                      80
They may have graced
In Africa before they came,
Stolen away, to this land
To serve as dark slaves.

We arrive in the evening at Billy's plantation
In this wild and exotic land but not touched
With a bracing wind of season's colorful change

I visit with him for two days, and my eyesight
Improves greatly for it, but do I see what is here
Before me or does it see me? Restless as he is,                              90

We agree to visit Point Coupe, French settlement
On the Spanish shore of the river, and we come to
The White Cliffs; heat sunders us; we set off to see

On horseback the White Plains and I take note
Of many species of never-timbered trees; we pass
Beneath the high painted cliffs then sail back

Across the Mississippi, and all the while I am filled
With unspeakable delights even though my body
Weakens perceptibly in the afternoon of each day.

Fear ignites small sparks with me, and I make order                100
From it or try to; I resume my collections, mark
The miles of our adventures, plot the days I have
Toward home. The disorder of my nights now tears
Me mildly apart, and I want to place the full stops
Demanded by propriety in every sentence or step.
"Billy," I say one day, "my eyes—I am so so sorry
To tell you, but the least light torments me in a way
More hellish that I can describe." He chastises himself
For pushing me to travel so hard and finds us a resting
Ground so I can breathe deeply and cloak my eyes                   110
With wet cloths. I love this land so deeply but when
Sick and lost among earth I have never seen, terror
Sometimes tears me apart. But who do I deceive now?
If I am to live an ample life I must begin to think
Of my route back to Carolina before cold weather
Sinks in with her frosts and bone-cracking cold.
I find the Company's schooner is ready to set sail

Back to Mobile, and Billy books me passage. Pale,
Sitting up with apologies, I feel suddenly old,
And wish I were at Kingsessing in the heather                      120
Field behind the house, not here in heat, on a brink
Of blindness or worse, illness that time allows.
Yet coming this far west was truly no error,
For I have seen the River that even greater men
Than I have defined inadequately. Majesty lies
In knowing such grandeur. And for my questing
I have received great gifts of value for my shelf
Of memories and intellectual pursuits only. Day
Strikes my eyes like Cherokee arrows. I worry
That by the time I reach Mobile I'll have wept                     130
My sight away. Rain begins in small pearl-drops.
I find myself conquering those ancient fears
And unfolding like a message-bearing dove.

The contrast of all Nature's lives are stark;
I range back and forth along that silken border.

Before I board the schooner I tell my friend
Goodbye, clasp Dunbar on the shoulders
And thank him with strong gratitude for all
His patient welcome to me. "The joy was mine,
Billy," he says gladly, "for I have been able                    140
To speak of wondrous things none other here
Understands in the way we can." And I know
What he means: shell bluff, fruiting plain,
The aborescent aromatic vine, the day we chased
A swimming bear to land and landed after
Him and still were not able to have sight
Of that rambling and curve-clawed creature;
And much more of color, shape, nature's forms
Gone gloried in the morning's bathing light.
He means the snow-haired Frenchman we sailed                     150
To see, the tale he told us of the tyrannical conduct
Of white men toward the Indians; he means our
Simple conversations of mind and lovely matter.

Focus fails my tired eyes. Spangled sun scatters
Light beneath the moss-proud trees as I scour
The scene one last time. We embrace, he ducks
Beneath a branch and is gone, and I am hailed
To board by the Captain, and my water-flight
Upon the Mississippi begins again; can harm
Come to anyone as enthralled with all Nature                     160
As I? Of course. And I feel no pain or fright
As we come current-bound, American drifters
On the life-wide back of water, past erased
As if it never moved past me. I am more sane
Than priest or seer, skin the color of a rose,
Pale fire, while bend to bend the vessel shears
Me from nothing, for permanence is a table
At which I shall sup for decades yet, the sign
Of my salvation, the migrating bird's clear call.
We steer around the channels and all boulders                    170

And I know the meaning now of water and of wind.
We arrive in Manchac in the evening and next
Day I take my leave of the Company and set off
For the forks of the Amite River with others,
And come evening we anchor in the shallows
And fish and shoot for pleasure wayward fowl,
Though the more I understand the less I think
It is my place to take the life of any creature.
Next day, now mid-November, we sail out into
Ponchartrain and skate before the fresh wind                          180
Far into the starry night, and I say softly: home!
What I have seen stumbles through my mind
With aberrant and quite splendid disorder: seas
Of cinnamon-colored bark with a spicy smell,
A new species of verbena with decumbent branches
And lacerated deep green leaves which terminate
With corymbi of violet blue flowers. A sudden
Jarring shakes the boat to a shuddering stop
And I know we have run aground near midnight.

All night our crew beats the hard sandy blight                        190
Of stricture. I know that here we are a crop
For the harvest of wind and flood, and scudding
Clouds float across the lake in reflection, fate
Waiting to decide our destination. By inches
We begin to move with strong wind, swell
Off the sandbar next day, and shedding disease
Of immobility, miraculous cure, a shout finds
The surface of Ponchartrain. Now we roam
Onward out in the middle of the lake, defend
Ourselves against ground in the deep and blue                        200
Mirror on which we reflect our image-rapture
South. On and onward, demarcation to links
In the navigational chain, we glide and prowl.
We stream toward Mobile again. The gallows
Of my illness recedes, my head-throbs bother
Me less each league. The sunset is pinkly soft.
With each moment I am less and less vexed.

Now I gather each collection I have finely made
And leave them all to Swanson and McGillivray
To ship for Fothergill in London. Because it is                                210
Too far to sail back past Florida, the only way
Back to Augusta is through the Creek Nation.
Much danger lies among the Seminoles and Lower
Creeks; there is no choice. They tell me of killings
By them at the Bay of Apalache. Fearful, still sick,
I join a caravan of traders now setting off to trade
In the Creek Nation. Early on departure day
My eyes fill with sick-blindness, and I weep, rub
My sight raw. For a moment I despair, but then
Clarity comes to me, and I all but dance to see                                220
The bright bay before me, to hear the loud chatter
Of rough men, the stamping of impatient horses.
November is near her end. Can I truly mend
On such a long ride home? I set out with them
Knowing I have seen the river of men's dreams.

*Friend, some kind of exhaustion bends me*
*Toward the couch against the study wall.*
*I did not know then I would never be free*

*Of the disorder in my eyes again, that all*
*Miles we travel stay on our traveled backs.*                                  230
*Now I hear the wild geese swim air and call*

*Out their destinations like feathered sacks*
*To others who follow, even far behind.*
*I know what my story finally always lacks:*

*The truth that even those like me gone blind*
*Can love the well-traveled country of time.*
*I would not change a second of my life's design.*

I have stood and seen the river as he did
          with its imperial disdain, seen it from
Memphis and New Orleans, such power,                                           240
          so slow it seems to be unmoving.

I have stood on its steamboat banks
       and held flocks of upswarmed seagulls
in my eyes while I dreamed away thousands
       from nearby dives and casinos,

from the cathedral behind which Faulkner
       lived. I have stood in my motel room
window and watched it lordly slip the country
       north to south, simple as a floating farm,

complex as my memories of those who                  250
       traveled it in the fur days, who drove on
west to find flowers or one thing fundamental
       enough to live and then to die for.

But, Your Majesty, you are nothing, not a glint
       of sun, a silver stretch of perfect dreams,
compared to the Keowee River, the ford we crossed
       in our youths, the sound, the sound, the sound

of all water, all history, personal and too precious
       not to share with what comes after:
pistil, stamen, sepal, petal, and the old journey         260
       back upstream through all pain

to the point of all creation, the intersection
       of passion and biology, of sun and moon
and that brief trembling of all Nature
       that is the bright witness of our days.

HE THAT OBSERVES THE WIND SHALL NOT SOW;
HE THAT REGARDS THE CLOUDS SHALL NOT REAP.

# CANTO TWENTY-TWO

*L*ATE November now, a chill in the northern wind,
And we set out east in a large boat and get off
At Taensa where I join a group of packhorsemen
Heading toward the Creek Nation. The jingling caravan
Has near thirty horses, sixteen loaded, three traders,
And myself. I still have the faithful horse on which
I have ridden so many thousand miles, and he cannot
Bear more weight, and so they loan me a mount
Which I laden with my effects. Now in Indian file,
Shouts and commands to stock and men, they head                10
Us east and with a crack of a whip and a cry,
The Chief drives us onward, and I want to shout
Back my elation but I just feel my friend bear on
With them all into the wilderness. We are kept
At a trot, and each horse has a set of bells that
Rings and clangs without ceasing, a strong clattering,
And the smack of the whips, the shouts, the bells,
And the trod of the horses are nearly deafening to me.

In three days' time my old horse Tom is on the point
Of giving out, and I halt the caravan to see what            20
Can be done for him. "Aye God, Bartram, there's
A group a traders a piece ahead of us with horses
To sell, cain't say what they do with yore old nag,"
Luke says, spitting tobacco. I nod, do not say I will
Die before I let one hair be harmed on my friend.
I pat his long sweating head and lean down to whisper
Endearments. Order does not hold here. Some wrong
Attends us, some misrhyme, some out-of-sorts
Motion through the cold and colder woods-world.
And yet though they are hard, the packhorsemen           30

Show evident signs of humanity and friendship
And grant they will not leave me to die in the woods
As I protect my staggering old horse from burden.
"Left, you'd be kilt by the Choctaws, don't take
Kindly to strangers trespassing on their properties,"
Spits old Timmons, grinning to show a mouthful

Of black teeth. "I'd not leave no man to them people."
Soon we come to a grove of surpassing beauty
And my illness fades, fears falter, and every bush
Seems buoyed with an aromatic scent as rich                40
As that from cloves or nutmeg. Ride, we ride on,
And my horse's steps grow shakier, weary, perhaps
Ill, too, as I have been, and yet he will not halt
If I ask him to walk on, and my heart rends for it.

"There!" Jack Wilkerson cries in mid-afternoon,
And far ahead I can see the other trading company
With its large herd of horses. He turns to me, smiles
"Tol' ye, so, Willy-am. Hee." He loves to be right,
Which he rarely is, so I let it be, and anyway my joy
Is redoubled. I lean down and whisper to old Tom:         50
"We will find you retirement ahead to rest and grow
Strong again." Before dark, I meet with the leaders
Of the other group and buy a fine, young horse
And then go to my old friend and lead him to a wide
Cane pasture by a river and hug him well and say:
"You'll be free here for a season, and they will pick
You up on their way back when you have fattened
On this grass and slept. You can huddle in the trees
When the cold is worst, stand out in the bright sun
As heat returns. What great adventure you saw!           60
What impossible importance you bring to the world,
Dear friend!" Now, so shaken, I embrace him
One last time, unstrap the bridle, slap his rump,
And watch him run with fair delight toward grass
Still green though the cold season has now come.

Next morning we set off, and I look for old Tom,
But he has vanished into freedom, and I know I
Have seen the last of him except in my memory.

Days, we ride days, and my new horse is strong.
Ox-steady, haughty with the muscular arrogance           70
Of the young, and I nearly laugh at his belief
In eternal life. "Coming in!" young Luke cries,

And we see moving slowly toward us a freezing
Group of emigrants from Georgia: a man, his
Thin and fearful wife, several ragged children,
And three stout young men herding onward
A dozen horses bearing everything they own.
The woman's face is pale, sickly, and so afraid
That she trembles head to foot. I smile kindly at her
To show we mean no harm, doff my hat, speak                              80
Softly, cannot outshout Wilkerson who asks aloud
Who they are and if they have seen any danger.

"Whar you headed?" Timmons asks. The husband
Swallows hard and says, "West," and that is all
He can manage as they pass us, and I ache for them
In the sure coming deaths of at least one in winter

To come. Now John in our company lights out
To announce our presence to the Creeks lest they
Send out a party to slit our throats in a screaming
Battle on the banks of some unnamed creek.                               90
We ride, we ride on, and my bones crack with ache.

Late in the day we come to a branch of the Alabama
River, and strong storms have swollen it so greatly
That to cross here is impossible. We scout for fords
And find no shoal where we could do more than
Drown quickly and quietly. The water is so cold
It frosts my hand to the touch but must be crossed
If we are to get east before winter. "Got to build
A raft to ferry over them goods!" cries old Sam,
And I doubt the wisdom, but they begin to chop.

100

Of proper trees for such a raft there's a fine crop,
And so we take our axes and hack down a span
Of them then gather dry canes while in our guild
Of companions Thomas gathers vines embossed
With sharp sunlight. Soon they show me an old
Trick of travel: nine-foot tree lengths, and a span
Of canes sewn on top tightly. It shines like a sword,

Fourteen feet in final breadth, caned, then lately
Tied with vines. A boy named Benton now slams

Into the water with a stout tendril and swims across                    110
In water to his chin, and we tie other vines by hand
To its end until we have a rope that he secures to
A sheltering oak. We secure the other end to our raft,
And with a shout and a cry we push and pull the
Craft into the strong current and all the way over,
Losing nothing in its route. We do this several
Times, and on its last trip I put all my belongings
Except my trousers, and we exult, but now come

The horses, a problem I am unsure of: they run
Up and down the bank, wild to cross, longing                           120
For the other side as we are. I see now the feral
Bank begin to fill with alligators, snakes, a fever
Of a nightmare moment. I will not wait to bleed.
As wild-wind driven as is the seasonal chaff,
I am all motion: water white and the sky so blue
It hurts to see, I drive horses off the edge of land
Into the flow, and I plunge in after them, the loss

Of some stock likely. And yet I find I am stronger
Than my late disease, and they are mad for strokes,
And we all reach the other side, men wild, clapping                    130
For my feat, me shivering, horses shaking off water,
And a cold sun setting. We turn to see, with disbelief,
That we must now cross *another* stream to reach land,
And a great groan goes up, but they unpack their axes
Again and begin to chop trees, laughing when I say
I have never heard of a woodsman's "raccoon span."

                    Built, bridged, slow-going,
            my eyes burning with disease:
        we cross the stream before us and
by nightfall reach the banks                                           140
                    of the Tallapoosa River:
            my weakness drives me mad

my illness ebbs then flows back
wild for vengeance and to destroy
           my mind: by fire-frame
     a young white man appears
out of the darkness, terrified,
weeping, turning in fearful circles,
    and two men catch him
       as he collapses crying and               150
           I sit up, remove the wet cloths
     from my eyes and see he is
trembling terribly: cannot hold a
tin cup of water to slake his cracked
    lips. His hands dance dumbly
       by the raking firelight, and I
         come to his side and put my
    arm around his shoulder, he
    then stutters out: I was I was I was
riding north north from Pen-Pensacola         160
    and come up-upon some pilgrims
      a man man and his pale thin wife
        and three children, three stout
     boy boys b-oy, uh, and just as we
just as we joined, joined, Choctaws
come at us from twin a-angles, circling,
    taking the horse horse horses from under
      them and and and, they come for me, and
        and I kicked my mount & rode rode
     fast & down low not to get knocked      170
   down by low branches and O dear God
was it the horror of all life
    and I thought they was going a
      leave me leave me be but but but
        these two these two chased me
    miles and miles, screaming cursing
all all the while and I swum my horse
across a big river and they shot shot shot arrows
    at me and cried Choctaw madness curses at
      me and I I I couldn't stop riding riding    180
        and I seen your light and I said in mind

God hope they be white men
or or or or or or I am I am I am I am—

THE LOVE THAT ROSE ON STRONGER WINGS,
   UNPALSIED WHEN HE MET WITH DEATH,
   IS COMRADE OF THE LESSER FAITH
THAT SEES THE COURSE OF HUMAN THINGS.

I hold him in my arms:
He weeps softly, saying:
They was screaming.                                                     190
They was screaming
*They was all screaming,*
Indian and pilgrim, and I
Could not tell which was which
Or why fear or rage took them
So far from any humanity.
I could not could could not.

      The other hard men shake it away
      The other men shrug as if to say
      Life is not for granted, will disappear               200
      In an unguarded moment, they bear
      No obvious ill-will toward Choctaw
      Or pilgrim: in the woods one is claw
      And one is fresh meat, and to know
      Is to be God and God would show
      The path out: Here, we have no God
      But luck and a strong arm. We've trod
      A thousand miles safely, and I'm stuck
      To know it's only through sheer luck
      That, sick as I am, I fare better than            210
      Some pilgrims now beneath the sod.

He pulls away from me, takes dried meat
   from our stores, stuffs his saddle bag,
      and remounts, and thoughtful Luke says:
         In the name of God you ain't riding on
            in the dark tonight, you think you less

likely to be kilt there than here tonight?
I'm going going I'm I'm I'm going on
my way my way I'm I'm headed I'm going
east toward toward: Here his speaking stops            220
as he kicks his weary mount and rides out of our
firelight, Wilkerson crying out to come back! come on!
But he is gone and Timmons cries: Goddamned fool to
ride on in the night away from to what he cannot see, but
I know that is the worst phantom, the one we cannot
find with our eyes but is there anyway to take us
at the point of our greatest fear, to tear us apart.


\*


Morning: it is very cold, and the earth appears
As hoary as a fallen snow. The fire's been kept
Well-kindled all night, and, my eyes clear now,            230

I recall the doomed family, the boy and how
He sat terrified in my arms and how he wept
Against what did not chase him into tears.

I stand and see in the mist across the river
A white trader naked but for a breech-cloth,
Encircled by Indians who wave and climb

Into a large group of canoes. In good time
They paddle over, take us back (north?)
Across the flow. Light comes in a sliver

Of golden-silver shine. They are taking us            240
To the town of Mucclasse, a mile or two
Distant, and we arrive to find that friends

Welcome us here. This is not the ends
Of the Earth after all but a sky of new blue
And fine vermillion, leaves now gone rust

And yet with a few ochres and reds to sway
The attentive eye. Rest, audience, and now
A wedding to attend in all its loveliness.

A Creek called Corn Tassel, with us, the best
Tracker on our journey, is to wed by vow                            250
A native girl of the town. The end of day

Begins the dancing and feasting, singing
From all, the bonfire's warmth washing over
Me, and I watch the young couple's eyes

As they look at each other with soft surprise
That this has happened to them. As clover
Covers a slope, their joy set me thinking

That I will never share such a happy day
But I do not feel pity for myself, for I am
A gatherer of roots, Earth-man, petal-boy                           260

With sick but grateful eyes. Now the joy
Is withdrawn to their simple room. I am
Filled with transcendent happiness for them.

Dance, dance: feast on plants from meadow
And house-side garden. It is my own wish
That others know what has come to pass

Me in the night.

                                *

All night then NIGHT mares of the fearful

        and what COMES for me in the guise of flowers
                                                                    270
    mares of the night coming FOR William to break

            his soul with sickness, MY days done or not done

and O my SOUL let me float away from that poor pilgrim

GRANT me bear the unbearable plot of stories

of blood, let me rise in the penitence of MERCY

and TO ME and the stammering failure of the sun to rise

O give me the time of flowering

even in the hideous pantomime of dreams, LORD,

give me a way out of wisdom or into it

\*

Come to the village, come to the trail,
Death to the pillage and strike to the nail.
Torment my sadness, sails for the sea
Echo all madness that whispers to me.

280

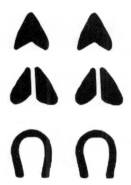

We are not yet ready to take the trail east.
We roll up our bedding and sup a snail's feast.
We ride for a new town that's named Alabama.
Frost coats, like dead-sheets, strikes as a hammer

All land where the dancing has already begun.
The horses go prancing right into the sun.

We see like a rumor remains of Toulouse,
Four-pounders tumored with rust and with use.                    290

It sits in a fork in between two large rivers,
Tallapoosa and Coosa wing wind with its shivers.
Night in the town shows us music and dancing
As sun settles down on their shouts that go lancing.


                              *


Morning: the rhythm of horses and town stampers is gone
Morning: we ride slowly through the frosty fields back
         to Mucclasse where I hear a company of traders
         will soon ride out from nearby Tuckabatche
         for Augusta so I ride there, learn they have gone,
         and return to hear another caravan will leave from        300
         Ottasse town in two or three weeks:
Morning: slow preparation in waiting for time to pass

         I arrive back to find the trader's store shut
         the town in edgy waiting ḥeyꞌa, ḥeyꞌa, ḥeyꞌa
         Creeks wild for revenge and the quick rage
         of battle, and the story is revealed in reδ strokes
         quick as the dart of a hummingbird to the next
         blossom on a spring morning, and yet shuddering
         cold has come and cannot break even with fires
         that scream and slice the shivering air with fright:      310

The trader's son has
loved the slender wife
of a hunting chief, and
when the Creek returns
home from his scout,
he is told of this love;
he and his warriors then
intrigue to ask outside
the trader's son as if
friends. He comes, is                                      320
knocked down, and
stripped to his skin,
and the Creeks with
knotty bludgeons beat
him half senseless and
plan to cut off his
ears in ritual punishment
(I imagine the howling
mob, the frost-blackened
blood on the town earth)                                    330

Now the trader's son writhes in the bloody soil
Played dead in the earth and holds the handle
Of his knife in the bloody soil and when they come
To slice off his ears he leaps up screaming and

dances around them                    in the bloody soil
screaming like mad                      breaking free, running
off into the swamp                         filled with thick snakes
vines, thickets,                              and sulfurous mud; he
wanders there all                          night, lost and chased
until his hunters give                   up in the cold and          340
come home vowing                       revenge when he
sneaks back in as                        he surely will,
not able to stay in the         swamp forever;
no man can stay there forever in
the place that makes mad
the sanest strong
man ever
known.

\*

Now the boy is in his father's house and terror—
A circle of village men screaming that he lose                    350
His ears—dances round and round it while the chiefs
Gather in parlay to mete justice. They come to the
Door of the trader and say: "The boy must lose his
Ears or you all your goods, which we guess must
Be worth a thousand pounds." The trader and his son,
Who says he dearly loves the girl with whom he
Was found, let me inside, and both are weeping
Bitterly and say I must see the head of their trade
Group, Mr. Galphin, and ask for his help, or they
Must starve or the boy lose his ears.                            360
                              Not waiting
Two weeks now, for I cannot, I depart early
The next morning, oddly strong, my eyes clear,
My work made plain to the Creeks who do not
Hold me guilty of any breech as I ready for
The long ride that pours out before me.

**Alone and alone on the road and alone:**

And suddenly the shattering silence of my life
Where am I going—by way of beautiful Coolome
*In frost-white days the color of my beard and hair*            370
After this I looked, and behold, a door was opened

When I realize my own *Travels* are in the past
I tarry there with Mr. Germany, elderly trader
*He was not as old as I am now, active, agreeable*
In heaven: and the first voice which I heard

Day by day I slow on the trail and yet find joy
His wife is a Creek woman, worthy and amiable
*They wanted to send their children for education*
Was as it were of a trumpet talking with me;

Each morning I rise twisted with pain all over　　　　　　　　380
I recross the river at Tuccabache, an ancient town
*Waiting for traders was agony then, wasn't it?*
Which said, Come up hither and I will shew

Am I William or Williams and is there a difference
I join the chief in the areopagus with Casine and smoke
*Each morning I rise twisted with pain all over*
Thee things which must be hereafter.

Many voices, many pasts: find the stem and blossom
And they bring me to their vespers and mystical fire
*The glassy fragility in my chest begins again, friend,*　　390
And immediately I was in the spirit, and behold, a throne

I near my sixtieth year with a silvery anticipation
Now comes the Black Drink, aged chiefs sit in classes
*But it fades again, and I will be with you till the end*
Was set in heaven and one sat on the throne.

Fair companion and companions, bless your steps
And they raise conch shells filled with Black Drink
*Oh yes: Aꞏhoo—ojah, aꞏſu—yah they sang in circles*
And he that sat was to look upon like a jasper

I have danced these steps on the hills of Keowee　　　　400
The skin of a tyger stuffed with tobacco is brought
*I must write a paper on the genus of those plants*
Or a sardine stone: and there was a rainbow

I have danced these steps in the town's Old Gym
And laid at the King's feet, the great pipe adorned
*And I must say adored, smoke to the cardinal points*
Round about the throne, in sight like unto an emerald.

And the Council House—Mark's site in Greene County
Sanctuary, priest, eagles' tails, cabins, otters, piazza:
*Their paintings with much more meaning than mine here*　　410
And round about the throne were four and twenty seats

Where Daddy found the pattern of the hidden posts
Then the fasting begins here to prevent sickness
*It was cold and they ate only a meager gruel, I recall*
And upon the seats I saw four and twenty elders

Phantom companion packing with Bartram now
Their monuments are antiquities with no known meaning
*And what meaning does my life have in it now?*
Sitting, clothed in white raiment and they had

My journey just begins now and I ride for the road                    420
I observe as I ready to leave the quiet solemnity
*It was their Sabbath: what is sacred is gold to all*
And they had on their heads crowns of gold.

                              *

The second day of January, and the day is cold
And clear and white with a sparkling frost.
I ride toward Augusta with a company of traders:
Four men, thirty horses, twenty of which are loaded
With leather and furs. We set out beneath a sky
Of cobalt blue, our horses glad, gliding in motion
For the warmth and the natural motion their species                   430
Craves. I ride with a young man named Isaac
For awhile, but we have so little to say he sways
Away back to his friends, and I am content to stay
Back and alone, feeling the land beneath me
In its cold and friendly rolling. We ride all day,
We cross small streams, fording them, sloshing
Up freezing water our animals ignore or seem to;

We camp, build great fires, eat our meager meals,
And I want to tell them of the Mississippi River,
Of the Cowee Valley, and of the Crystal Basin                         440
But words ruin that world for me, and so I lapse
Into a silky silence, and they do not mind, for they,
Too, are quiet men. In three days we arrive once
More at the Chattahoochee River and see on either

Side the towns of Chehaw and Usseta: they almost
Join each other and yet speak two languages,
Perhaps as different as Muscogee and Chinese.
We cross without incident, the river being low;
We are not molested or harmed in any way
But hailed in passing with a friendly wave                                   450
And I wonder: Are we coming back into the world
Again now or have we been in it all along?

Ride to ride, we finally reach Ocmulgee and its
Ancient mounds and expansive old fields,
And something mysterious and withdrawn hovers
Over it and around it and through it, and I walk
After we have set our camp and look at the river
Which is foaming from recent floods and raging
Over its banks. We meet two companies of traders
From Augusta bound for the Nation, men, horses:                              460
And the traders tell a terrible story of losing six head
In the crossing, the steeds becoming tangled in vines
And cried out their suffering as they sank beneath
The water and drowned. I think of my own lost horse
And step away from them into a dark place and weep.

Is there a labyrinth into which all experience fits?
It is night and I am lost in the cardinal points of Earth.
I am going back I do not want to go back; nightmares
Frighten me insensibly, and I awaken from the labyrinth
Lost in it; I imagine the ceremonies once held here,                         470
Dancing, rituals, dread promises, and love of images
With bright meaning for the Ancients. What is my order,
And do I dare offend it? I have taken a dangerous
Trip to reticence. I have stepped into the monster's lair
And gone in too far some nights, turning to find
My way blocked from passage to passage, filled
With boulders and misbegotten promises, with eyes
That shade mine for a few delicious moments
And then fade into the private histories we bear
To bear this world. My suffering is beyond light,                            480
Beyond seasonal shifts, beyond the last compass point

All men may bear. And yet O the fragrance of petals
In April, the feeling that soon I may escape from it
All, that, one more turn, and I can brighten all
That I see for others who can also see life through
The lens of one who loves Nature for herself alone.

We break out the leather boat,
Eight feet long and propped
Open with stout limbs,
Will use it to ferry goods                                    490
Across the river in a few
Dropping days. So I wander,
Since our boat is ready,
Horses turned out to pasture.
We cannot leave yet and so
I roam the old fields, find
Dejection beyond bearing,
Ask myself: what happens
When the Great Adventure
Is over? Can another day                                      500
Dawn that would make me
Shout in green rapture
As these in the South have?
I say, half in jest: send to me
An incontestable sign, drama
Of the winds and ruin of rain.
And to my shock air opens,
And an eagle dips down
Riding on a shaft of sunlight,
Haughty beak arched for food,                                 510
And it races along the water-
Course, bright talons out,
And I imagine its kind kill,
Offering a body in exchange
For the magnificence of rising
Over the Earth in blue splendor.
And down and down he comes
Until he's scratching the water
Wing-beat to wing-beat then

He splashes in a sharp white　　　　　　　　　520
Cry and takes up the fish
With its sun-white scales
Flapping in death and glory
And I think: God! That is
The clue to my healing,
That I am a beautiful victim
Of this gorgeous wildness;

*That is the clue to my healing,*
*That I am a beautiful victim*
*Of this gorgeous wildness;*　　　　　　　　530

That is the clue to my healing,
That I am a beautiful victim
Of this gorgeous wildness.

# CANTO TWENTY-THREE

CROSSING day! Cool and pleasant, order
Restored, tides of the river restrained by
Clear, warm weather, we launch, cross
Over time and time again with our goods.
We load and paddle, load and strongly row
White ripples in the bright river, leaving
The Ocmulgee mounds behind us; I feel
Stronger than I have in days, no longer lost
In the labyrinth of my brooding. Now we
Go back over, and I wait, round up our horses
And **drive!** them into the water. They swim
Like brown-backed whales, manes up,
Spirited and snorting, and we cry them
Over, and soon they dash out of the current
On to dry land, not one lost or even hurt.
Now our large group splits, and only three
Of us with many bundled packs of leather
Ride toward Augusta: we will make it.

When a river comes, we swiftly take it
Easily: Oconee and Ogeechee. The pleasure
Of a river crossing is the same as a sea,
I think, flowing, flooding, then to dirt
Again on the other side. We are unhurried
Even though my heart races now to skim
Off days and nights. We camp, we sup,
We ride until the daylight starts to dim,
And then camp. We follow old courses
Set by trappers through woods and lea.
A happy man does not add up the cost
Of his mileage; my soul begins to heal.
Once I fall into water that is freezing
And suffer from it, but fire can show
Salvation from cold. We ride the woods
Oak to oak with pleasure, without loss.
And the studded and cerulean sky
Lights our way; moon full or quarter—

No matter if we stay on a straight way.
The traveling is hard, but soon we ride
Into Augusta, and I can scarcely believe
The streets and women in their swaying                                40
Stride from store to store. Children cry
In play, and I realize how much we miss
The kindness of our own kind, the voice
With known words and customs. And yet
Part of me remains in that red land, and
I turn toward and then back, a jocund
Janus finding pleasure either way I go.
I rest and visit Dr. Wells, my friend, who
Lives near the city on his plantation.
He give me fine food, says, "You're thin,                             50
William, let's put some fat back inside
Your clothes!" I laugh. I *am* thin, my eye
Is still not entirely well I know now,
For it weeps and blurs at odd times.

But what victories I celebrate! His limes
And oranges lift me, his venison, sow,
And steer barbecued slowly are delight
To my palate. "You should not yet ride,"
He says. "Something of your eye-rims
Is wrong." I tell him of my late sedation                             60
For a month in the West. "If that is true,
Then certainly you could stay, know
Rest for a few weeks." I decline, rocking
By the fire and smoking, drink in hand.
"I am now surely in your gracious debt,"
I whisper, and he says, "William, I rejoice
In your presence so greatly you guess
Wrongly to be indebted!" No reply
Is needed to such hospitality. Delaying
As long as I can, I ride back and retrieve                           70
My goods from Augusta and now glide
Beneath the sun south toward Savannah.

Days are still cold, but inside by each mile
I warm. I realize how hard these months
Have been on me. My bones ache, brass
Cracked from miles and cold. I hear clops
From behind catching up and quickly turn
To see a fine fellow at a jaunty canter
Coming toward me, arm up. He's Irish
And quite voluble, asks if he may travel          80
With me, and I express my true delight.
 "I want to see if the climate here is good
For Mediterranean vegetables and fruits,"
He says, "especially vines for fine wine,
Mulberry for silkworms, citrus, lemon."
I tell him while our winter has been hard
I have ridden across the rugged span of all
America and know it will bear much bounty
Year to year and in all seasons. He is
Astonished and tells me of Ireland, cold          90

That breaks bones, ice, but also the old
Songs of deep green landscapes, a mist
That sings over lake and bog. Counting
On his hands, he names ten species, tall
As summer, from Ireland that would regard
Carolina with delight. I describe persimmon
And wild grapes, all of this land's design,
And he is astonished. I show him how roots
I collect sail back to London. Deep woods
Also cause his eye to roam, since night          100
There falls on moors that range and ravel
Up the countryside. As we are tiring,
We stop to rest near Great Springs, banter
Halting when we see the gush that burns
Upward, transparent and cool then drops
Back down and flows in rocks and grass,
Sinuous and lovely. "To have seen it once
Is magnificent!" he shouts with a smile.

"To live near it would be quite sublime!"
The fountain fills with multitudes of fish,                                    110
Bream, trout, catfish, gar, and it is amusing
To watch them rise and fall in the rocky
Apertures. My friend and I share names
Of the nearby plants: *Laurus Borbonia*,
*Callicarpa*, *Magnolia grandiflora*, and
Nearby I take him to the usual gathering
Of ancient mounds and explain what lies
Inside them and that Cherokee and Creek
Indians have no more idea of who built
Them than we do. We ride on south, see                                        120
Fields of chipped jasper or agate which
The Ancients used to make arrowheads
And knives. I kneel and pick up two
Misshapen implements, perhaps spoiled
In the making. "To think they are here
Still after such a long time makes one

Feel an insignificance." The brief sun
Settles. We camp, we talk in the clear
Sharp starry night. The heavens unroiled,
My heart now misted with the calm blue                                        130
Of a coming spring, are we being led
By a Greater Power down the ditch
That carries this river? Or can it be
That we are mere flotsam, no guilt
Necessary for any act? I do not speak.
We rise, we ride, he sings and sighs
For Ireland, weeps openly, lathering
Creeks fordable, the bars of fine sand
Easily crossed. With no groaning you
Learn to suppress emotions the same                                           140
As the friend with whom you flock, he
Suffering to sing but with no abusing
Of himself or others. I have no wish
That is not granted, no unmade rhyme.

We stop in several days at Silver Bluff,
And I tell my friend George Galphin
The sad story of the trader boy and his
Indian love. Galphin sighs and says,
"No good can come of this, William,
And no true right can clear this insult                    150
To them. The boy may well be forced
To lose his ears, but I'll move all of hell
And heaven to salvage things." He claps
Me on the back to seal his word. We dine,
We tour his plantations, but I am edgy
With the need to reach Savannah, though
When I think of Philadelphia, when I
Recall my journey in Florida, I still yearn
For one last ride in that hot land before
I leave. My Irish friend and I separate              160
When we reach town, and I tell him fare
Thee well in God's good grace and care.

Sentimental, unguarded, he weeps, bears
His soul without shame. I do not now fear
For him; he *will* fare well. I am not desperate
To leave just yet, and I cannot quite ignore
That I want to see my old haunts and turn
My eyes to their loveliness with a sigh
One last time. I want to ride, glide, know
Once more what I have seen: not cagy                 170
Enough to lie, I do not write home, line
My saddlebags with food, take two traps,
Powder, horn: Like the ocean when it swells
Before a storm, my heart is full for sources
Of my solitude. Crystal Basin! The tumult
Of emotions when I think her, a million
Rhythms rolling me at once. I cannot rest
Until I go once more and see if this
Vision still lives. Like a scudding dolphin
I ride south and do not even feel the rough          180

Road beneath me. My cantering horse hoofs:
*Her eyes, her eyes, her eyes, her eyes.*
And from first light to roseate sunset, time
Indulges me with tender warnings.

                              *

Spring and the unfolding of flowers and their bright and tender cups
Spring and the sound of my horse's beat on the hard-packed road
Spring and amiable excursions, new friends, health restored
Spring and I am dismounted and kneeling to look
            Upon a new flowering bush resembling the Gordonia

What is it that is in perfect bloom and bearing ripe fruit?                    190
            (The month? The day? The weather? The latitude
            And my dismounted jealousy over any other day.)
What is it that is a flowering tree of the of the first order
            For beauty and the fragrance of its blossoms?

Whose leaves are oblong, broadest toward their extremities
Whose leaves are reflected and slightly serrated
Whose flowers are large and snow-white
Whose flowers are ornamented with a crown or tassel
            Of gold-colored refulgent stamina in their center—
            The inferior segment of the corolla hollow, forming            200
            A cap or helmet and entirely includes the other four
            Until the moment of their expansion
Whose fruit is a large, round, dry, and woody apple
            Opening at each end oppositely by five alternating fissures
            Containing ten cells and replete with woody cuniform seed

I saw it first when traveling with my Father
I saw it first in the late fall when its leaves were gone
            And I could not judge beyond the stems what it might be
I saw it first when my eyes were not half-sickened
            Or my bones and muscles broken from distance and grief         210

By right of being its first descriptor
By right of being here in its blossom time

By right of time and latitude and heat to make it open
       Its eyes just for me

I name it                    *Franklinia Alatamaha*, honor
My illustrious                Benjamin Franklin
I name it and              break one off and snug
It in a buttonhole          and ride on ride on
South knowing now        where I am being led
    And where I           must go and why.             220

\*

Morning: we sail onward now, boat and boat in-river
Toward Spalding's Upper Store, and my pain drives

Me nearly mad with exaltation, a hidden shuddering of all
Fear a man can know. I have come by sail and horse,

Have stopped at the homes of friends I may never see
Again; I pause one time to draw a quick sketch of buds

And flowers and the face of a Seminole who stands
Before me impassionate and powerful, as immutable

And warful as any lovely part of all Earth. High summer
Now, and it burns my skin and burnishes me, my eye        230

Pouring film again, and yet I would have to die to forfeit
Where I must ride. I pause beside the lakeside, canter

Across creeks, and ford small clear riverine systems
And I am alone, quite solitary, and I bathe in the heat

And build a campfire and think back over my life
And want to praise with gratitude for my failures

In business but not for my own personal industry for I
Have seen things no white man has yet described.

I still recall the trip behind me, eyes then blooming
With memorial monuments: mounds of the Ancients,                    240

The ball game dance in Cowee, how alone I felt there
When I came to know I must turn back. I have been

Quite mad, an irrational creature in his Quaker calm
Turned too human to bear. I have felt my bones dance

With an ecstasy invisible to all others, for to share it
Would derange me from its necessary powering.

I am a man with all senses attuned to a perfect season
Simultaneously, honed so finely that each sound,

Each light, each aroma, or taste defines and torments me
At the same time. And yet now as I sit by this crackling fire       250

I have never been more alive or in love with living
And cannot think that some day I must leave it all behind.

*Though what we are meant and bound to do is leave*
*It all behind when we pass away, leave the blossom*

*And the rose, leave the crystal basins and the tearing claws,*
*Leave the gardens and their perfectly mannered plants*

*So unlike that wilderness I tramped as a younger man*
*That I am like a dam holding back the greatest tide on Earth*

*For one last day, long enough to let it swell me higher*
*Than death, so that death will be ashamed in his trumpeting.*       260

And I join him, phantom of campfires and petioles,
Sip the summer air, knowing, to where he is bound and why

And thinking: Yes, yes, and yes, William, touch what
Touched you and what will keep you home-bound

For decades from now; touch it with your inestimable heart
And eyes, the tools of your trade, the diamonds of all light.

A meteor signs across the open sky: it scrapes like a gem
On an invalid's last window as I cook the fire with my stick,

Stir the coals and watch brands blossom before me.
Next day now, and I pass a Seminole standing by the trail                    270

And his eyes narrow, head cocks once, and his hand rises
And I read the silent message from his lips: Puc Puggy?

Puc Puggy? And I nod to let him know I have returned
And he defers, nods once, backs away to let me pass

With great and noble appearance, and I honor him
With a hand held high, and soon I am alone

Once more, and each step my horse makes is more familiar
And I think yes, and yes, and yes, and I know: It must be

Near or rather *I* must be near, and once perhaps I see it,
But these are the tumuli of the Ancients, and I despair                      280

And find myself wondering if I have become fatally lost
When I arrive: unforgettably ahead of me in the clearing

And I ride into its presence. My heart shatters. I climb down,
Turn my horse out to graze and walk to and kneel by

Patrick's grave. The terrible day comes back, how he
Descended to me down in the sinkhole, how the vine

Snapped, and he fell and cracked, how his eyes knew
For one long fatal moment, how happiness came into his

Eyes knowing his life had been a good one. I sit down
On his grave and stare, touch the rocks with my hands                       290

As if to beg him to awaken, untimely no more, but
He still sleeps. Of course he will safely sleep. I tell

Him he was my friend, that I will never know such days
Again and will live off them as a starving man parcels out

His food to last as many hours as possible. I stand, brush
Off my clothes and whisper his name and see my horse

Stamping, well-fed and impatient, and mount him and do not
Turn back, for I know now where I am headed, what I must see

Or die in the trying. Heat nearly suffocates us, but I bear it
Without notice, stopping at bubbling springs of clear water                    300

To sip and bathe. Once I come across two sunburned white
Traders, and they look at me as one sees a fleeting phantom

Say little, look sick and lost, and yet pass me and stumble
Inward in all things and are gone. Birds cry. I ride between

Huge mounds flecked with stored mica and the cool glint
Of shellwork gorgets or beads; I feel Cuscowilla near,
Feel its shape and woodsmoke dances, know that soon

Its embrace will pull me in, magnetized by all memory
And precious heat before the country of all cold comes.

                            *


Now I feel the earth shiver as if it asked                                       310
            a question of me, hear the rainwater shake off
                    flowers like the welcome of small silver bells
                            and realize how close I am to seeing and knowing.
                    A light rain breaks the sky and patters through
            the dense greenery. Even in this time there are
more signs of white people here, but I will not
            let their insightless presence ruin me
                    or wreck my resolve. A fluid need fills

my veins as I ride on hard ahead and full of pain
and yet a kind of rural profundity as well.                    320
If God allows me: that is the canter I hear
in my horse's slow gallop: *if God allows me, if God allows me.*
And soon I have come to Cuscowilla, and I see
alarm on the face of a child but then his eyes
go wide and he smiles, his hand comes up,
and I see his mouth shape ᴘᴜᴄ ᴘᴜɢɢʏ, and
I nod and say: I am the Flower Seeker, the rain
and the sun and the root and the stem, but where
is she? My horse's hooves: *Where can she be?*
*Where can she be?* Villagers come out to greet            330
Me, and I dismount, and two fine warriors
recognize me, and I smile, and they call my name,
and one old man walks out with a blossom he has
just plucked and hands it to me and raises an eyebrow.
I bow and laugh, knowing I must be ritually
welcomed before I can ask, but I glance
around and do not see her, and several of the people
speak some English now, and they ask if I
have captured other flowers since I left,
and one mimes the firing of a gun, and the others        340
howl with mirth but not derision.
They want to sit for a welcoming meal,
but I take aside one of the friendliest men
and ask as well as I am able (and sign) about
the girl I met in the dark, and before the words
escape my mouth, his face turns tender and solemn
and he says, "Come," and I follow him, knowing
the pale inevitability of sorrow in his slow tread.

I cannot breathe. My eye turns
On me, half blinds my sight.                                350
I stumble in the disinterested light.
My Quaker soul slowly burns,

Sunshine spangles the clearing
We enter in the forest, breaks

Shade to shade like wide lakes
In a plain. We are now nearing

What he seeks, for he goes slow
Then slower, and he puts an arm
On my shoulder and to disarm
My grief, touches me to show                    360

An oval pile of shining stones.
I say quietly, "No," but he speaks
Softly, and my composure breaks
As he whispers one word: "𝕭𝖔𝖓𝖊𝖘."

I hold myself hard in his shadow
And do not speak. "𝕾𝖍𝖊 𝖍𝖆𝖘 𝖉𝖎𝖊𝖉
𝕺𝖋 𝖈𝖔𝖚𝖌𝖍𝖎𝖓𝖌 𝖘𝖎𝖈𝖐𝖓𝖊𝖘𝖘," he sighs.
I walk away into a green meadow,

And he does not follow me, instead
Walks back to the village, and I,              370
Loved well once in the dark, fly
Half away and think of the dead.

What we love unblossoms too well
To bear even though we know it will
Come to us all. I imagine a windowsill
Where I will be long from now, can't tell

Of my sorrow to one who might ask,
In passing, of my health. I return
To her stones and cannot discern
The shape or grace of her, a task             380

For God in His wisdom to create.
I walk into the edge of the trees
And seek a flower in the breeze
To place upon her sleeping slate.

It is then I realize I cannot bear
It. I cannot bear the world
Without her, the hot uncurled
Vexation of loss in this air.

I glance back at her once, walk
Slowly away forever, ride on                                                    390
From the village then glide on
The river back and barely talk

To anyone. Isle to isle, wave
To shuddering wave, I feel
The shave and the sudden peel
Of sunburned surf, see the grave

Before me no matter what I do.
I feel dead inside to roaming.
In a rose-brief southern gloaming,
I feel I have done nothing new,                                                 400

That I have discovered only old
Certainties, fragile eternities, quiet
Groves, and the kindly patient riot
Of death that herds us all to fold.

Yet slowly I begin to refill with the badinage of friends
Yet slowly I see a quick glimpse of unexpected beauty
        In the fields and the edge of the forest;

Savannah! I head upriver to the home of my friend
        Jonathan Bryan who is returning from Savannah
        To his villa eight miles up the river                                   410
        With its spacious gardens, fruit trees,
        And flowering shrubs, and once again
        I luxuriate in my love of Linnæus:
        *Arum esculentum* with its turnip-like root
        Which makes an excellent food like the yam;

Its leaves large and beautifully green, the spatha
large and circulated and the spadix terminates
With a very long subulated tongue.


Miracle of the flora and risen sun, my purchase
    For this world and reason for life before me               420
Miracle of blooms off the drawn page and leafed book
    Before me in the fragrant light of my days
Miracle Savannah and now Charleston and now north
    Toward the home I have not seen in four years
Miracle of memory and imagination, of our ability
    *To sit at the window and prepare to rise, go outside*
    *Into the garden with its fresh bravura green and gold*
Miracle of time and transit, crossing the Cooper River
    Crossing the Winyaw Bay near Georgetown
    Then nearly losing track in my eagerness for home      430
Miracle of a boyhood in Bartram's steps and our excavation
    Of the fort where he visited, of my father recording
    The Keowee River at the ford where Bartram crossed
    To the village and then to head up into the Overhills
    And to listen to it here and now in exaltation and light
Miracle of Wright's Ferry on the Susquehanna where I begin
    To anxiously look toward home, but now it is cold
    And I see the seasons have turned upon and without me
    And the river is clogged with ice and I cannot cross here
    And I feel sick with anxiety that I am so close and cannot    440
    Get across to travel back home and see my loved ones
Miracle that Anderson's Crossing five miles north of here is open
    (And that I have driven over our Anderson's Crossing
    In Morgan County near Bostwick a thousand times)
    And so I set off again in the company of some travelers
Miracle that we gather now at the ferry, traders, travelers,
    Those going away and homeward bound, some with
    Packhorses loaded with leather and furs, and for a moment
    I am back in the mountains northwest of Keowee


And I see that it is not the water we will cross but the frozen river    450
    Itself: a gleaming white bridge of ice, and after testing
    What weight it will bear, our caravan sets off over it

And I see that it shall not crack or splinter and that I will
      Cross over to the other side, and I am riding it now
      With jingling traders and their packs, riding it now
      With travelers and one more fearful than I of the fall
And I see that I am near the other side that I will reach the other side
      And we do not ride close so as to equally distribute the weight
And I see I am across. Time, time. That this is my best and final voyage
      That it is evening and I have reached Lancaster          460
      That it is morning and I am eagerly riding again before light
      That I see the buildings of Philadelphia now in the distance
And that now I travel along the frozen Schuylkill River
      within four miles of the city and that *I am I am I am*

Inside by the fireside my father sits.
I stand steaming before him
His disappointment, his regret
His son failed in business and routine
And I half-fear what he will say,
But when I see him fragile and now old          470
By the flicker of delirious flames.

Morning arises stormy and pale,
No sun, but a wannish glare
In fold upon fold of hueless cloud;
And the budded peaks of the wood are bow'd
Caught, and cuff's by the gale:
I had fancied it would be fair.

A silvery light swims through the window.
The fire crackles and rubs its hands
Against the season, and we stand here          480
For the rest of his life, and I do not say to him:
I am the Flower Seeker and could
Have done nothing else with my life:
I bring this gift to you in our last days
Together on this earth and pray your peace.
I say nothing. I sense the moment of blossom
And how it begins beneath a high sun
And how short a time our plumage spans that light.

I sense the silence of spring, the bare hum
Of blossoms in their budding wonder.                          490

# CANTO TWENTY-FOUR

*H*ERE *in the last summer of my last year,*
*Here in the moontide garden of my lives*
*I stand to walk before I lie. My friend,*
*You are heir now to the truth of my life, you know*
*The incalculable tale of all the mounds before me.*
*Summer drones outside my open window. Heat*
*Blossoms along the unscribed-on parchment*
*Of my skin. America was in war when I returned*
*From my travels and is now a country of promise*
*And defect. I feel breathless. I remember his face*    10
*When I came to this room, when in his old age*
*He saw me return, just seven months before he died,*
*And I drew for him facts in the air, the ambrosia*
*Of nomenclature, the rare luxuries of unnamed species.*
*He would clap and say: O, how wonderful, William!*
*But that was a lifetime ago, and in that lifetime I have*
*Gone nowhere else beyond a day's ride from this place.*
*Now I know I must shuttle into the garden for breath.*

*Not these long lines*
    *But the memory of rapture*    20
        *Not winter's memorial bareness*
            *But the rupture of buds into delight*
                *Not my unskillful bones but those*
            *To come after me, if the* Travels
        *Stays in print or is not entirely*
    *Forgotten: for we bear the skill*
*Of plant husbandry well*
    *For we bear our adventures*
        *With gentle memories and a need*
            *For the magnificence of truth*    30
                *For eyes to fill up valleys*
            *And crystal basins and sinkholes*
        *For the gifts of fireside madness*
*We must save what Nature bears*
    *For us. Not a need for words*
        *But for learned eyes and hands*
            *To pick up and pick out life*

*In its inexplicable grandeur*
*And variety, to keep going when pain*
*Breaks us but does not break us down*                    40
*And then, like a flowering world*
*In its perpetual meadow, we will*
*Turn into light itself and shine*
*Lux æterna on pivoting Earth*

*This garden is my Penelope, love of return,*
*Center of the Known World, but it has no*
*Traveled boundaries, and its effervescent hum*
*Is unwreckable even in the desiccation to come.*
*I feel the subtle geology of old age slip away;*
*I feel pleasures beyond all darkness. What enfolds,*    10
*Desires; what desires, embraces; what embraces,*
*Resurrects. Already I am singing into the pollen air*
*With fruitful messages of days more delectable*
*Than mysteries from the rain. I am an ant rising*
*After a storm to the surface of its conical mound,*
*Covey settling between the garden and the river.*

*I am what does not endure and yet refuses to shiver*
*In the still-life winter. I recall as I walked around*
*The Ancients' hills beside the rivers and realizing*
*These were men with passions as uncorrectable*        10
*As my own. These women cooked and made fair*
*Necklaces of beads from mussel shell. All places*
*Become one then: one high site, one who holds*
*All in her warming arms. Night becomes new day.*
*Numbers all add up to the same inviolable sum,*
*The same vector, same One.*
*In the air, petals catch a northwest wind and blow*
*Southeast: that is what direction always earns.*

*I have not found the edge to my garden.*
*I have walked halfway round the world*
*And lost my health and desire to wander*              10
*In the process. I began with all order then*
*Felt it fall to pieces in my fragile keeping.*

*And yet when I returned it came again*
*And I did not dare leave lest it abandon*
*Me to a place where gardens cannot grow.*
*I walk across the room to keep it so.*

*What in the end can one man know?*
*Enough, I say, to be alive and grow*
*Equally in knowledge and the random*
*Rituals of rivercourses after heavy rain.* 10
*In the end there's no real need for weeping*
*Over what is sacrifice and what is sin.*
*Our mission is to sail and not to founder*
*On the reef of fear no matter what is hurled*
*Our way. Our resolve must ever harden*

*But not the imperial demands*
*Of love, which must be pliable*
*As roses from beginning to end.*
*We must learn the names of all*
*We see and pass the names along.* 10

*Lux æterna on a pivoting song,*
*Spring, summer, translucent fall,*
*Breaks that shear our arms but mend*
*The mill of memory: it is all liable*
*To drive us into desert's moon-sands;*

*Now I stand and need my cane*
*To slowly unsulk out the door*
*Into all paradise. I feel unmoored*
*From necessity and all breath,*
*Auger agony from my soul* 10
*And rush into what lies between*

*Here and the river, unseen*
*And yet opening buds whole*
*As the sky. There is no death*
*To take one who has soared*
*Above Keowee; there is no roar*

Of regret, only the riper grain
Of eternal summer. O Father,
In the end of things did I please
You well enough? Has my life                                    10
Given you peace to know teaching
Lasts? Words endure, scenes last,
Typha latifolia *arise near water.*

Son, sister, brother, daughter,
Garden of ancient bones now past
Understanding: arise now, reaching
Out, and be a kinsman or a wife,
Dance where no terrible disease
Can harm the love of our mothers.

Circle in the council house, dance
The stamping rhythm of all life,                               10
Fling wings open in the sweet air
To turn once and lift above geography
With the Pegasus dash of the young.
Come with me into every shape of Nature.

We can step each day into nurture
From the growing world, first rung
Of that eternal scaffolding stratigraphy
Of earth and stars. And on this stair
We touch clouds and learn to loaf                              10
As our successors will, like the ants

Unchallenged by rain or sudden threat.
Age begins to shed its claim on me;
Once again I am setting out for Fothergill
Into the unfictive world of blue birdsong
And green nations. I climb the brigantine
Ladder heading south, sail into storm

And season. I fear no evil. The warm
Green pastures restore soul, each scene
A path into the world for which I long                         10

*Each second every day. I hear the trill*
*Of fine friends in the grove of full trees.*
*My cup runs over; my eyes are not wet.*

*The earth is the Lord's and the fulness*
*Thereof; who shall ascend into the hill*
*Of the Lord or stand in his holy place?*

FOR NOTHING IS SECRET, THAT SHALL NOT BE MADE
MANIFEST; NEITHER ANY THING HID
THAT SHALL NOT BE KNOWN AND COME ABROAD.

*Clean hands, pure heart, spritely grace*                    10
*And a lack of vanity; all is now still*
*As a painted world. No more illness*

*Can track me down, no more harm*
*Descend or threaten me with loss.*
*I will not wane or grow any weaker*

*Day by silken day. I, the Flower Seeker,*
*Stand and step into the shimmered gloss*
*Of last light; wind is my final charm.*

*Take my arm to steady me as we go.*                         10
*Let us see what no one has ever seen.*
*Let us learn what we can never know.*

*I feel the rock and I fall into the flow.*
*Let me lie forever in all shades of green.*
*Let me push into that current. I will row*

*Hard for no shore. I will seek no rooms,*
*Be reaching for what warms and blooms*
*When you find me curled as if for sleep.*

*I have been a pilgrim roaming deep to deep*
*With the penitent's unstable ecstasy, looms*
*Spinning dreams away from those tombs.*                     10

*I reach for a flower that lies exulting*
*From a liquid sun. I take loveliness in hand.*
*I feel the pulse say goodbye to my arms.*

*Higher now, above the rivers and the farms,*
*I rise until I come into the quilted land*
*That has a name beyond this exalting.*

*Take my words to steady me as I go.*
*Let us love what we will not redeem.*
*Come with me into the flow and take*

*Back the isles of paradise, the wide lake*                    10
*On which they still lie. I have seen*
*Glory in a garden, roses in the snow.*

*And yet there is still one lovely light*
*That I would love to shape again and know.*
*I will be sailing south toward that glow*

*If you call my name.*
*When you call my name.*

*

William Bartram died on Tuesday, July 22, 1823, at the age of 84 while walking in his garden. He was buried there the next day in an unmarked grave.

# POSTSCRIPT

*I* FIRST heard of William Bartram more than fifty years ago when I was a boy, and my father first began his lifelong study of the glorious Keowee River valley in northwestern South Carolina and the Indian and white men and women who made it their home in frontier days. There was something magnificent about the name: *William Bartram*—it sounded important and memorable.

Some of my awe melted away years later when I found out he was called "Billy" by family and friends until he was grown, and that he was a failure in almost everything he did until his epic trip across the American South that led years later to the book that made him immortal. Most people simply call his book *The Travels*, and it really needs no other words.

Still, it's worth remembering the complete title: *Travels Through North & South Carolina, Georgia, East & West Florida, The Cherokee Country, the Extensive Territories of the Muscolges, or Creek Confederacy, and the Country of the Chactaws; Containing An Account of the Soil and Natural Productions of Those Regions, Together with Observations on the Manners of the Indians.* Little wonder it's just called *The Travels*.

Before I go further, I want to say that I hope those legions of Bartram fans out there—and there are *huge* numbers of people who love Bartram as much as I do—will forgive my turning his life into the material of fiction. Many of Bartram's "memories" in this poem simply never happened, but in the interest of shaping a story, I took liberties that I believe shows us a more well-rounded character than we can find in *The Travels*.

For those who don't know the book, the best edition to get is the companion volume to *The Flower Seeker* published by Mercer University Press and edited by Dorinda Dallmeyer. It's the first new edition of the book in years and has marvelous essays that place Bartram in the context of today. If you want more specific in-depth knowledge, you might also buy *The Travels of William Bartram: Francis Harper's Naturalist Edition* (University of Georgia Press, 1998). It is one of the few genuinely essential books that any educated person in the United States should own—especially those in the South. You will recognize the story, even much of the exact language Bartram used.

I grew up with the fabled Dover edition of *The Travels*, and I read it for the first time from beginning to end when I was a young teenager, probably about 1964. Since that time I have read it many times and even taught parts of the book in my nature-writing course at the University of Georgia.

ALL OF MY LIFE, I HAVE BEEN obsessed with the epic poem. I first read the Robert Fitzgerald translation of *The Odyssey* in high school and was more deeply affected than I can explain. When I was a freshman in college I encountered the John Ciardi translation of Dante's *Divina Commedia* and that kicked off a lifelong obsession with that great epic poem, though I now prefer other translations. Many others followed, especially Ezra Pound's *Cantos*, a poem with which I have been wrestling for well more than forty years now. In fact I met Pound's daughter, Mary de Rachewiltz, a fine poet and author in her own right, and she graciously signed my pristine copy of the 1970 edition of *The Cantos* that I bought as a young journalist in 1974.

I have spent much of my life planning for my own epic poem, but I found it terribly difficult to nail down a narrative project that interested me. Pound, at the end of his life, came to regard his own epic as a "botch," which it is in many ways because of its method of collating fragments and using them to imply meaning that must remain elusive. It is also marred by Pound's admiration for fascism and for the anti-Semitism for which he apologized (too) late in life. To me it shows a lack of artistic discipline—he came around to that opinion, too. And yet it is a wild and magnificent beast.

Other epics have just as many problems. Charles Olson's *Maximus Poems* follows Pound's working method into the same power and the same impenetrable obscurity. James Merrill's *The Changing Light at Sandover* is more to my taste in many ways, but it also lacks a cohesive narrative and much of it was "written" by a Ouija board, and that oddness hangs over it like a fog.

I began a lifelong study of other epics: Virgil's *Aeneid*, Ovid's *Metamorphosis*, Homer's other masterpiece, the *Iliad*, *Beowulf*, *The Seafarer*, and especially Milton's magnificent *Paradise Lost* which I read in its entirety on Milton's 400th birthday in 2008. (I've probably read it 20 or more times.) There were also *The Odyssey: A Modern Sequel* by Nikos Kazantzakis and *Omeros* by Derek Walcott. Of those two, I've never been able to get through the Kazantzakis book because there is no variation in presentation through 33,333 lines. I love *Omeros* and got to meet Walcott during the Cultural Olympiad at the Georgia Governor's Mansion, where I was a guest, as a Georgia writer, when all living Nobel laureates for literature gathered at the time of the 1996 Atlanta Olympic Games. And finally, I couldn't leave out *The Canterbury Tales*, which I adore and first began to learn in high school under the tutelage of my brilliant English teacher Florence Wagnon, who had an enormous influence on my life. I learned it first in Modern English and later in graduate school in Middle English, that gloriously musical variant I'm sorry that we lost along the way.

Still, the narrative epic poem as it was once practiced, has, with a few brilliant exceptions, appeared dead and buried for a century or more. It seemed to me that I needed to find a way to acknowledge the great 20th century poetic epics while using my background as a novelist to establish a plot and give it a shape.

It was only about three years ago that the light went on for me. In what was a genuine Eureka moment, I suddenly realized that the object for my poem had always been right before my eyes: William Bartram.

Just why I had not thought of this years ago astonishes me. In many ways, the American South has its *Iliad* in Shelby Foote's magnificent Civil War trilogy. But it still needed its *Odyssey*. I grew up in love with the natural world and spent much time in the fields and woods. I have for the past 25 years been a professional science writer at the University of Georgia as well as an adjunct professor of creative writing. And as a child and then a young man I tramped the wonderful Keowee River valley in South Carolina—a place to which Bartram came and that he loved when the famed Fort Prince George, built by the British in 1753, was no longer garrisoned and had turned into a trading post.

In 1967-68, I even helped excavate the fort as a volunteer with archaeologists from the University of South Carolina and made what was the single most important discovery in the whole dig: the cornerstone of a building in the fort with the dates 1761 and 1770 carved on it. I was 18 years old, and it was one of the most thrilling days of my entire life.

The sites of the fort and indeed the entire valley are now gone, inundated by a project of what was then the Duke Power Company (now Duke Energy). I will never, until my dying breath, forgive them for it. They bulldozed down and then flooded one of the most beautiful places on this Earth.

For years, I associated Bartram almost exclusively with the Cherokee town of Keowee and Fort Prince George. And yet, as the years passed, I began to understand better the depth of Bartram's work as a "flower seeker" (more on that name in a moment). When I said at the outset that the Keowee Valley has been a lifelong area of study for my father, I wasn't kidding: he probably knows as much as anyone alive about the history of that now-lost paradise.

I should also point out that while I have not traveled the entire route of Bartram's *Travels*, I have been along much of it and once lived in Mountain City, Ga. He came very near the first house in which my wife Linda and I lived after our marriage in 1972. Right now, we live in the country in southern Oconee County, Georgia, and less than 20 miles away, across the Oconee River into Oglethorpe County, is one proposed site of the great Buffalo Lick that Bartram wrote about. So I know this land well.

When I realized I could use Bartram's *Travels* as the jumping-off point for an epic odyssey of the American South and its flora and fauna, I was immediately faced with problems. The most important is that the *Travels* are a chronological and sequential mess. As Francis Harper found out years ago, Bartram relied on memory to recreate his four-year journey across the South and in doing so got dates confused, combined one trip with another, and often just apparently did the best he could to recreate what he remembered.

He also crafted what was then seen as a very strange combination of scientific reportage and rapturous, sometimes almost purple prose about such unscientific topics as beauty. These two kinds of writing often hit each other in the book like colliding trains, and Bartram switches back and forth between them as if he were putting the book together from two different manuscripts.

My own idea is that *The Travels* embody another collision that happened about then between the Age of Reason and the Age of Romanticism. It's as if Bartram has two glasses before him, one filled with each, and as he drinks from one, he writes from its effects, but when he switches glasses, he switches approaches, too.

In many ways, it makes for a stylistic mess. It also creates one of the most powerful reading experiences ever penned about America or the South. It has an uncanny power to stay in the memory for a lifetime. Coleridge apparently based his poem "Kubla Khan" on passages from Bartram, for instance, and scholars say other Romantic poets were strongly influenced as well. Long after many other writers are gone and forgotten, *The Travels* will be sailing happily on and deservedly so.

At first, I saw no way around the self-imposed mess Bartram made of *The Travels*. After all, there is no standard biography of Bartram—something that seems completely indefensible until you realize the man never left home for the last 46 years of his life. There is also the reverence with which Bartram fans hold him: he is one of the few 18th century Americans who still has groupies.

I should know because I'm one of them. And yet I had to find some way past the almost saintly image of him we see in the *Travels*. After all, he *was* a Quaker, and that sect is known for its austere and peaceful ways. That's when I realized I could have Bartram narrate the poem himself in extreme old age as a kind of confession—filling the blanks. It's something I've done before in fiction because I've always been interested in old age and have written a great deal about it. And yet what was he *really* like?

The facts of his biography are somewhat thin and I won't recount them. Go online and poke around. I also realized that I could conflate my own experience as part of the poem to stand in for those of us who have spent our lives grateful to have had Bartram as a friend and companion. When I saw this path, the poem almost exploded in my mind.

I wrote much of it in a state of wild and grateful rapture. Many days I finished my work in tears. Sometimes I would cringe when I was creating incidents whole cloth from my imagination, but I knew it was necessary if I was to fill in motivation for his actions and to ferret out a deeper reason why he didn't leave home for the last half century of his life. (The standard reason is that he was injured in a fall in 1786 when he was 47 years old while pruning a cypress tree and that he suffered from the eye troubles he contracted on the western leg of the *Travels*—I didn't invent that part of *The Flower Seeker*.)

Another issue was the use of language in the poem. I could not write it as if Bartram were speaking 21st century English, but it was equally impossible to use the mannered locutions of 18th and early 19th century usage. It would be unreadable. So I tried to create a stylistic place between the two, something that mimics both the quotidian scientific passages from the *Travels* and its moments of ecstasy and even epiphany. I do not know if I succeeded. I know I did the best I could. (Since 18th century orthography was, shall we say, creative, I have standardized the place-names Bartram used with their modern equivalents, so readers will, I hope, be less confused. There is also a slight inconsistency in how Linnaean names are used, since in places I used Bartram's versions, some of which remain standard and some of which have been slightly altered in spelling over the years, and in some places I use modern equivalents. I did this on a case-by-case basis, and I can only say that I hope no one comes to this poem as a primary source for botanical information.)

I also knew from the first that I wanted to use artwork and maps as part of the poem, and the shaped lines that hold artwork were written that way first and the artwork found second. First of all, Bartram was a fine artist, and I knew I could not give a true picture of his character without it. Second, the entire idea of this poem is the intersection between Art and Science, and as he includes both life and earth sciences all through the book, I wanted to include more than just words.

There are many passages from *The Travels* that are used verbatim or rewritten slightly to change the emphasis or color of a passage. And I frequently invent whole scenes and episodes that never happened. Indeed, it would be easy to argue they simply *couldn't* have happened.

But Bartram was a human and not a saint. He had the same desires and weaknesses all of us have. I wanted to portray him as a man not as a perfect oracle.

We *do* know that he was a kind and gentle man, and I suspect he was tortured by conscience as many men like that are. There are few precedents for one who travels this much on horseback or on foot for four years and then goes home and almost never leaves for an overnight trip for the rest of a very long life.

I will admit that from the first day I began writing, I *became* William Bartram—as much as one man can "become" another. The day I finished the poem I nearly fell to pieces. The experience was that intense.

I knew from the beginning that I also intended to create a work that operated on several levels because I wanted *The Flower Seeker* to take in many worlds, not just the one Bartram saw on his *Travels*. To this end, I studied the great poetic epics from *Gilgamesh* on, and deconstructed writing methods and approaches. I was struck by such things as the now-well-known use of so-called "Homeric epithets," the repetition of such phrases as "much-enduring," "great-hearted," and "wine-dark" in *The Odyssey*. Scholar Milman Parry understood early that these were not simply repeated phrases that are used when the hero of the poem appears. (Bernard Knox's introduction to the Robert Fagles translation of *The Odyssey* explains this beautifully.)

But there was much more I wanted to accomplish. Even though I have only one other language, French (and I have it poorly, at that), I wanted to find ways to link Bartram to the great world of scholarship of the past in all areas—science, art, literature, religion, and more.

To accomplish this, I did something akin to what owners of some ruby mines in North Carolina's Cowee Valley do to lure paying customers. (Bartram ended his journey into the Cherokee country at about that spot, so the comparison is apt, I think.) These mines do what's called *enriching*—putting pretty stones, some of value, most not, in the buckets that customers screen in water flumes. It's not a bad idea at all, and it certainly isn't deceptive—giving customers a chance to find *something* for their work, even it's not a native stone such as the ruby or sapphire. A gem hunter there simply chooses, to screen in a flume, buckets with only native stones or ones that have been enriched.

So I enriched my long poem with words, lines, selections, and excerpts from numerous other sources, none of which I choose to make public as notes with *The Flower Seeker* (though my editor knows the source of them all). It isn't necessary to understand them to comprehend the poem, but they do add another level of meaning so that those who wish to do so can read the poem as a scholarly text. James Joyce famously said of *Ulysses* that "I've put in so many enigmas and puzzles that it will keep the professors busy for centuries arguing over what I meant, and that's the only way of insuring one's immortality." I don't make any such fanciful claim, but I did want to write a poem that could not be completely "gotten" with one, two, or even three readings.

I NEED TO EXPLAIN THE CD THAT is included in the hardback limited editions of *The Flower Seeker*, too. The sound in the background—the running water—is to my knowledge the only extant recording of the Keowee River at the ford between the Cherokee village of Keowee and Fort Prince George. My father took a battery-operated reel-to-reel recorder there on April 13, 1967, to record the sound of that glorious river's flowing water. Now part of a hydroelectric impoundment, the river is gone, though, one hopes, not forever. This astonishing recording is a treasure. As I am a composer, too, the music on the CD is mine.

IT IS STANDARD PROCEDURE TO LIST WORKS consulted when writing about the past, even in fiction or the epic poem. And there are dozens of books about Bartram, and over the years I have read many of them with the greatest pleasure. My brother, Dr. Mark Williams, also knows a great deal about Bartram and as an archaeologist of Southeastern native cultures understands the world that Bartram saw far better than I ever could. I have benefited hugely from the insights of Mark and my father. But there are only a few books I want to cite that helped me the most, though I read and studied dozens over a period of three years.

The first is *William Bartram on the Southeastern Indians* (University Nebraska Press, 1995) by Gregory A. Waselkow and Kathryn E. Holland Braund. This wonderful book is a compilation of all Bartram's writing about Indians from *The Travels*, along with deeply insightful commentary from two seasoned anthropologists. If you're a Bartram fan, buy it immediately.

The second is *Guide to William Bartram's Travels* (Fevertree Press, 2002) by Brad Saunders of Athens, Ga. This interesting book, which Sanders wrote, illustrated with photos he took and maps he created, is a good place to start for anyone interested in Bartram. It connects past and present and visually stands out among the many books retracing Bartram's *Travels*. Anyone wishing to know the historical background of Bartram's book and all important names and places should buy the Saunders volume.

Two other books that have had a great impact on my life were essential in writing *The Flower Seeker*. The first is *Documents Relating to Indian Affairs, 1754-1765*, edited by William L. McDowell, Jr. (South Carolina Department of Archives and History, 1970, reprinted 1992). The letters in Canto Fifteen are verbatim from this book. I would like to thank the Department of Archives and History for permission to use these excerpts.

The second book is *Myths of the Cherokee and Sacred Formulas of the Cherokees* by James Mooney. First published in 1900, the volume was republished in 1982 by Charles and Randy Elder, booksellers in Nashville. My own well-worn copy is the Elder edition. Mooney's scholarly volume is one of the single most important books ever published in the United States, and I beg of you to buy a copy for yourself or to give to friends. I have known this book since I was a boy, and the status it holds in my house is one of near-reverence. Section O on page 301 is from this book.

My own thanks are vast, but I'd like to thank Marc Jolley at Mercer University Press—a wonderful man and first-rate editor. He invited me several years ago to edit a volume of nature writing by Georgia authors, and though I didn't quite do that, I hope this book is a suitable substitute. I also send great thanks to Jim and Mary-Frances Burt of Burt & Burt Studio in Macon, Ga., for the design of *The Flower Seeker*. Their brilliant work is vital to the book.

I owe a special thank you to archaeologist Tom Charles of the University of South Carolina for his drawings of petroglyphs. These are part of the multimedia approach I used to telling this story. While I moved these petroglyphs to western Georgia in the poem, they actually can be found in what is now Oconee County, South Carolina, not far from the now-lost sites of Keowee and Fort Prince George. While I moved them for narrative purposes, they really belong in a different part of Bartram's *Travels*.

Finally, I want to say a word about this book's title. Bartram himself was told that the Seminole honorific *Puc Puggy* meant "the Flower Hunter." Still, I don't care for the parallel that translation draws between the search for botanical specimens and hunting animals. It has nothing do with animal rights or welfare, though. I simply believe I needed a title that by implication delves deeper into what Bartram sought. While he clearly was hunting specimens, I believe he was seeking much more—insight, beauty, spiritual elation, and meaning for his life.

People who love Bartram do so for many things, but I doubt anyone misses the vast canvas on which he painted his interests and longings. To me, he was a seeker in the broad sense, and it is that belief that underlies my decision to call it *The Flower Seeker*.   In the very first lines of the preface to Francis Harper's "Naturalist Edition" of *The Travels*, which was originally published in 1958, Harper recounts a comment from a professor at then-Clemson College (now University) who heard about Harper's project. Dr. William Mills said to Harper, "I hope you will make Bartram live again."

That, too, has been my goal in this book.

Philip Lee Williams,
Watkinsville, Ga.
June, 2010

## ABOUT THE TYPE

The greater portion of *The Flower Seeker* was set in LTC Caslon, a typeface designed in 2005 by the American type designer Paul Hunt. LTC Caslon is a modern remastering of the original Caslon—created by William Caslon in the early 1700s—which was widely used during Bartram's time.

Tiepolo Book was used for sections expressing the author's thoughts in present day.

In contrast, Lucida Blackletter was employed for portions spoken by native characters in the time of William Bartram.

Documents and correspondences were set in Adine Kirnberg Script.

Other typefaces, used sparingly throughout *The Flower Seeker*, were applied to specific words to enhance their meaning.